FIFTH EDITION

The World of Music

David Willoughby

McGraw Hill

Boston   Burr Ridge, IL   Dubuque, IA   Madison, WI   New York   San Francisco   St. Louis
Bangkok   Bogotá   Caracas   Kuala Lumpur   Lisbon   London   Madrid   Mexico City
Milan   Montreal   New Delhi   Santiago   Seoul   Singapore   Sydney   Taipei   Toronto

McGraw-Hill Higher Education

A Division of The **McGraw-Hill** *Companies*

THE WORLD OF MUSIC
Published by McGraw-Hill, a business unit of The McGraw-Hill Companies, Inc., 1221 Avenue of the Americas, New York, NY, 10020. Copyright © 2003, 1999 by The McGraw-Hill Companies, Inc. All rights reserved. No part of this publication may be reproduced or distributed in any form or by any means, or stored in a database or retrieval system, without the prior written consent of The McGraw-Hill Companies, Inc., including, but not limited to, in any network or other electronic storage or transmission, or broadcast for distance learning.
Some ancillaries, including electronic and print components, may not be available to customers outside the United States.

This book is printed on acid-free paper.

2 3 4 5 6 7 8 9 0   DOW/DOW 0 9 8 7 6 5 4 3 2

ISBN 0-07-249150-7

Publisher: *Christopher Freitag*
Developmental editor: *Nadia Bidwell*
Marketing manager: *Lisa Berry*
Producer, Media technology: *Todd Vaccaro*
Project manager: *Ruth Smith*
Production supervisor: *Carol A. Bielski*
Manager, Photo research: *Brian J. Pecko*
Supplement producer: *Nate Perry*
Cover design: *Srdjan Savanovic*
Interior design: *Elise Lansdon Design*
Typeface: *10/12 Gill Sans*
Compositor: *UG/GGS Information Services, Inc.*
Printer: *R. R. Donnelley & Sons Company*

Library of Congress Cataloging-in-Publication Data

Willoughby, David.
　　The world of music / David Willoughby.—5th ed.
　　　p. cm.
　　Includes bibliographical references (p.) and index.
　　ISBN 0-07-249150-7 (acid-free paper)
　　1. Music appreciation.   I. Title.
　　MT6.W533 W7 2003
　　781.1'7—dc21
　　　　　　　　　　　　　　2002025459

www.mhhe.com

Contents

PART One

Preparation for Listening   2

CHAPTER 1

Introducing the World of Music   4

Preparing to listen perceptively to this globally diverse and culturally rich art form

CHAPTER 2

Vocabulary for Listening and Understanding: The Nature of Music   15

What is music?

CHAPTER 3

Vocabulary for Listening and Understanding: The Elements of Music   22

Words and symbols sufficient to improve listening skills, formulate opinions, and communicate effectively

PART *Two*

Listening to Vernacular Music   36

C H A P T E R   *4*

American Folk Music Traditions   38

From traditional folk and blues music in rural America to urban revivals in Chicago, Memphis, and Greenwich Village

C H A P T E R   *5*

American Religious Music Traditions   63

From psalm singing in Colonial times to the contemporary popular religious music of today

C H A P T E R   *6*

Jazz in America   84

From ragtime to swing to fusion, a look at America's own art form

C H A P T E R   *7*

American Popular Music   114

America's commercial, popular music from Tin Pan Alley to the Nashville Sound, the Motown Sound, rock and roll, and rap

PART Three

Listening to World Music 148

PART Four

Listening to Western Classical Music 211

CHAPTER 13

Music of the Romantic Period (Nineteenth Century) 279

Romantic genres: the symphonic poem, art song, program symphony, and solo piano pieces—and the music of Schubert, Chopin, Tchaikovsky, and many others

CHAPTER 14

Music of the Twentieth Century 296

Major developments from traditional sounds to the avant-garde: impressionism, serialism, neoclassicism, minimalism, electronic music, and chance music

CHAPTER 15

American Classical Music 321

A discussion of the context, composers, and styles of classical music in American culture

CHAPTER 16

Music in American Society 346

Ways that music functions in industry, the media, and the community

Preface

The World of Music is a music listening book. Going beyond the traditional limits of repertoire used for music study, it is designed for that growing number of teachers who want to focus on perceptive or analytical *listening to music as it exists in the real world*. In addition to western European classical music, this text includes folk, religious, jazz, popular, ethnic, and world music. These "nonclassical" repertoires, given substantive coverage in early chapters, provide appropriate material for introducing musical concepts and for gaining an understanding of the nature of music, how it is created, and how it functions. This approach affirms that no repertoire is too small for the study of music and that all repertoires are important, differing only in style and function.

The World of Music does not seek to study cultures and repertoires in depth, nor does it seek to teach repertoires as much as to use them. Its primary purpose is to use these sources to increase musical understanding. A goal of the textbook is to *capture the essence of each repertoire*. Students will recognize the different styles, appreciate their different functions, and develop a solid foundation for continued learning in areas of personal interest.

In a comprehensive book such as this, there is a trade-off. By giving added attention to nonclassical repertoires, western European classical music has of necessity been reduced. Again, the goal is *to capture the essence of the nature of classical music in its varied styles*. Therefore, all that is sacrificed is the quantity of information.

The World of Music presumes no prior musical training on the part of the student. It is a textbook for any introductory music listening course whether it is entitled Music Appreciation, Introduction to Music, Survey of Music Literature, or Music Listening. Its broad scope and introductory nature make it ideally suited for lower-division music literature courses designed for those not majoring in music as well as for music majors. In fact, when considering the global nature and the complexities of today's society, the attention the book gives to music from many traditional and contemporary musical styles may provide a much needed philosophical and curricular foundation for music majors early in their professional preparation.

Two broad, related statements underlie the philosophy and approach on which this book is based:

- The core of the approach leads to the development of listening skills, including the ability to describe and comment on the music heard.
- Listening skills can be taught through music of any time or place.

Listening Skills

The sequential development of substantive listening and descriptive skills is the central purpose of the text. More than the study of specific repertoires, it is the study, through listening, of musical concepts common to nearly all repertoires that ties the chapters together. Learning strategies are more clearly and frequently stated in this fifth edition than in previous ones. In addition to the elements of music presented in chapters 2 and 3, listening goals, musical concepts, and terminology are introduced throughout the book, as needed, particularly at the beginning of each chapter's Goals for Listening.

All chapters other than 1, 2, and 16 include Listening Guides, each of which is comprised of a recorded musical example from the full set of CDs that accompany the text. Listening Guides, as much as possible, explicitly reflect musical concepts discussed within the chapter. In previous editions, all guides were included as summary material at the end of chapters. This fifth edition now has them incorporated within the text, placed close to directly related content.

Also new to the fifth edition is "crossover" music, defined as music that reflects more than one genre or is sufficiently unique to defy classification. Crossover Additional Listening guides are included at the ends of chapters 4 through 15.

The purpose of each guide is to reinforce printed information and concepts. Each musical example includes a variety of strategies to assist in the listening process. Thus, for each recorded example, there is a listening guide that includes the following:

- Background information.
- Goals for developing listening and descriptive skills.
- The listening guide—an outline of or commentary on the music and its structure and style.
- Reflections on the listening experiences.

The goals for each listening experience have been developed sequentially so that, as students progress, their listening and descriptive skills and use of vocabulary grow gradually and consistently. The guides help lead this listening experience. However, since listening can to some extent be subjective, listeners may hear music in a different way than a guide indicates; thus, multiple perceptions may be entirely valid. The reflective comments and questions are presented to enhance perceptions, particularly from repeated listening, and to use as catalysts for discussion.

The goals and reflections are meant to be flexible, intended only as possibilities and as models. Teachers can modify them as desired and can have students create their own reflective statements or questions for discussion.

Repertoire

The choice of repertoire for music study is comprehensive and presented, as much as possible, without bias. Such an approach includes and reinforces the importance of cultural backgrounds that are not western European. It also acknowledges the musical validity of using music other than western European classical music in the curriculum.

The expanded repertoire for music study represented in this text symbolizes several important notions:

- At the dawn of this new century, it seems logical that substantive attention should be given to recent and current classical and popular music—the *music of our own time*.
- The United States of America is comprised of diverse cultures, and curricula should reflect this diversity as it is; thus, a strong emphasis should be given to *music of our own nation*.

- Music exists in faraway, exotic places—in other cultures. However, much music, derived from non-Western cultures, is close to our home and is important to American society—American ethnic music. Thus, we acknowledge the importance and the study of *music of the world*.

The United States is part of our global culture; thus, in this sense, its jazz, folk, popular, and classical music is part of "world music." To sustain the notion that American music is part of, not separate from, world music, we include a variety of repertoires within American music that have non-Western roots or influences. These repertoires include the music of native Americans, American ethnic and immigrant groups, and creators and performers of Latin America and the Caribbean. This broad coverage affirms that all repertoires can contribute in important ways to the study of music.

Because of the emphasis on expanded repertoire, choices of content and musical examples obviously had to be made. The text is organized so chapters, sections, or pieces can be omitted or given emphasis different from the text's to suit an individual instructor's interests and needs. In such a case, modifications can and should be made to the goals and descriptions in the Listening Guides to retain the sequential development of listening skills.

Photographs throughout the text are essential to its philosophical basis, depicting music as it is—performed by people everywhere, serving many valid purposes, and enjoyed and valued in many different contexts. Music is an active art, and people are seen making and responding to music.

This book focuses largely on the roots of a musical repertoire that includes: (1) background, history, and relationships to a culture (context), and (2) significant influences and contributions of creators and performers to a society and to musical development. This background, however, has been balanced with contemporary elements of various music, including its more contemporary sounds. Thus, this fifth edition of *The World of Music* is both historical and contemporary and can be a viable musical resource for the early years of the twenty-first century.

David Willoughby
Elizabethtown, Pennsylvania
Professor Emeritus, Eastern New Mexico University

Acknowledgments

The World of Music is an outgrowth of influences from many professional colleagues in music. I wish to acknowledge three individuals who influenced my early career direction and professional involvements relevant to the philosophy shaping this text. They are: Dr. Donald Shetler of the Eastman School of Music who in 1967 changed the direction of my professional thinking by rejecting all five possible dissertation topics that I presented, by advising me to go to Sibley Library and read about the Contemporary Music Project (CMP), and by suggesting that I come up with one more proposal; Dr. Robert Werner who, as a result of my subsequent dissertation, took a risk in 1970 and hired me as the assistant director of the Contemporary Music Project (CMP) with specific responsibilities in the area of comprehensive musicianship; and Dr. Barbara English Maris who, as president of the College Music Society (CMS), launched my continuing responsibilities with the society by naming me director of the 1981 Wingspread Conference on Music in General Studies. This led to a CMS "career" centered on improvements in the teaching and learning of college-level general music in classes for both music and nonmusic majors. I am grateful for the confidence these individuals had in my capabilities.

Having an abundance of opportunities for observing and participating with outstanding scholar-teachers through CMP workshops and CMS institutes and conferences significantly shaped my thinking regarding the need and responsibility to encourage a comprehensive approach to the selection of repertoire for music study.

Regarding the writing of *The World of Music*, I am very grateful to the William C. Brown Publishing Company for being willing to take the leap of faith in originally producing this text and particularly to Karen Speerstra, then music developmental editor, for having the confidence in my potential as a WCB author. I am particularly grateful to Meredith Morgan, the music editor for my first edition, who gave me encouragement when I needed it most and motivated me to give that extra effort; to Christopher Freitag, first with Brown and Benchmark and now with McGraw-Hill, whom I have found very helpful and stimulating in our many exchanges of ideas about the world of music; and to the "Book Teams" of each of the five editions of *The World of Music* for their willingness to offer constructive and supportive suggestions. I continue to appreciate their professionalism and competence.

I could not have researched the material without the resources and cooperative personnel of many university libraries, particularly the Golden Library of Eastern New Mexico University, the Hornbake Library of the University of Maryland at College Park, and various libraries in Pennsylvania's Susquehanna Valley, particularly at Susquehanna University, Messiah College, Franklin and Marshall College, and Elizabethtown College.

The contributions of students in music appreciation classes over many years are standard yet critical in the development of these texts. The students in my classes, particularly while preparing the first edition, cannot know the extent to which their experiences stimulated innumerable corrections and modifications and also affirmations of strategies and materials used and, in fact, tested. I shall always be grateful for their tolerance of all the disadvantages and logistical problems associated with a textbook in progress.

Finally, I must express my deepest appreciation to those who reviewed various drafts of *The World of Music*. Their comments and suggestions contributed immensely to the refinements in writing style, philosophical and cultural considerations, and information. In many cases the most critical reviewers were the most meticulous in their commentary and the most helpful in my refinements of the text. I thank them most sincerely. Those who reviewed the fifth edition are: Floyd Slotterback, Northern Michigan University; Robert Aubrey, University of Mississippi; Stephen Shearon, Middle Tennessee State University; Alicia Kopfstein-Penk, American University; Robin Armstrong, Western Maryland College; and Bill Shepherd, University of Northern Iowa.

Musical Examples

AL indicates an Additional Listening example

indicates the selection appears on the student CD set as well as the Instructor's CD set

*AL 16 appears only on the student CD set.

The World of Music

David Willoughby

One

Preparation for Listening

ignificant musical experiences can happen with or without formal training. Not everyone creates it or performs it, but we all listen to it. Music is a part of our experience from childhood through adulthood—in games at recess, in the shower with no one listening, in churches and schools, in movies and commercials, and on a stereo at home or in the car. Many people have become musically sophisticated by learning to play instruments and perhaps even to read music.

The World of Music is a book about music as it exists in the United States—our world of music. It is a book that encourages the study of music from a global perspective or a worldwide view. A global perspective can enrich our lives by helping us develop a greater respect for the music of other cultures and for the various cultural or ethnic groups within the United States. This global approach can also enrich our lives by deepening our understanding of the predominant or mainstream musical styles of the United States.

The primary purpose of *The World of Music* is to enhance the students' experience of listening to music by giving them more knowledge of music in general. To help students become more perceptive listeners, the text seeks to:

- Develop skills in listening to music intelligently. Listening is the core of the book and also the link which ties the chapters together.

- Cultivate an awareness of repertoires and musical styles representing a variety of cultures and regions of the world.

- Stimulate growth in an understanding of musical context, that is, the historical background and the social, political, and economic environment of a society that influences the creation and performance of music.

Part 1, "Preparation for Listening," consists of the first three chapters:

- Chapter 1 draws attention to the enormous variety of music and the place of music in various cultures, as examined from a global perspective. It discusses the advantages and disadvantages of using labels to categorize music and musicians in a multicultural, stylistically diverse world. It also discusses the varying and sometimes contradictory uses of the words *artist* and *artistry*. Perhaps most importantly, this chapter sets the stage for developing listening skills throughout subsequent chapters.

- Chapter 2 explores a vocabulary derived from the nature of music and how we use this vocabulary to describe music's acoustical and aesthetic qualities.

- Chapter 3 presents a beginning vocabulary derived from the elements of music. It stresses how creators of music organize these elements to create styles. This chapter will help students describe and understand the structure and style of music: what it is that makes up a piece of music. Additional vocabulary is presented as needed in later parts of the book.

The goals of chapters 1 through 3 (and the remainder of the book) include helping students do the following:

- Develop listening skills by intelligently using basic musical concepts and terms to describe music.

- Understand the structure of music by examining a variety of ways it is organized.

- Learn how sounds are chosen by individuals to create a personal style.

- Recognize stylistic differences—those characteristics that distinguish one piece from another.

To achieve these goals, students need to understand certain musical concepts and terms—a musical vocabulary. All **boldfaced** terms in each chapter are defined in the glossary. The glossary can help students understand new concepts, so consult it often.

1

Introducing the World of Music

Goals for Listening

- **Respond to** diverse styles.
- **Identify** musical preferences.
- **Look for** patterns in pulse and meter.
- **Describe** qualities of musical tones.
- **Identify levels of** musical restlessness and calm.

Listening Experiences: A Collage of Musical Styles

Summary

Terms and Concepts

Global perspective

American mainstream

Immigration and ethnic diversity

Cultural characteristics

Labels

Artists and artistry

*T*hroughout *The World of Music,* we discuss the roots and development of a variety of musical styles having the greatest impact on American society. These roots lie in the music of other **cultures** and nations, notably those of southern Africa, Asia, and Europe. The music presented is derived from the cultural mainstream (the historically predominant culture) as well as from the diverse subcultures within the United States. This text acknowledges and respects the similarities and differences among these various musical **styles** that make up the composite we call "American" music. Thus, the purpose of this chapter—and this book—is to convey the diversity of the world's music, particularly the musics important to large or small groups of people in American society.

The course begins by encouraging the development of listening skills through a sampling of the seemingly endless styles of music from many parts of the globe. One goal is to acquire a sense of what exists beyond our own experience.

We live today in a "global village" that is becoming smaller and smaller. With advances in transportation and communication, and with increasing social mobility, it seems not merely appropriate but actually necessary to approach music from a **global perspective.** Using this book, you can gain a sense of the lifestyles, traditions, values—and the music—of several nations and cultures. You will also gain an awareness of the diversity within our national boundaries that has contributed significantly to the cultural richness of our land.

The Infinite Variety of Music: A Global Perspective

The diverse musical styles in the United States include western European classical music (art music) and much of our folk and popular music that is also based on European traditions. Other styles, however, including jazz, blues, and various ethnic musics, have resulted from a blending of cultures and traditions. All these styles are an important part of music in American society and constitute what we call American music.

The first factor in the development of America's cultural mainstream was the predominance of English (or Anglo-Saxon) settlers in the New World, mostly in the seventeenth and eighteenth centuries. As our society and our government were taking shape, English culture defined America's politics, religion, and language. All succeeding immigrant groups had to choose **assimilation** with the Anglo-Saxon mainstream or isolation from it.

The American Mainstream and Ethnic Diversity

Groups that retained a substantial part of the language, customs, or social views of their original cultures became what we call **ethnic** minorities. Part of the cultural richness of our nation is derived from its ethnic diversity and its large number of ethnic groups. Some immigrant groups have partially assimilated into the mainstream of our society while retaining the songs, dances, instruments, languages (or at least accents and inflections), fashion, food, and lifestyles of their native cultures.

In many cases, new styles and modes of behavior have been formed by the merging of cultural traditions. For example, jazz evolved in the early twentieth century, in part from a merging of songs and dances of Anglo-Americans with songs and dances of Creoles (people of mixed French or Spanish and perhaps African heritage who were born in the West Indies and the southern United States)—and in part from a further merging of these two strands with the songs and dances of African Americans (descendants of black slaves).

The predominance of European influences in early American music evolved in part because (1) most early religious, folk, and popular songs were derived from traditions and styles from the British Isles and mainland Europe; (2) Americans, particularly throughout the nineteenth century, were exposed to European classical music by traveling to Europe or by listening to music performed by visiting or immigrant European musicians; and (3) European Americans rejected the music of Native Americans as primitive and unworthy. Thus, most of America's popular and classical music is based on the melodic, harmonic, and rhythmic practices of western Europe. The instruments we have traditionally used are, for the most part, the same as or derived from those used in mainland Europe and the British Isles. In this century, however, the American mainstream is becoming less European and more global.

Music in Culture

In all cultures, music is one form of human behavior, but it varies widely from culture to culture. Scholars may approach the study of music from these different yet overlapping perspectives. The study of music of other cultures, as well as our own, involves describing it in musical terms. The problem with this approach is that our musical language is not universal. It is based on western European musical concepts and cannot necessarily describe other music equally well. Furthermore, studying music of a culture implies much more than simply describing music. It also involves considering the **context** of music in a society, music as it relates to human behavior, and the general attitude of a people toward their music.

Scholars of music in cultures—of "world music"—are known as **ethnomusicologists.** They do the research on the music of a culture, write about it, and teach others about it. They live for a period of time in the country or region where that music is produced. They record the music, talk to the people who make the music, and find out why and how it is created, performed, and heard. They try to understand the music the way it is understood by the members of the culture. And this is true not only when they study the music of faraway places, but also when they study music in the Western Hemisphere and within their own national boundaries.

Social Aspects

Ethnomusicologists, through their research, seek to learn about musicians in a culture, asking such questions as Who creates? Who performs? and Who listens? These scholars try to determine what the life of a musician is like and what this person's status is, whether a musician is highly respected or more like a servant, professional or amateur, formally schooled or unschooled. They also discover how the musician acquires and develops skills.

This research produces information about a culture's ideas concerning music, such as how music ties into a belief system and how music relates to the fabric of that society. Researchers consider whether music is intended for immediate consumption or preserved in some way for future generations. They explore how a group perceives music in relation to nature and to society. Ethnomusicologists observe a culture's musical preferences. Do the people consider music beautiful or is beauty a concern at all? What sounds are considered to be pleasing and satisfying? Is there "good" and "bad" music? Does the culture have popular music and classical music?

In addition, ethnomusicologists ask where music is performed, how musicians dress when they perform, and on what occasions music is performed—for rituals, entertainment, concerts, ceremonies, sports, dance, drama, or religion. They examine the relationship between performer and audience: what the audience does during a presentation and whether the spectators are active or inactive, quiet or noisy, attentive or inattentive.

Ethnomusicologists study a society and its music to determine musical styles, genres, and forms, and the history and theory of its music. They also try to discover what can be learned about the culture from the texts of its songs, what the music sounds like, and what linguistic problems arise in describing the music. They find ways to describe the creative process, the use of melody, the tonal framework, the rhythmic organization, the choices of instruments, and the preferred qualities of vocal and instrumental sounds. These scholars determine how music is learned, taught, and passed on from one generation to the next, and whether it is notated or transmitted mainly by oral tradition (by example, by imitation and memory).

Ethnomusicologists discover what tangible things a community uses to produce music: instruments, equipment, printed music, or recordings. They also study to what extent the technological and urban, perhaps Western, influences are evident: mass media, sound reinforcement, concert and touring performances, professional musicians, and the music industry.

Musical Aspects

Ethnomusicologists also observe the extent to which a society is affected by outside political, economic, and cultural factors. They study to what extent its people accept or accommodate outside influences, making such influences a part of the culture—and to what extent people reject or conquer these influences to preserve the purity of the culture. In other words, they examine the extent of acculturation—the process by which a culture assimilates, blends with, or adapts to characteristics and practices of other cultures.

Acculturation

Cultures change, sometimes rapidly, sometimes imperceptibly. In this modern technological age, few cultures have not been affected by outside influences, accepted some of these influences, and changed their behaviors and practices as a result.

Ethnomusicologists have taught us much about music of non-Western cultures, subcultures of American society, and Western-influenced cultures in other parts of the world. They have taught us to take a global rather than an ethnocentric perspective; that is, they have taught us to be interested in more than our own culture and our own music.

Music is part of a culture; but music also resides outside the culture, reflecting and commenting on it. We learn much about a culture or a subculture from its arts: its songs, dances, and other expressions that depict or suggest feelings, attitudes, and important events.

When we take a global perspective and examine diverse musical styles, the problem of labels arises. How do we identify different types of music? Categories or labels are sometimes useful in organizing knowledge, information, concepts, styles, and people, and this book does use them for that purpose; but ambiguity and overlapping frequently occur, and stylistic distinctions are often blurred. Consider, among many influences, the current popularity of crossover and fusion styles, overlapping sales charts, classical composers who incorporate jazz or ethnic music, and jazz musicians who incorporate classical or religious music. Here are a few examples of ambiguous labels:

Labels: A Help or a Hindrance?

- George Gershwin is a composer of classical music and popular music—in the same pieces! *Rhapsody in Blue* (symphonic music) and *Porgy and Bess* (an opera) contain elements of both classical and popular styles. Gershwin also wrote songs for Broadway that were later arranged for string quartet. Does this make them art songs and a part of the classical music repertoire?

- A folk song typically grows out of a cultural group, and its composer or creator is often unknown. Yet the writers or composers of many well-known contemporary folk songs are known. Woody Guthrie, Pete Seeger, and Bob Dylan wrote songs that seemed very personal, were learned by memory, and at the same time became commercially successful. These composed songs were originally part of popular music genres but then became part of the folk music tradition.
- A popular song falls into the category of commercial music, that is, music intended to become commercially successful, even a hit. But if such a song doesn't become popular, it still remains in the category of popular music.
- Classical music is not popular or commercial music, yet contemporary composers want their music to sell and be performed.

What is the difference between a popular song and a pop song? Between pop music and soul or rock? Between blues, rhythm and blues, and soul? Does soul include blues or

Ravi Shankar: the world's best-known sitar player.

Eric Clapton, a legendary rock guitarist.

Joan Baez and Bob Dylan, folk musicians.

A guitarrón player.

Andrés Segovia, a
classical guitar player.

rap? Are there differences between rap and hip-hop? What labels will we use five years from now?

How do we classify new age music? As jazz, classical, or pop? As all or neither? What is alternative music? Is it a separate and distinct category? What is it an alternative to? As alternative artists or albums become more popular and move into the mainstream, does their music continue to be alternative music?

When is a popular song traditional and when is it contemporary? When is a song pop and when is it rock? When is a song gospel and when is it contemporary Christian? When is a song soul and when is it rhythm and blues (R&B)? And on and on.

Stylistic differences are sometimes very obvious, so designating a label is clear. Frequently, however, labeling is not so easy. Within the category of popular music but also between classical and popular or jazz styles, considerable overlap should be expected, particularly with today's propensity for crossover and fusion styles. Many artists reflect characteristics of more than one style from album to album, from song to song, and even within a song, and some music defies any label.

What matters and what doesn't? To repeat, labels can be helpful in organizing information and classifying music. Use labels and benefit from them, but do not adhere to them rigidly. Do not spend much time and energy defending one label or another. Do not assume that another person—particularly the instructor—is wrong about a label!

Artists and Artistry

An artist is one who paints or sculpts—a visual artist. An artist also is one who performs in whatever medium with creativity and sensitivity and with the ability to communicate with an audience. In this context, one plays artistically, that is, in a manner that is expressive, consistent in style, and based on musical, cultural, and historical knowledge. Artistic performance in music applies to all styles but is too often used only in the context of "high art," that of the western European classical music tradition.

In another context, one who performs music regardless of style is usually referred to as an artist, a usage common in the popular music industry. "She's a great artist." "Many artists show up on 'Billboard' charts."

Many of the artists included in this book are well known; others are little known or their identities are unknown. Artists are well known because they have gained national and international reputations from recording sales, tours, prestigious performances, rave reviews, and awards and honors. Yet many outstanding artists live in your communities and regions, perhaps never attempting national or international careers. They play at street festivals and county fairs and in churches, symphony orchestra halls, and night clubs. Active local artists often have excellent CDs to sell. Read the performing arts calendars in your local or regional newspapers. Get to know and support your local artists.

Goals for Listening

Representative pieces of recorded music are included on the complete set of five compact discs that accompany this book, and each example has a guide in the text to illustrate applicable concepts and information to assist in the listening process. Collectively, these pieces provide an overview of the vastness, richness, and diversity of music.

Begin now to develop **perceptive listening** skills. Concentrate when listening, and make a commitment to hear all that there is to hear in the music. Develop curiosity and a desire to know why it came to be, what its purpose is, how it serves the people who listen to or otherwise use it, and what one needs to know to understand it better. Think about the music and what you are hearing, and use words to describe what you hear. Think and write about your reactions to this music and how it is similar to or different from music that you already know and enjoy.

No prior musical skills are necessary to understand that music exists throughout the world and has existed for many centuries, that people make music a part of their lives for many different reasons, and that the world's musical styles are as varied as the world's people. Also, no prior musical skills are necessary to listen perceptively—with concentration, interest, and energy. Since you most likely already listen to music, maybe extensively, you can build on your own skills in order to listen perceptively.

The musical examples below are brief excerpts from a variety of musical pieces, each of which is presented in a fuller version in a later chapter. Collectively they provide a sense of the magnificent diversity of music and illustrate its infinite variety. These initial listening experiences will serve you well throughout this book since the skills that are needed will become more sophisticated. Concentrate as you listen, and remember that these first examples are only the beginning of an enriching music listening experience.

Listening Experiences: A Collage of Musical Styles

Consider each example and describe the music as you think about these questions:

- How do you respond to the diversity of musical examples? Which ones do you like the most? The least? Why?
- Which ones have the strongest beat? The weakest? Is stronger better? Describe any patterns you perceive in the organization of beats.
- Describe the quality of sounds you hear that are common in all examples. On one or only a few? Which sounds did you find most interesting? Why?
- Describe the levels of musical activity—from calmness and quietness to restlessness and high energy. Which pieces are consistently at one level or the other?

ollage of Musical Sounds

"Sylvie"

A composed folk song
Performed by Sweet Honey in the Rock
Composed by Huddie Ledbetter ("Leadbelly") — **CD1, Track 1, :45**

"Bourgeois Blues" (excerpt)

Blues
Performed by Taj Mahal
Composed by Huddie Ledbetter ("Leadbelly") — **CD1, Track 2, 1:05**

"Taking a Chance on Love"

Big band jazz
Performed by Benny Goodman and His Orchestra with Helen Forrest, vocal.
CD1, Track 3, 1:04

"Backtrackin' "

Traditional bluegrass
Performed by the Nashville Bluegrass Band — **CD1, Track 4, :47**

"Magonde" (Song for the Chief) (excerpt)

Traditional mbira music of Zimbabwe — **CD1, Track 5, 1:06**

"Yo Le Le"

Popular music from Senegal
Performed by Youssou N'Dour — **CD1, Track 6, 1:03**

String Quartet, op. 33, no. 2 ("The Joke") (II—Scherzo) (excerpt)

Classical chamber music
Composed in 1791 by Franz Joseph Haydn
Performed by the Tátrai Quartet — **CD1, Track 7, 1:06**

Symphony No. 1 (III)

Contemporary symphonic music
A three-movement work composed by Ellen Taaffe Zwilich
Performed by the Indianapolis Symphony, John Nelson, conductor
CD1, Track 8, 1:13

What is unfamiliar music to some can be profoundly important music to others. Music exists to serve different purposes: to entertain, to uplift, to stimulate feelings and responses, or to enhance certain rituals, from a football game to a high mass.

Summary

Music exists throughout the world. It is part of all cultures, and we learn about other cultures from their music. Ethnomusicologists help us learn about musical acculturation and assimilation. They also help us realize that many cultures, traditions, and ethnic groups produce an infinite variety of music, of which any one person can come to know only a small part.

People make judgments about music and develop their own attitudes, tastes, and preferences. Most of us have a relatively narrow range, preferring styles we know well, perhaps grew up with, and feel comfortable with. This book will help you build and expand on what you already know, so that you can gain an understanding of what is less familiar and examine relationships, similarities, and differences among different musical styles. Additionally, *The World of Music* may stimulate you to find new music you like and value and may help you acquire a sense of what exists beyond the limits of your own experience.

When we recognize the diversity of music and acquire a global perspective, categorizing music, defining terms, organizing musical styles and genres, and giving them labels can be useful; but labeling can also be problematic when applied too rigidly. Musical styles frequently overlap, and lines of distinction frequently are ambiguous.

2

Vocabulary for Listening and Understanding

The Nature of Music

Summary

Terms and Concepts

Definitions of music

Music as science

Music as art

Silence

Movement through time

Expressive quality

Artistic quality

Functional quality

Universality

Psychological aspects

Creative process

Performance process

Listening process

As your exploration of the world of music proceeds, your sense of what music is and what music is to you will probably become more clear, more understandable, and more inclusive. This exploration begins with a consideration of three possible definitions of music. The core of this chapter is a look at the nature of music according to its physical or acoustical characteristics and its aesthetic, expressive, and functional qualities.

What is music? Music eludes easy definition, as can be seen from the following possible definitions

"Music is sound that is pleasing to the ear." Most of us respond well to sounds that we like. But if pleasing means only pretty or beautiful, then much music is excluded under this definition. Music can be noisy, loud, raucous—anything but pleasing. Music does not have to be beautiful or pleasing to be music, unless one's concept of what is beautiful or pleasing is very broad. And what about music that may sound pleasing to us but not to others or music that may have a larger purpose than to sound pleasing. Such a definition excludes much western European art music composed in the last 100 years as well as much music representative of some non–western European cultures.

"Music is sound and silence organized in time." This definition is relatively objective, because it includes all music from any place at any time. It avoids the subjective. But a person listening to music that may seem to be noisy, weird, displeasing, and ugly may judge: "To my ear, this isn't music!" We cannot really define music without subjective factors—taste, judgment, and personal reactions—as exemplified in the common expression, "I don't know anything about music, but I know what I like."

"Music is sound that you want to hear as music." Sound that is not organized in some fashion typically cannot be called music. Yet the roar of a waterfall, the sound of rain falling on a tent, or the chirping of birds can be "music to my ears." These sounds are music not in the objective sense but as pleasing and, thus, perhaps musical sounds. In fact, the sounds of birds, water, whales, and other sounds of nature have been taped and used in "organized" music. Conversely, all sorts of drums, cymbals, and gongs; harsh, dissonant harmonies; and abstract, totally unsingable melodies have been organized into music. However, are such creations really music? As at least one student has asked, "What would prompt a person to write something like that?" Still, incorporating sounds that might be perceived as noise can be music if you want it to be. If one does not like a certain style of music, one can still respect it, value the creative process that produced it, and learn from it. Perhaps you will want to create your own definition of music.

Definitions of Music

The physical characteristics of music involve principles of **acoustics,** physics, mathematics, and engineering. People who are aware of the scientific aspects of music include those interested in specifications (specs) of stereo components, in sound reinforcement at recording studios and concerts, in the creation and performance of electronical or computer-generated music, and in the acoustical design of rooms and concert halls.

Physical Characteristics

Acoustics is the science of sound and the physical basis of music (see appendix A). It is applied to the construction of musical instruments, audio equipment, auditoriums, recording studios, homes, and offices and to medical technology through sonar (sound-related) diagnostics and treatment.

Music as a Science

Audio enthusiasts refer to principles of acoustics when they use such terms as *frequency range, echo, graphic equalizers,* and *signal-to-noise ratios.* For example, the quality of

The interior shapes of walls, floors, and ceilings affect the sound heard by the listener.

audio speakers is measured in part by their frequency response as specified by the range of frequencies they can produce. To produce music, an audiophile will want a speaker system with the widest frequency response.

Acoustical engineers design recording studios and auditoriums according to certain principles, such as resonance and reverberation (echo). The shapes of interior walls, floors, and ceilings all affect the sound heard by the listener. For example, saying that a room has good acoustics means that the degree of resonance and reverberation is suited to the purposes of the room. Thus, a facility that is constructed of a considerable amount of porous material will absorb sound waves and create "dead" acoustics. Conversely, a facility constructed of hard, dense material will bounce the sound waves around the room, resulting in "live," or highly resonant, acoustics. Computer technology has taken most of the guesswork out of sound design and acoustical treatment of auditoriums, sanctuaries, and other facilities.

Music as Sound and Silence

Music is an aural phenomenon; we listen and respond to it as sound. Yet silence—from short rests to long, dramatic pauses—is also very much a part of music. Many composers of classical music recognize the importance of silence as a compositional technique with its own aesthetic and dramatic effects, rather than silence being merely a rest from sound.

Music as Movement through Time

Music, like motion pictures, moves from one moment to the next. To appreciate music (or movies), it is important to remember what happened before and to anticipate what is about to happen. By contrast, photos, paintings, and pottery are static. What is seen at one moment will still be there the next moment.

Much music moves forward with energy and momentum, in a predictable progression, to a clear conclusion such as the end of a phrase (similar to how a phrase functions in prose and poetry). Other music may move through time with less noticeable forward energy; such music may seem static, suspended in time, without a clear phrase structure.

settings that ranged from labor halls to the White House. Their performances included songs about abolition and women's rights (especially women's suffrage). In developing this repertoire, the Hutchinsons helped establish a new genre of American music and a radical tradition in American folk and popular music that has been continued by Woodie Guthrie, the Almanac Singers, Pete Seeger, Bob Dylan, and Joan Baez. More recent popular artists have also created songs to describe, reflect on, and perhaps advocate the improvement of social conditions; such artists include Bruce Springsteen (the working class), Willie Nelson (farmers), Elton John and many other artists (AIDS), and many rap performers (urban conditions). Contemporary performers often participate in benefits for their favorite causes, using their music to mobilize support and especially funds.

Rally songs have been used to promote union organization, political candidates, and patriotism. Protest songs have promoted causes (prohibition, civil rights) and condemned wars (the Mexican-American war; the Vietnam war). A rally or protest song may have been composed, or someone may have written new words to a well-known folk or popular song, in effect creating a new folk song.

Composed folk songs are also discussed briefly in chapter 7 as a form of popular music; which reflects the ambiguity of music composed in folk style. A composed folk song may have been published in printed form, recorded, and sold commercially, and then learned from memory (transmitted orally). Thus, at times, the line between a folk and a popular song is not very clear. Examples of familiar, composed folk songs include "So Long, It's Been Good to Know You" and "This Land Is Your Land," written by Woody Guthrie; "Blowin' in the Wind," written by Bob Dylan; and "Where Have All the Flowers Gone?" written by Pete Seeger.

Dancing has always been an important part of the lives of Americans of all backgrounds; thus instrumental dance music is a vital part of traditional folk music. The fiddle has been the primary melody instrument in virtually all instrumental folk dance traditions, and fiddle tunes were a common genre of folk dance music. These tunes were arranged for various instrumental groups, notably the string band, which in the nineteenth century featured fiddle and banjo. Today, they are performed by many bluegrass bands (see chap. 7). The guitar became popular only in the twentieth century. Listen to Listening Guide 7 (page 50) for examples of two popular fiddle tunes.

Dance Music

"Negro **spirituals**" typically are Europeanized versions of the religious folk songs of southern blacks that emerged in the early nineteenth century. These songs may have been created by slaves or may have been adaptations of camp meeting hymns or existing folk songs from the white culture. Notated concert arrangements of spirituals made this music famous worldwide; to this day, they are popular pieces in the repertoire of professional and amateur soloists and choirs, regularly performed in churches and concert halls. But western European notation cannot adequately reproduce the slides, "tone bending" (slight lowering of the pitch and then returning to the original pitch) and other fluctuations in pitch and rhythm that were and are an integral part of the performance style of black folksinging and that more accurately reflect the black experience that inspired this music.

The secular counterpart of the spiritual is the **blues**, a style of music that was to have considerable influence on jazz, rhythm and blues, soul, rock, and other forms of more recent American popular music. Some performers specialize in "singing the blues." This is one of the most powerful means of musical communication; the feelings evoked by the music and the text may be mournful or melancholy, but the intent is to lift the spirits of

Spirituals and the Blues

L istening Guide

Two fiddle tunes

A. "Soldier's Joy"

Performed by Gid Tanner and his Skillet Lickers, a rural string band from north Georgia—two fiddles, banjo, guitar, and vocal.

Recorded in 1929.

B. "Soppin' the Gravy"

Performed by Nashville Bluegrass Band—fiddle, banjo, guitar, mandolin, bass.
From the album *Waitin' for the Hard Times to Go* (1993) — **CD1, Tracks 17–18, 5:19
(SCD) CD1, Track 7, 2:25**

Goals

Describe the melodic style of each fiddle tune.
Focus on the bass line to help recognize chord changes.
Identify phrase patterns.

Guides

A. ("Soldier's Joy")

In duple meter. Count in a moderately fast two. The first two themes (a and b) are instrumental. Theme c is vocal. All phrases have eight bars and the following basic chord progressions; but concentrate on hearing the tonic (I) and dominant (V) chords:

```
a  I  --   --   V  I  IV  V  I
b  I  IV   I    V  I  IV  V  I
c  I  --   --   V  I  --  IV  I
```

| 0:00 | Intro | One guitar chord and commentary designed to get the listener into a mood for dancing |
| | Verse 1 | Instrumental |

			1	2	3	4	5	6	7	8
0:13	a a	Descending motive at the beginning	I	2	3	4	5	6	7	8
			I	--	--	V	I	IV	V	I
0:29	b b	Ascending motive at the beginning	I	IV	I	V	I	IV	V	I
0:44	Verse 2	c a b b (c is vocal) The chords to the c theme are:	I	--	--	V	I	--	IV	I
1:15	Verse 3	c a a b								
1:45	Verse 4	c a a b b								
2:23	Verse 5	c a a b—ends with tag (each a phrase is modified)								

B. ("Soppin' the Gravy")

In duple meter—in a moderately fast two. Theme a, theme b, and theme c each have one phrase (eight bars) and a repetition of that phrase (eight bars).

The form is a b c a b c a b c Tag.

—Continued

Listening Guide — *Continued*   *No.* 7

Reflections

Can "Soldier's Joy" be perceived as duple meter with four beats to the bar instead of two? What are the advantages and disadvantages of the many repeated patterns and phrases? Each phrase of the first example begins and ends on the tonic chord (I), with midpoints (fourth bar) ending on the dominant (V); listen for these sounds. Which are the chords of movement? Which are the chords of rest?

Describe the similarities and differences between the styles of the two fiddle tunes and the fiddle playing. In "Soppin' the Gravy," what do the other instrumental parts (guitar, banjo, mandolin, and bass) add to the style?

people who are "feeling blue." It is significant that the blues is discussed or at least referred to in chapters 3, 4, 6 through 8, and 15 of this book, suggesting the importance of its role in American folk, jazz, popular, and classical music.

Blues evolved into specific forms: the three-line poetic stanza form of poetry and the 12-bar blues form of music. These are common structures, but each has many exceptions.

The first line of poetry is usually repeated and followed by a contrasting third line (a a b form). The poetry most frequently has a sense of mistreatment or injustice—the misery of an oppressed people or of someone who has lost or been abandoned by a lover or a loved one.

The original Fisk Jubilee Singers (1873), who helped make the Negro spiritual universally popular.

I got a brownskin woman, she's all right with me.
I got a brownskin woman, she's all right with me.
Got the finest woman that a man most ever seen.

Lord, I can't stay here, and my lover gone.
Lord, I can't stay here, and my lover gone.
Sometimes I wonder, my brownskin she won't come home.

The music reflects the poetic structure, with four bars of music to each of the three lines of poetry, adding up to the common 12-bar blues. Over time this 12-bar musical structure has evolved into the following:

- A regular pattern of chords—a relatively consistent chord progression.
- A blues scale created by alterations to certain pitches, known as "blue notes."
- A blues feeling that performers enhance by bending tones or sliding into or out of pitches to enhance their moaning, mournful "bluesy" quality. A gifted blues singer uses all these patterns and alterations to create the feel of the blues. Listen to Listening Guides 8 and 9 below and others.

The 12-bar blues form is found in all styles of jazz and in much popular music, including rock. It forms the basis of boogie woogie and much popular music of the mid-twentieth century, such as urban blues; popular forms of early rock and roll (rockabilly), and the zydeco style (the music of the French-speaking African Americans from southwestern Louisiana). Listen to Listening Guide 35 (page 00).

istening Guide   *No.* **8**

"Death Letter" (excerpt)

Traditional country blues—in this case, an example of delta blues (blues from the Mississippi delta).
Performed by Son House, vocal and guitar.
Recorded in 1965 — **CD1, Track 19, 1:46**

Goals

Describe guitar timbre.
Identify places in the music where chords change.
Recognize the sounds and patterns of the blues, especially the phrase structure of the 12-bar blues and a typical chord progression.

Guide

Count the pulse in a moderate four. I = tonic sound, V = dominant sound, IV = subdominant sound.

Intro	A three-bar vamp
First	1--2--3--4--5--6--7--8--9--10--11--12--
chorus	I -- -- -- IV -- I -- V IV I --

Three more choruses with the same structure.

—Continued

Bluesman Son House.

Reflections

Recognize the sounds and patterns of the blues, especially the chord structure and vocal style.

Recognize interpretive qualities in the singing and the guitar playing that help define the blues: pitch bending, slides, and blue notes.

Which are the chords of movement? Which are the chords of rest?

Compare Son House's guitar playing with that of bowed string instruments. How are his sounds different from folk guitar, rock guitar, and classical guitar sounds?

Compare House's vocal quality and style with those of other singers.

L i s t e n i n g   G u i d e   *No.* **9**

"Bourgeois Blues"—two versions

Words and music by Huddie Ledbetter.

  A. Traditional blues
      Performed by Huddie Ledbetter (Leadbelly), vocal and guitar.
  B. Urban blues
      Performed by Taj Mahal, vocal, 12-string guitar, piano; Ralph Rinzler, mandolin.
      CD1, Tracks 20–21, 4:20 (SCD) CD1, Tracks 8–9, 4:20

—Continued

Leadbelly.

Taj Mahal.

Huddie Ledbetter (1885–1949) was born in Louisiana and became a world-renowned singer and songwriter. Although he was first recorded for the Library of Congress by John and Alan Lomax, most of his recordings are with Folkways Records. His songs reflect the African American culture in the first half of the twentieth century. "Bourgeois Blues" is a song about black immigrants in large cities, in this case, Washington, D.C. Other well-known songs by Leadbelly include "Grey Goose," "Good Night Irene," and "Sylvie" (see Listening Guide 1).

Taj Mahal, a blues singer from New York City (born in 1940), uses elements of other cultures, particularly elements from the Caribbean (such as reggae and West Indian), in his music. His music ranges in style from country blues, sometimes electrified, to soul and rock.

Goals

Describe the blues vocal and instrumental style, the blues form, and the blues chord progressions.

Guide

Duple meter in four. Strong rhythmic impulse. The chord progression for each chorus is common:

  A. (Leadbelly)
     Eight-bar guitar intro.
     Three vocal choruses.

—Continued

B. (Taj Mahal)
   Spoken intro followed by a one-bar vamp.
   Five vocal choruses and two choruses with mandolin lead.

Bars: 1   2   3   4   5   6   7   8   9   10   11   12
       I   -- -- -- IV -- I   -- V   IV   I   --

Reflections

Compare the two renditions. Notice Leadbelly's rhythmic flexibility and increase in tempo.

Notice Taj Mahal's accompaniment—guitar, mandolin, and piano. Describe the style and the respective contributions of the performers.

Folk Roots: An Expanded View

Only a thin line separates certain genres of American popular music from their roots in folk music. For example, there is a close relationship between the traditional folk music of the Appalachian Mountain area in the southeastern United States and hillbilly music; between string band folk music and early bluegrass, and between camp meeting and revival songs and southern gospel music. Thus, to some extent, the roots of certain contemporary genres of American popular music—especially country, blues, and gospel—lie in America's southern folk music.

A significant impetus for this broadening of the sources of folk music was and continues to be the thousands of concerts and festivals of folk, blues, bluegrass, and jazz festivals that take place each year, many of which are huge commercial enterprises. Among the best known are the Newport Folk Festival, the Newport Jazz Festival, the New Orleans Jazz Festival, the San Francisco Blues Festival, and the Smithsonian Folk Arts Festival.

Ethnic Traditions

In the United States, the folk songs and dances of immigrants began in the traditional folk manner: They brought their own. Then, as they became assimilated, they allowed composed folk music and music borrowed from other American subcultures to become their own. This description applies to the folk music and dances of the white Cajuns (French Canadians) and the French-speaking black immigrants who settled in southwestern Louisiana; to the Mexican Americans (*tejanos*) who settled along the Texas-Mexican border; and to the Puerto Rican, Mexican, Polish, and Italian immigrants (among others) who created urban ethnic neighborhoods. American ethnic (immigrant) music is discussed further in chapter 8. (A textbook like this one cannot be all-encompassing, and so the music of the increasingly important Asian immigrant communities and cultural traditions is not discussed here; but perhaps a future text can include these and others, for example, the indigenous music of Alaska and Hawaii.)

A Folk Revival

A revival, in this context, is a resurgence or a return to popularity of a previously existing, perhaps once popular, genre. Examples of revival genres include ragtime, klezmer, Native American songs and dances (through pow-wows that are popular tourist attractions), and folk music in the United States and elsewhere. A revival usually involves the

Bob Dylan at the
Newport Folk Festival,
1965.

Newport 1963.

interest and participation of performers outside the tradition that originally produced the genre. The revival discussed here is the folk song revival of the 1960s.

This revival, according to some scholars, began in 1958 with the recording of a version of an old folk ballad, "Tom Dooley," by an aspiring pop group called The Kingston Trio. In that year, this song soared to number 5 on the charts in the United Kingdom and number 1 in the United States. In the music industry, that kind of success generates interest by other artists and other record companies. By the early 1960s, recordings of folk songs and, more commonly, songs composed in the manner of folk songs became an extremely important part of the music industry and of popular culture. Many of these songs were versions of traditional folk songs and ballads; others served as rally and

istening Guide   *No.* **10**

"The Night They Drove Old Dixie Down"

A song from the folk music revival of the 1960s

Performed by Joan Baez, vocal—with guitar, bass, drums, group singing (added to the choruses).
Composed by J. Robbie Robertson.
From the album *Blessed Are . . .* (1972).
Also on other Baez albums, most recently on *Ring Them Bells* (1995)
CD1, Track 22, 3:21 (SCD) CD1, Track 10, 3:22

Joan Baez is a folksinger who first became famous while singing in the coffeehouses of the Boston area in the late 1950s. She was a hit at the Newport Folk Festival in 1959. Baez became a peace activist and humanitarian and received many awards, including honorary doctorates. Through the years, she always tried to balance her activism and her music. "The Night They Drove Old Dixie Down" was the title track of her successful album in 1971; it reached the American charts at number 5 and was in the top 40 for 15 weeks. Her most recent albums include *Diamonds and Rust in the Bullring* (1989), *Play Me Backwards* (1992), and *Ring Them Bells* (1995)

Goals

Describe the rhythmic impulse—weak, moderate, or strong.
Describe the differences between verse and chorus.
Describe how repetition contributes to the effectiveness of this song.
Identify the instruments.
Define a vamp.
Describe the vocal quality of the singer. Compare the singing style of Baez with other folksingers and with singers in other genres.

Guide

This song is a narrative ballad (a story) in verse-chorus form. The instrumental accompaniment features drums, bass, and guitar. A brief instrumental passage (vamp) precedes each verse.

Intro
Verse
Chorus
Vamp
Verse
Chorus
Vamp
Verse
Chorus

—Continued

Reflections

Does the "sing-along" in the choruses of Joan Baez's song add to or detract from the music?

What is most striking about this piece?

How is it a folk song? How is it not a folk song?

Is this song strophic? Why or Why not?

Discuss the symbolism and meaning of the text.

protest songs; still others were contemporary ballads and more lyrical folklike pop songs. Most were recorded with minimal instrumentation; often the singers were accompanied by a guitar. Typical settings were hootenannies (gatherings at which folksingers entertained and audience members frequently joined in), coffeehouses and small clubs in Greenwich Village, and eventually similar places in other urban areas. Newsletters, magazines, books, and radio shows were devoted to this new folk music. That was the typical popular music environment of the early 1960s—urban folk music, until Bob Dylan added the electric guitar in 1965, confounding the devotees of folk and stimulating a new genre: folk rock. Among the best known urban folksingers of this time, in addition to Dylan, were Arlo Guthrie; Joan Baez; Peter, Paul, and Mary; and Simon and Garfunkel.

Traditional folk music is, by definition, created anonymously, learned through the process of oral tradition, and performed by amateurs in nonprofessional settings. But the music of the 1960s was none of these, especially after electric instruments were added. Was it, then, not folk music? Or had the definition of folk music changed?

Urban Blues   Scholars and others who studied the blues created labels, such as folk blues, country blues, classic blues, rhythm and blues, Chicago blues, urban blues, and even urbane blues. In the early part of the twentieth century, country blues singers, particularly from the Mississippi delta, moved to northern cities, and classic blues singers, notably Ma Rainey and Bessie Smith, performed with jazz and blues bands and paved the way for later jazz-blues singers such as Billie Holiday, Ella Fitzgerald, and Sarah Vaughan. (See "African American Influences" in chap. 7.)

In the 1940s and 1950s, blues singers added electric guitar, a rhythm section, and sometimes horns; their new style came to be known as *urban blues,* one of several categories of blues. (A related genre is zydeco, or Cajun blues—see chap. 8, p. 165). Urban blues had moved beyond traditional folk blues; the songs were now composed, recorded, and sold, though they were not produced and distributed by mainstream record labels until the second half of the twentieth century.

In 1949, *Billboard* magazine gave this genre the name *rhythm and blues,* or R&B. It has become a recognized and important genre of American popular music and of the music industry. The king of R&B (urban blues) is B. B. King. However, today, R&B seems to be a label for a wide spectrum of African American pop music rather than only blues-based music (see "African American Influences", chap. 7).

Bessie Smith.

Other prominent artists include Muddy Waters, T-Bone Walker, Lightn'n Hopkins, and Howlin' Wolf. Several early rock artists based much of their repertoire on the blues, including the Rolling Stones, Jimi Hendrix, and Cream (with Eric Clapton). Contemporary rock-oriented blues musicians include Etta James, Robert Cray, John Hammond Jr., and Eric Clapton. Blues bands are currently popular; they are heard regularly at blues festivals and at clubs and community events in almost any city.

Listening Guide   No. 11

"Call It Stormy Monday"

Early rhythm and blues (urban blues).

Performed by B. B. King and the B. B. King Orchestra.

Features Albert Collins, vocal and guitar.

Composed by Aaron T. Walker.

Recorded in Memphis in 1993 — **CD1, Track 23, 7:17 (SCD) CD1, Track 11, 7:17**

B. B. King, born in 1925, began as a plantation worker in Mississippi and became an international superstar as a blues guitarist and singer. He started his career in Memphis, has been recording since 1949, and has been a national figure since 1952. He always wanted to give the blues a higher status, and made it more acceptable. He moved it into the mainstream of American popular music, but at the same time he maintained close contact with his roots.

—Continued

B. B. King.

Goals

Besides 12-bar choruses and the standard chord progressions, identify those elements of music and style that make this a blues song, vocally and instrumentally.

During repeated listening, follow the bass line that supports the chord progressions, the guitar and its varied sounds, the piano and how it is used, the backup instrumentalists and how they are used, and the words—to find out how B. B. King describes his week.

Describe the roles and prominent patterns of various instruments or instrumental combinations (such as background instruments, drums, and keyboard).

Guide

10 blues choruses:	1	Instrumental
	2–4	B. B. King, vocal
	5–7	Albert Collins
	8–10	B. B. King, vocal

Reflections

Compare this performance with those by Leadbelly, Taj Mahal, and Son House (in this chapter) and with those by Little Richard (chap. 7) and Clifton Chenier (chap. 8).

Does this performance illustrate the style and the feel of the blues? To the extent that it does, how important is strict adherence to the traditional 12-bar chord progression (I -- -- -- IV -- I -- V IV I --) as revealed in previous examples. What is lost in the phrases that deviate from traditional patterns?

How is Albert Collins's singing and playing different from B. B. King's?

The study of traditional American folk music and the blues provides two important benefits: (1) an insight into America's musical history through an understanding of the styles that have been an important part of the lives of many Americans and (2) an understanding of how music evolves and of the contexts in which musical styles change—for example, from traditional to commercial urban folk music, and from country and urban blues to rhythm and blues (R&B).

Summary

Additionally, the relatively simple folk music and blues forms provide a foundation for the study of more complicated music. The musical characteristics and techniques of folk and blues contribute to the development of listening skills. By now, musical perception should include recognizing meters and phrases, counting the number of bars in phrases to discern form, recognizing cadences and whether they are open or closed, hearing changes in chords, and recognizing the sound and function of the most familiar chords.

Additional Listening

Example   No. 1

Appalachian Spring: Suite (Doppio movimento—excerpt)

Ballet music that incorporates a Shaker folk tune.

Music composed by Aaron Copland; originally a ballet.

Performed by the New York Philharmonic; Leonard Bernstein, conductor.

First performed in 1945 — **CD1, Track 24, 3:02**

This excerpt consists of five variations on the Shaker tune "Simple Gifts." The Shakers were a religious sect that formed around the time of the American Revolution. They produced thousands of songs, of which very few survive today. "Simple Gifts" is the best-known Shaker song that has survived. Here are the words to this simple folklike tune:

> 'Tis the gift to be simple, 'tis the gift to be free,
> 'Tis the gift to come down where we ought to be;
> And when we find ourselves in the place just right,
> 'Twill be in the valley of love and delight.

> Chorus:
> When true simplicity is gained,
> To bow and to bend we shan't be ashamed;
> To turn, turn will be our delight,
> Till by turning, turning we come out right.

Goals

Describe the melody.

Identify instruments.

Recognize changes from one variation to the next: melodic and rhythmic characteristics, tempo, loudness, mood, texture.

—Continued

E x a m p l e   *No.* **1** — *Continued*

Aaron Copland.

Guide

0:00	Theme	Statement of theme: upper woodwinds, clarinet melody
0:32	Variation 1	Slightly quicker tempo. Oboe melody; bassoon countermelody.
0:58	Variation 2	Full orchestra; melody enters at different times in different registers
1:36	Interlude	Nonthematic material between variations
1:44	Variation 3	Brass: brilliant, solid; violin flourishes heard in background
2:09	Variation 4	Slower and quieter
2:29	Variation 5	Full orchestra; full texture; majestic

Reflections

Describe ways Copland varied the Shaker melody.

What is the purpose of including the interlude?

Consider reasons for the order of the variations. Would other sequences be more, or less, effective?

How effective is a folk tune (or hymn tune) when placed in the context of symphonic music? Does it lose its original character? If so, does that matter?

American Religious Traditions

Goals for Listening

- **Describe** melodic character.
- **Describe** melodic patterns.
- **Recognize** interpretation and embellishment.
- **Describe** rhythmic impulse.
- **Recognize** chord progressions.
- **Notice** changes in loudness.
- **Describe differences in** vocal and instrumental tone qualities.
- **Identify** basic elements of musical structure.
- **Identify** cadences.
- **Identify** phrase patterns.

Summary

Additional Listening

Terms and Concepts

Early American hymns

Hymnody and hymn books

Singing schools, shape-note system, and fasola

Composers and writers

Revival music—the old gospel songs

Black gospel

Southern gospel

Popular contemporary styles

This chapter focuses on American Protestant religious music that developed from the rural and small-town folk culture of white and black Americans. That music was important in the development of American culture. It is emphasized in this book, not because music from other traditions did not exist or was not important, but because the various styles of Protestant music have been prominent and have made a deep impact on American culture. Music from two other traditions is discussed elsewhere in the book: the religious music of the Jewish people in chapter 9 (p. 202), as part of world music; and the liturgical music of the Roman Catholic Church in chapter 10 (p. 215), as part of western European classical music.

American religious music, like folk music, can be examined in both Anglo-American and African American traditions. Until the twentieth century, hymns and songs for revival services and camp meetings belonged to both traditions. As the two styles evolved, differences emerged, and by the mid-twentieth century the two styles were known as black gospel and southern gospel (sometimes called white gospel). Today, much of the music used in churches retains these styles, but much contemporary religious music has taken on more characteristics of pop and rock and has become part of our popular culture.

White gospel music (like Anglo-American folk music) was originally influenced by British hymns and songs. As people moved southward and westward from New England, their religious music took on a distinctive, folklike character that separated it stylistically from the more refined, formal British music.

The distinctive black gospel music was derived largely from the musical expressions of freed slaves and their descendants in the Deep South, combined with British-influenced hymns and songs that became Americanized as they moved into the South from New England. By the mid-twentieth century, popular elements had crept into traditional black gospel music. Today, as with white gospel, much black religious music outside the church incorporates elements of pop and rock.

Goals for Listening

The primary purpose, as before, is to increase your awareness of and your ability to describe the following individual and interactive musical elements:

- *Basic characteristics of melody.* Describe melodic character: simple, singable, and conjunct. Begin to recognize musical lines other than melody. Describe melodic patterns (ascending or descending; repetition in other voice parts) and recognize themes or motives. Recognize personal interpretations and melodic embellishments.
- *Basic elements of rhythm.* Identify characteristics of tempo, downbeats (bars), and meter. Describe rhythmic impulse: the character of the rhythm (a driving beat, a fluid rhythm, or a weak or uneven pulse).
- *Basic elements of harmony and tonality.* Recognize harmonic style, chord changes, chord progressions, and modulation. Become more skillful at recognizing the three primary chords. Their names signify their relationship to one another: The tonic chord is a chord of rest, and the dominant and subdominant are chords of movement.
- *Degrees of loudness.* Describe varying loudness, noticing any changes within a piece of music.
- *Qualities of tone production.* Increase your skill at describing differences in vocal and instrumental qualities and identifying instruments.
- *Basic elements of musical structure and style.* Identify open and closed cadences and question-answer phrase patterns. Identify style and the elements that contribute to it. For example, what musical characteristics give black gospel its sound?

Listening examples in this chapter include two hymns from *The Sacred Harp*, a white southern gospel song, a traditional black gospel song, three variants of a well-known southern spiritual song, and an example of contemporary Christian popular music.

This is a brief discussion of some highlights of the early years of mainstream American Protestant religious music.

Early American Hymn Singing

Psalm Singing

America was settled in the early 1600s by English, Dutch, and French immigrants; and the English Pilgrims and Puritans who first settled in Massachusetts brought with them the practice of singing psalms. Both groups had fled religious persecution and wanted to establish colonies where they could observe their religion in freedom. The religious practices of these early immigrants included the unaccompanied singing of metered and rhymed versions of the psalms. Two widely divergent styles of **psalm singing** emerged during this nation's first 100 years; a European, refined style found among the more urban and more musically literate populace and a less sophisticated folklike style found among rural people and the less musically educated.

The refined style involved singing hymns in harmony from printed music. It was part of the notated tradition; the singers had to be able to read music. The folk style became a popular part of the oral tradition and led to the creation of a body of traditional folk hymns.

Psalm singing had a profound effect on the development of American religious music. It was preferred by the early settlers over the liturgical music of the Roman Catholic Church and over Lutheran chorales because these English immigrants were averse to state religion and ecclesiastical power.

Psalters

The Puritans and the Pilgrims both used English **psalters**—hymnbooks that provided settings of the psalms to be sung during worship. The Pilgrims used Henry Ainsworth's psalter, *The Book of Psalmes: Englished both in Prose and Metre*, published in 1612. This book included 39 melodies, one of which was the "Old Hundredth," commonly known today as the "Doxology" (see fig. 5.1). The Puritans favored a psalter by Sternhold and Hopkins, published in several editions; its third edition in 1553 included 51 psalm settings but no hymn tunes. For the music, the Puritans used a published collection of 97 four-part harmonizations of psalm tunes by leading English composers of the day. It was compiled and published in 1621 by Thomas Ravenscroft.

In 1556, a version of the Sternhold and Hopkins' psalter with music was published. A version published in 1562 contained all 150 psalms and became the standard hymnbook for all Protestants in America and for many in England. More than 600 editions appeared, the first in 1562 and the last in 1828. The first American psalter was published in 1640 in Cambridge, Massachusetts. Printed on a press that had been brought from England, it was the first book of any kind published in British North America. It was known as the *Bay Psalm Book* and included no music. Seventy American editions were published through 1773, 18 editions were published in England, and 22 editions were published in Scotland. The first edition with music appeared in 1698.

Lining Out

The music in the psalters did not benefit people who could not read music—and there were many such people, particularly in rural areas. To sing the hymns, many rural congregations practiced **lining out**, a technique that involved their own memory and the leadership of someone with a powerful voice; the leader would sing one line at a time, and the congregation would sing it back. Lining out, a form of call and response, was not a new idea; it had begun in England and Scotland. In fact, it is still a common practice today in some rural regions of the United States, such as eastern Kentucky.

Like most music practices derived from oral tradition (in which music is perpetuated by memory rather than notation), lining out did not ensure consistency or accuracy. However, consistency and accuracy were not necessarily desired. Local variations developed, fragments of one tune would find their way into others, and the number of tunes in common use diminished.

Lining out created a style of singing, common in folk traditions, that included florid lines and vocal embellishments (slides, turns, note bending, and other ways of ornamenting the melody) sung by various members of the congregation. People, in effect, changed the melodies according to their own musical taste and ability. Without strong direction, singers tended to sing in their own way at tempos that accommodated the slowest singers. Another reason for slow tempos was that the leader, in singing each line, interrupted the flow of the congregation's singing.

Singing Schools

Psalm singing began with notated music, but the oral tradition eventually became prevalent. By the early eighteenth century, dissatisfaction with the state of psalm singing was being expressed, particularly in New England. Essays were written and sermons preached decrying this folk style and the practice of lining out. It was felt that the "proper" tradition of psalm singing had been lost. The critics urged a return to singing from musical notation, and this led to the establishment of **singing schools**.

In New England around 1720, a few ministers decided to do something to improve this "deplorable" state of psalm singing. The singing school was created to get people to sing together "decently" and with "some semblance of art." More specifically, the participants, many of whom were teenagers and young adults, would come together for an evening or, in some cases, for two or three days to learn to read music and to learn more hymn tunes. The leader was usually an itinerant "singing master." The young people also came to make friends and to have a good time.

In eighteenth-century America, religious life took on dual functions: the church served not only as a place for worship but also as the town meeting place, the center of community life, both sacred and secular. However, psalm singing took place in homes, in taverns, and outdoors as well as in churches. In some cases, psalm or hymn tunes and secular folk tunes became closely related or interchangeable. Therefore, it was logical to have an important need of the church met by a community activity not affiliated with any particular denomination, and that activity was the singing school. The need for improved singing grew from the church, but the singing schools—like the church—also met the social needs of the community.

Church music was meant for the performer rather than the listener. The idea was to participate in singing, not to be sung to. How the music sounded to a nonparticipant was of little importance. What was important was the experience of performing, which allowed the congregation to be active participants in worship.

The impact of the singing school movement was threefold: (1) it raised the general level of musical literacy, (2) it greatly expanded the repertoire, and (3) it encouraged native composers.

The Fasola and Shape-Note Systems

In Boston in 1721, John Tufts published the first music textbook in America. It was called *Introduction to the Singing of Psalm-Tunes* and included an experiment designed to help people read music. Instead of placing ordinary notes on the staff, Tufts substituted the initial letters of four syllables—fa, sol, la, and mi—which were part of a system known as the **fasola system**, then in wide use in Great Britain. Each syllable represented a different pitch. A full scale would use the syllables as follows:

```
1    2    3    4    5    6    7    8
fa   sol  la   fa   sol  la   mi   fa
```

The purpose of these syllables was the immediate identification of scale degrees. In learning to read music, for example, at singing schools, people would learn a hymn tune using these syllables before adding the words (listen to Listening Guide 12, p. 69). However, Tufts's system was only moderately successful. *The Easy Instructor*, published in Philadelphia in 1801 introduced a **shape-note system** (see figs. 5.1 and 5.2), whereby each pitch of a hymn tune was notated on a staff, but each note head had a distinctive shape that represented a specific pitch. A triangle represented fa, a circle sol, a square la, and a diamond mi. This system used standard notation for rhythm but added the graphic, quickly comprehensible note heads so that people could recognize and sing the correct scale degrees. *The Easy Instructor*, along with other shape-note hymnbooks that soon followed, contained hymns and anthems by New England composers, usually including some pieces by William Billings. These books were used in the singing schools that were organized throughout the South, and so the shape-note system spread. However, new collections that appeared in the next several decades contained pieces that were different from those of New England.

These new collections included three- and four-part hymn settings of melodies that resembled the ballads, songs, and fiddle tunes of the southern oral tradition. The composers were presumably arrangers of indigenous folk melodies. In effect, they captured in notation hundreds of these traditional melodies, arranged them as "folk hymns," and published them in shape-note hymnbooks. The best-known of these hymnbooks were *The Southern Harmony* (1835) and *The Sacred Harp* (1844). Both collections were used widely in singing schools, by church congregations, at social meetings, and at conventions. Conventions and all-day "sings" were organized around these hymnbooks; examples are those sponsored by the United Sacred Harp Musical

Figure **5.1**

A hymn from the oldest known shape-note book, *The Easy Instructor*. The melody is the familiar "Doxology" on the second staff from the bottom.

Source: *White Spirituals in the Southern Uplands*, by George Jackson Pullen.

L istening Guide   *No.* 12

Figure **5.2**

A well-known fuguing tune (listen to 12.A below). It was published in a collection called *The Easy Instructor* (1801), which was printed in shape notes (also called buckwheat notation).

From Music Division, Library of Congress, Washington, D.C. Reprinted by permission.

Two shape-note hymns from *The Sacred Harp*

A. "Sherburne"

An early American fuguing tune from *The Sacred Harp* (see the section on William Billings).

Composed by Daniel Read.

"Sherburne" is an example of a fuguing tune from the early New England period. It was included in *The Sacred Harp*, a collection of four-part settings of folk hymns first published in 1844. This rendition was recorded in 1959 in a country church in northern Alabama at a weekend meeting of the Alabama Sacred Harp Convention.

B. "The Promised Land"

Performed by Dare to Breathe, a contemporary St. Paul–based a cappella vocal quintet.

"The Promised Land" was included in the 1991 edition of *The Sacred Harp*, although, like "Sherburne," it appeared in the inaugural 1844 edition.

These two examples reveal a singing style that was common in singing schools, *Sacred Harp* conventions, worship services, and other gatherings throughout the nineteenth century — **CD1, Tracks 25–26, 3:13 (SCD) CD1, Track 12, 1:42**

Goals

Recognize and describe the texture of each hymn.

Recognize four-part chordal hymn style and strophic form.

Describe the meter and rhythm.

—*Continued*

Guide

A. "Sherburne"

The meter can be felt in two at a moderate tempo. The first time through, the participants use the fasola style of reading the shape notes. After singing the syllables, they use the hymn text. The phrase structure is the same with the hymn text as with the fasola. Refer to the notation (see fig. 5.2).

The first phrase is in chordal style, like a hymn. In the remaining phrases, you hear the same melody sung independently (like a round) except at the cadences of the third and fifth phrases. Both times, the first two beats of the first phrase are not in strict time; start on the downbeat but hold it slightly before feeling the second beat.

1--2--3--4--5--	While Shepherds watched their flocks . . .
1--2--3--4--5--6--7--8--	The Angel of the Lord . . .
1--2--3--4--5--6--7--	The Angel of the Lord . . .
1--2--3--4--5--6--7--8--	The Angel of the Lord . . .
1--2--3--4--5--6--7--	The Angel of the Lord . . .

B. "The Promised Land"

Verse 1
Chorus
Verse 2
Chorus
Verse 3
Chorus
Chorus

Reflections

In "Sherburne," the singers make no attempt to "pretty up" their voices; they sing at full volume at a quick tempo. One hears no embellishments or ornamentations.

The rhythm can be described as steady and straightforward. Notice the four-part vertical structures (harmony) common in hymn singing, but in the second phrase of each verse, the treatment of both harmony and rhythm changes. At first, all the vocal parts (soprano, alto, tenor, and bass voices) move rhythmically at the same time. At the sixth bar, the music shifts texture. Each voice then moves separately, one in imitation of the other; thus each vocal line has the melody (like a round), and melodic fragments are passed around from voice to voice.

In "The Promised Land," the singers convey the elegance and sophistication of trained singers, and the recording benefits from advancements in modern technology, yet retains a straightforward, unswerving manner characteristic of the singing in the "Sherburne" example.

Association, the Chattahoochee Musical Convention, and the Southern Musical Convention. Listen to Listening Guide 12, p. 68, two hymns that were published in *The Sacred Harp*.

The singing school was the main vehicle for disseminating shape-note music, and to this day annual sings keep the shape-note tradition alive, particularly in the rural South. Many of the hymns sung today in Protestant America, such as "Nearer, My God to Thee," "Rock of Ages," and "Sweet By and By," were by urban composers and later became part of the shape-note repertoire.

Composers and Writers

Singing schools and efforts to teach people to read music created a demand not only for hymnbooks but for new poetry and harmonized tunes. Three men who were especially creative, productive, and influential in the development of American **hymnody** were William Billings, Isaac Watts, and Charles Wesley.

William Billings   In order to read music, the people involved in singing school bought tune books. They wanted new tunes, composed and printed in America. As singing schools increased in number and spread throughout the colonies and into the South and Southwest, the demand for tune books increased. In 1770, William Billings (1746–1800) published his *New England Psalm Singer*. Its success stimulated an outburst of musical creativity. This was an ideal situation for those inclined to compose music. They could write music for which there was a clear demand and high appreciation.

Collections of Billings's music that followed the *New England Psalm Singer* were *Singing Master's Assistant* (1778), *Music in Miniature* (1779), *Psalm Singer's Amusement* (1781), and *Continental Harmony* (1794). This last collection included a number of anthems—extended, more sophisticated sacred pieces intended for trained singers. Billings's earlier collections, however, included "plain tunes" or hymns. These pieces are settings having simple melodic lines and four-part harmony, each part moving with the same rhythm. These settings are sometimes said to be in the "familiar style," a style common to most hymns (see fig. 5.3).

Some of Billings's settings were **fuguing tunes**, a style of hymn that was popular in England and achieved some measure of popularity in America. A fuguing tune is typically a four-part hymn with a short middle "fuguing" section in which the parts enter at different times, starting one after the other as shown in fig. 5.2. The parts have a similar rhythm and frequently similar melodic characteristics, and each enters "in imitation" of the preceding part.

Isaac Watts   One of the most successful and effective creators of psalm settings and religious poetry was the Englishman Isaac Watts (1674–1748). He was convinced that singing only psalms was too restrictive and, in 1707, published *Hymns and Spiritual Songs*, a collection of poems reflecting current religious attitudes. Watts's poetry stimulated a new kind of hymn, which was not dependent on the psalms. Vivid imagery, simplicity, and emotional intensity characterized his poetry. For two centuries, it has appealed to people ranging from urban New Englanders to white and black people of the rural South. Watts's words and sentiments contributed to the religious passion and fervor of the Great Awakening in the mid-eighteenth century.

This was a time that saw religious denominations, including large denominations such as the Presbyterians, Methodists, and Baptists, introduce mass public religious rallies conducted by evangelists who, as Charles Hamm describes it, "through impassioned oratory, roused people to emotional heights causing them to embrace or re-embrace Christianity, spontaneously and publicly."

The hymns of Dr. Watts were essentially his religious poetry set to well-known melodies. Among his best-known and most widely sung hymns are "When I Survey the Wondrous Cross," "Joy to the World," and "O God, Our Help in Ages Past."

Charles Wesley   Charles Wesley (1707–1788) was a prolific hymn writer, creating 6,500 hymns from the Scriptures on a wide variety of Christian experiences. Many of these hymns were set to popular tunes as a conscious strategy for attracting people's interest and to evoke an emotional response to the message. Charles Wesley and his brother, John Wesley (1703–1791), formed a team to spread the gospel throughout the United Kingdom, particularly among the poor. Their hymns—like Dr. Watts's—reflected Christian evangelism, revivalism, and the concept that individuals could make their own decisions about salvation. Their mission in life was to reach the poor and outcast in the United Kingdom.

Although they spent some time in Georgia spreading the gospel, their lasting influence in American religious life has come through their numerous hymns texts, many of which are in common use today, including "Jesus, Lover of My Soul," Hark! the Herald Angels Sing," and "Christ, the Lord, Is Risen Today."

Gospel music originally referred to hymns and songs with texts related to the Gospels rather than to the psalms. The term came to describe an extensive body of evangelical hymns and songs used at revival services, at camp meetings, in Sunday schools, and in churches. This music became prevalent in the early nineteenth century during the second phase of the Great Awakening, when itinerant preachers and evangelists stimulated a remarkable revival of religion. Present-day southern gospel music grew out of this tradition.

Twentieth-Century Gospel Music

The Great Awakening spread quickly throughout the South as preachers traveled and conducted mass meetings to spread the gospel and win converts to Christianity. These public religious rallies or revival services were often held nightly for one or two weeks. The momentum of great revival services as a way of promoting Christianity continued to build throughout the nineteenth century and the first half of the twentieth century, and these services became social and recreational as well as religious events. The evangelists, through their impassioned oratory aroused emotions and induced people to commit or recommit themselves to the Christian faith. These preachers understood very well the role of congregational singing and special music in stimulating the emotions of a crowd.

Revival Music

The gospel music sung at revivals and camp meetings in the early days of the second Great Awakening was to a large extent derived from the oral folk tradition. Familiar songs were adapted to religious poetry. Gospel music originally appealed to both white and black Americans, but by the second half of the nineteenth century distinct styles began to emerge, though mostly in performance practices rather than in the hymns themselves. That is, the hymns were frequently the same, but the style of singing them became different.

Tastes diverged dramatically in the second half of the nineteenth century, as can be seen in the various hymn and song collections used in revivals. The revival or camp meeting hymn, created out of the oral tradition, remained popular on the frontier and in rural areas. The gospel or church hymn, composed by writers and musicians, became important in urban churches, which wanted music that was more "classical" and more European, with good four-part harmony combining psalm tunes and the music of classical composers with more traditional folk hymns. Rural churches and Pentecostal or "holiness" denominations and sects preferred a more popular type of song, such as many camp meeting songs and hymns—what might today be called "praise songs."

istening Guide   *No.* 13

"I'm Headed for the Promised Land"

Southern gospel.
Performed by the Chuck Wagon Gang, a vocal quartet with guitar.
Recorded in 1956 — **CD1, Track 27, 2:29**

Goals

Describe the overall style: melody, harmony, rhythm, tone quality, form, and text.
Describe the vocal quality.
Describe the style of guitar accompaniment.

Guide

Duple meter in four at a moderate tempo; strict, regular rhythm; men's and women's voices with guitar accompaniment; two verses, each with two equal phrases; very repetitive; little melodic, harmonic, or rhythmic embellishment. The opening guitar arpeggio is a tonic chord; an arpeggio is a chord with each note sounding separately.

Intro	A short, tonic guitar chord (arpeggio); free rhythm
Verse 1	Quartet: eight-bar phrase, open cadence (four 2-bar segments) eight-bar phrase, closed cadence (four 2-bar segments)
Verse 2	Vocal solo with quartet: same structure as above and for the following verses
Verse 3	Quartet
Verse 4	Vocal solo with quartet

Reflections

Discuss the repetitiveness. Does it add to or detract from your appreciation of this song?

Compare the style of this performance with that of black gospel and other styles.

As the unique characteristics of black gospel music emerged, music in the white, rural churches sounded similar to what we know now as hillbilly music (see chap. 7), and black gospel music became known as southern gospel.

The interest in gospel hymns resulted in a tremendous number of compositions and published collections. Many hymns sung in American churches today came from these collections. Lowell Mason composed, adapted, and arranged hymns and published more than 20 collections; his *Carmina Sacra* alone sold half a million copies. Thomas Hastings composed 600 hymn texts, more than a thousand hymn tunes, and 50 collections of music. William Bradbury published more than 50 collections, one of which sold over 250,000 copies.

Toward the end of the nineteenth century, revivals were shifted from rural to urban settings. Great buildings called *tabernacles* were built to house the revival meetings. Preachers, to an even greater extent than before, became religious salesmen, sometimes establishing complex organizations. Realizing the importance of music at these revivals, they became associated with song leaders who conducted congregational hymn singing and sang solos.

One of the first influential pairings was Dwight Moody and his song leader, Ira Sankey. Sankey made the gospel hymn a popular song. Many hymns were in verse-refrain form—simple, repetitive, emotional, and memorable. At the turn of the century, Billy Sunday recognized the value of his song leader, Homer Rodeheaver, who helped make his revivals entertaining and popular. In recent decades, Billy Graham—with his featured soloist, George Beverly Shea; and his musical director, Cliff Barrows—has held revivals worldwide. Shea became a successful recording artist in his own right. Graham's crusades were urban and international and made extensive use of the media, particularly radio and television.

Enthusiastic and emotional involvement is common in gospel music.

istening Guide   *No.* **14**

Amazing Grace! How Sweet the Sound

John Newton, 1725-1807

AMAZING GRACE C.M.
Early American Melody
Arr. by Edwin O. Excell, 1851-1921

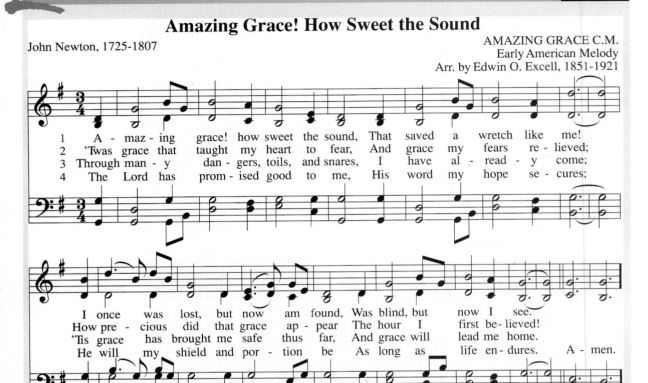

1   A - maz - ing   grace! how sweet the sound, That   saved   a   wretch like me!
2   'Twas grace that taught my heart to fear,   And   grace   my   fears re - lieved;
3   Through man - y   dan - gers, toils, and snares,   I   have   al - read - y   come;
4   The Lord has   prom - ised good to me,   His   word   my   hope se - cures;

I   once   was   lost, but   now   am found, Was blind, but   now I   see.
How pre - cious   did   that grace ap - pear The hour   I   first be - lieved!
'Tis grace   has brought me safe   thus   far, And grace will   lead me home.
He will   my   shield and por - tion   be   As long   as   life en - dures.   A - men.

Figure **5.3**

An early American folk melody of unknown origin. It appeared in the South during the nineteenth century in many of the oblong tune books under such names as "New Britain," "Redemption," "Harmony Grove," "Symphony," and "Solon." The earliest known collection containing it (found by George Pullen Jackson) is the *Virginia Harmony* printed in 1831 in Winchester, Virginia, and compiled by James P. Carrell and David S. Clayton (Lebanon, Virginia).

This arrangement by E. O. Excell, a Chicago gospel-songbook publisher, was included in his *Make His Praise Glorious*, 1900, no 235.

"Amazing Grace"

A southern spiritual song.

Two versions:

A. Black gospel version performed by Tramaine Hawkins. Adaptation and setting by Marty Paich and Tramaine Hawkins. With orchestra, keyboards, bass, and drums—with the L.A. Love Crusade Choir. Recorded in Hollywood in 1993.

B. Excerpt. A traditional folk version sung by Doc Watson and Jean Ritchie, both well-known traditional folksingers. It was recorded at Folk City in New York City in the early 1960s — **CD1, Tracks 28–29, 5:54 (SCD) CD1, Track 13, 2:22**

—Continued

Jean Ritchie, traditional folksinger.

Doc Watson.

Goals

Recognize and describe melodic embellishment.

Describe the various singing styles.

Compare the two settings of this song—how they are arranged and presented. Do they capture the spirit of this song equally well?

Guide

A. (Tramaine Hawkins)

Black gospel.

   0:00 Verse 1 A cappella; slow tempo; highly embellished; extended when orchestra enters on final cadence.

   1:28 Verse 2 Similar in style to Verse 1 but with orchestra playing an underlying, unchanging texture; chord changes begin near the end of the first phrase.

   2:39 Verse 3 In a new key; stronger rhythmic impulse, modulates to new key.

—Continued

B. (Doc Watson and Jean Ritchie)

Folk style.

This example is in triple meter at a slow tempo; each phrase or part of a phrase begins with a pickup (on the third beat). Some flexibility with the pulse (in other words, the pulse is not rigid).

Considerable melodic embellishment in an Appalachian or southern rural folk style.

This version has five verses, each verse made up of two phrases and each phrase having two fragments (half phrases). This excerpt includes the last three verses.

Verse 3   Two phrases, seven bars each (4 + 3). Two voices in unison (Doc Watson and Jean Ritchie); no accompaniment. Pause (or extra beat) at end of second phrase, before pickup to fourth verse. Remaining verses have the same structure.

Verse 4   Watson with humming harmonization.

Verse 5   All voices singing words. Some melody; some harmony.

Reflections

What is the musical interest in these examples? What is the cultural interest?

Describe the nature and extent of any melodic embellishment in the second example.

Describe how the interpretation in the second version is similar to or different from embellishments in the first version. Which example seems to be the most appropriate setting for "Amazing Grace"? Why or why not?

Traditional Black Gospel

In the mid-twentieth century, *gospel music* referred to a style of music that emerged from black worshipers and the way they worshiped—the manner of religious musical expression. This style has become a vital part of music in black churches and also in popular culture.

Black gospel music grew out of black congregations and had its origins in black folk music, but it became a music of professionals, with stylistic similarities to modern soul music or black popular music (see chap. 7).

The roots of black gospel music lie in black spirituals, camp meeting hymns and songs, adaptations of Moody/Sankey revival hymns, the lively services of black churches, and the songlike, intense sermons of black preachers—all combined with cultural and performance qualities growing out of slave culture and the black experience.

The infusion of ragtime, blues, and jazz into the religious musical expression of African Americans in the early twentieth century created modern, black gospel music. It became a style that comfortably merged sacred and secular influences. This music combines passionate religious feelings with effective showmanship. The more popular black gospel music grew out of the Church of God in Christ and other "holiness" or "sanctified" churches. These churches functioned as folk theaters, community centers, houses of worship, and "homelands of the soul."

The texts of traditional black gospel songs are typically about suffering and surviving from day to day. They are about poverty, segregation, unemployment, sickness, broken families, depression, betrayal, and isolation. They express dreams of "mansions o'er the hilltop," "vacations in heaven," and other visions of a better day.

Black gospel is emotional, vocal, physical, theatrical, and musically skillful, and it arouses an enthusiastic physical and emotional response in the audience. The sound of black gospel has been a dominant vocal influence in contemporary popular soul music and has contributed to the rhythmic and theatrical aspects of rock. Its appeal transcends sectarian boundaries. The style includes shouts, moans, and melancholy slurs (influenced by the hymn texts of Isaac Watts). The music has syncopation, rhythmic vitality, and blue notes. Singers decorate, embellish, and vary the music in all sorts of ways. They frequently use a wide vocal range and perform intricate melodic and rhythmic patterns with remarkable dexterity. Hard-driving energy is typical. The style frequently features interplay between a leader and respondents, who may be the choir, the congregation, or both.

The "father" of modern black gospel music was Thomas A. Dorsey (1899–1993), a former blues singer (he sang under the name of Georgia Tom) who became a successful promoter, composer, publisher, teacher, choir director, and organizer. Black gospel music influenced the development of jazz, soul, and rhythm and blues, and became known worldwide, mostly because of the efforts of Thomas A. Dorsey and the popularity of Mahalia Jackson and, later, Aretha Franklin.

Some of the most successful early black gospel singers were women. The best-known female artists included Roberta Martin, Rosetta Tharpe, Clara Ward, Marion Williams, and Mahalia Jackson (Listening Guide 15, above). Andraé Crouch, Shirley Caesar, and the late James Cleveland were later contributors to the advancement of gospel music. Such groups as the Soul Stirrers, the Mighty Clouds of Joy, and the Edwin Hawkins Singers have helped create the sounds of contemporary gospel music. Hawkins's recording of "Oh Happy Day" (1967) became the first big crossover hit (gospel-pop); yet, not surprisingly, it sounds very traditional today. Aretha Franklin, Sam Cooke, and Little Richard were among the artists who moved successfully from gospel to popular music. In recent years many singers who

Thomas A Dorsey.

Listening Guide

Mahalia Jackson.

"Nobody Knows the Trouble I've Seen"

Traditional Black gospel.

Sung by Mahalia Jackson, perhaps the foremost singer of commercial black gospel music.

Recorded in 1963 — **CD1, Track 30, 3:47 (SCD) CD1, Track 14, 1:54**

The titles of Jackson's successful albums illustrate the type of music in which she specialized and to which she was committed: "Make a Joyful Noise unto the Lord," "Great Songs of Love and Faith," "Every Time I Feel the Spirit," "I Believe," "Come On Children, Let's Sing," "Bless This House," and "Sweet Little Jesus Boy."

Goals

Describe the highly emotional, improvisational style of black gospel music.

Recognize question-answer phrases and their cadences.

Recognize chord changes and note when they occur. Practice remembering the sounds of the tonic, dominant, and subdominant chords. Hear the sounds of other chords as well.

—Continued

Guide

0:00	Intro	Piano and organ in free rhythm, improvisational
0:15	Part 1	Very slow, free rhythm; melodic embellishments and piano improvisations throughout

Nobody knows, Lord, de trouble I seen;
Lordy, nobody knows my sorrow.
Yeah, nobody knows the trouble I seen;
But Glory Hallelujah.

1:54	Part 2	Drums and walking bass are added, helping to establish a strong meter and a strong rhythmic impulse at a much faster tempo. (The symbol "x" means a chord other than I, IV, or V.)

1--2--3--4--5--6--7--8--

First phrase	I	--	IV	I	--	--	x	V	continuing energy in eighth bar (open cadence)
Second phrase	I	--	IV	I	--	--	V	I	closed cadence
Third phrase	I	--	IV	I	--	--	x	V	open cadence
Fourth phrase	I	--	IV	I	--	--	xV	I	closed cadence
Fifth phrase	I	--	IV	I	--	--	x	V	open cadence
Sixth phrase	I	--	IV	I	--	--	xV	I	closed cadence
							(holds)		

Reflections

Can each of the six 8-bar phrases in the second part, most likely to be perceived as 4 + 4, also be perceived as twelve 4-bar phrases?

Commercial gospel blends characteristics of traditional church music with characteristics that appeal to a wide, diverse audience. How is this musical example commercial? Not commercial? Does commercial always mean watered down?

Describe how you respond to this music.

remained in black gospel have incorporated elements of popular styles in their music. Black gospel remains in the church, but has also made its mark in the world.

Popular Contemporary Styles

Gospel music today seems to have transcended, to some degree, the stylistic distinctions between white gospel and black gospel. Black, white, and mixed groups are creating music in styles with which they feel comfortable and which they believe will sell to the widest audience, regardless of categories and labels. Much of this music consciously incorporates elements of pop and rock; as a result, the only difference between a contemporary white or black gospel song and a pop or rock style may be in the lyrics.

Listening Guide

No. **16**

"Lord of the Dance" (excerpt)

Contemporary Christian.
Performed by Steven Curtis Chapman.
From the album *Signs of Life* (1996) — **CD1, Track 32, 3:15**

Steven Curtis Chapman is one of the most successful singer-songwriters in contemporary Christian music. His recordings have been successful since his first album *First Hand* (1987). Among his many honors, the Gospel Music Association awarded him Artist of the Year, Songwriter of the Year, and Male Vocalist of the Year in 1990, 1995, 1997, and four other awards since 1997. He also won two Grammys, the most recent in 2000 for best pop-contemporary gospel album.

Goals

Identify instruments.
Describe the musical characteristics of the choruses—of the verses.
Describe Chapman's vocal quality.

Guide

0:00	Intro—instrumental
0:31	Chorus
0:41	Verse 1
1:04	Chorus
1:15	Verse 2
1:39	Chorus
2:00	Chorus extended
2:08	Verse 3
2:31	Chorus

Reflections

Consider the music in relation to the words: for example, verse 3 and the chorus:

I am the heart, You are the heartbeat
I am the eyes, You are the sight
And I see clearly I am the body
You are the life
I move my feet, I go through the motions
But you give purpose to chance

I am the dancer
You are the Lord of the dance

Does this song reflect pop, contemporary Christian, gospel, or something else? What aspects of this music would be considered sacred? What aspects would be considered secular?

A modern counterpart of the music of the revival movement, particularly southern gospel, is the music that is an integral part of the programs (services) of television's televangelists (perhaps now almost a remnant of the past). The purposes of the television's revival meetings and the "old-time religion" are the same: to win souls to Christ and to use music to help make that happen—music familiar in style to large numbers of people, simple, catchy, repetitive, easy to sing, and memorable. In recent years, this music influenced and was influenced by new styles of commercial popular music: contemporary Christian and Christian rock or gospel rock.

Music that incorporates elements from popular, rock, and R&B styles is increasingly becoming a part of the contemporary church. Popular styles, with electric guitars, electric bass, and drum sets (live or on tape), are becoming standard fare in many churches that seek new audiences (parishioners). Much of the taped music commercially produced for churches adds the sounds of strings and winds, usually synthesized.

The contemporary manifestation of white gospel music (southern gospel) can be found in the early gospel songs of many successful country artists, from Elvis Presley and Johnny Cash to the Statler Brothers and the Oak Ridge Boys, and to more recent artists such as Ricky Skaggs and Ricky Van Shelton. It has become acceptable (and perhaps commercially practical) to use popular culture to proclaim the Christian message.

Contemporary Christian music is promoted largely through Christian bookstores and Christian programs on radio and television, including Christian cable networks. The more popular Christian and gospel recordings are evident in any major full-service record store. The Gospel Music Association (GMA), through its annual Dove Awards, continues to influence the style of contemporary Christian music, having moved from its southern gospel roots to sophisticated, lush, sometimes symphonic arrangements of newly composed songs in a pop style. Since the early 1990s, when our culture became more inclusive, styles merged, and labels became less appropriate, GMA included and honored more music from the black community.

With popular singers like Amy Grant and Sandi Patti and popular music on religious television programs, Christian music has become important enough commercially that its sales are now "charted" by *Billboard* magazine. Amy has long since moved into the pop world, Sandi remains highly successful (she won or shared the Dove "Song of the Year" honors four times in the 1980s), and others have emerged such as Michael W. Smith and Stephen Curtis Chapman. Petra, probably the most popular gospel rock group, began performing in 1972 and is still recording. Acappella and Take 6 are groups that incorporate gospel, contemporary Christian, R&B, and jazz in their unique a cappella styles.

Summary

This chapter on religious music is based on generalizations about common practices of millions of churchgoing Americans from the beginning of our nation to the present. Music has been important in churches and to their parishioners, music that continues today in both style and substance. Some practices have not changed in the past hundred years. Others have adapted to recent changes in taste and style and to advances in audio technology, electronic music, and television.

The study of traditional American religious music, like the study of folk and blues music in chapter 4, has provided two important benefits: (1) an insight into America's musical history through an understanding of the styles that have been an important part of the lives of many Americans and (2) an understanding of how music evolves and what contexts allow change—for example, early American hymnody, traditional black gospel, and southern gospel changing to contemporary gospel, contemporary Christian music, and praise music.

Additionally, the relatively simple forms of religious music provide a way to study musical characteristics and techniques that will contribute to your development of listening skills as you prepare for more complicated music in later chapters. By now, your musical perception should include recognizing meters and phrases, counting the bars in phrases to perceive form and to recognize open and closed cadences, hearing when chords change, and recognizing the sound and function of the primary triads (tonics, dominants, and subdominants).

Like all American culture, particularly folk music and blues, American religious music is rooted in the traditions and styles of Europeans and was influenced later by African cultures. The story of America's folk and religious music is in its development and evolution as it moved from the northeastern cities to the rural South and West and merged with folk music, and sometimes with music of other cultures, particularly African-based music.

The white and black gospel music since the 1990s has, for the most part, become less differentiated. Black artists have been winners at the annual Dove Awards of the traditionally white Gospel Music Association. It is becoming more common to simply refer to pop-oriented commercial religious music as "gospel" or "Christian."

E x a m p l e   *No.* 2

"Troubled Water"

A classical composition for piano based on a traditional African American spiritual.
Performed by Althea Waites, piano.
Composed by Margaret Bonds (1913–1972).
From the album *Black Diamonds* (1993)—Althea Waites plays music by African
American composers — **CD1, Track 33, 5:23**

"Troubled Water," published in 1967, is a setting of the spiritual "Wade in the
Water." It reflects the influence of African American culture in music and the
infusion of jazz rhythms and harmonies in classical forms—evident also in the
musical example by William Grant Still (chap. 15, Listening Guide no. 4).

Goals

Recognize points of repetition and contrast.
Recognize thematic development through variation form.

Guide

0:00		Introduction
0:11	A	Section 1—main theme—minor key
0:37		Main theme—varied
1:01		Contrasting material
1:20		Transition to Section 2
1:35	B	Section 2—main theme—major key
2:05		Main theme—varied
2:36		Contrasting material
3:11		Transition to Section 3
3:23	A	Section 3—main theme—minor key
3:49		Main theme—varied
4:20		Transition to closing section
4:37		Closing section

Reflections

Notice that the piece is monothematic (one theme) with sections (ABA) identified
by shifts in modality (minor-major-minor)
Describe aspects of this music that are derived from European culture.
Describe aspects of this music that are derived from African American culture.
Compare the three transitions. What do they contribute to the composition?

CHAPTER 6

Jazz in America

Goals for Listening

- **Recognize and describe** swing rhythm.
- **Recognize and describe** syncopation.
- **Recognize and describe** improvisation.
- **Recognize and describe** thirty-two-bar chorus with bridge.
- **Recognize and describe** twelve-bar blues.
- **Recognize and describe** big band.
- **Recognize and describe** combo.
- **Recognize and describe** vibrato.
- **Recognize and describe** mutes.
- **Recognize and describe** comping.
- **Recognize and describe** scat singing.
- **Recognize and describe** walking bass.
- **Identify** sounds of instruments (individual and in combination).

Terms and Concepts

Jazz in America and throughout the world

Chronology

Styles and techniques

Swing

Instruments and instrumental combinations

Jam sessions

Sidemen

Women in jazz

Summary

Additional Listening

*J*azz is a twentieth-century American phenomenon, but jazz artists and styles are now recognized worldwide. Jazz includes widely divergent styles ranging from entertainment music to art music. It is ever-changing and defies simple definition.

Within the scope of this course, we will attempt to gain some understanding and awareness of the following:

1. How jazz fits into American society.
2. The cultural factors that contributed to its creation as an art form.
3. Its common instruments and their sounds.
4. What jazz is in musical terms.
5. The major artists who contributed to the development of jazz.
6. The various jazz styles.

The primary purpose is for students to develop the ability to recognize and describe the following elements of the jazz style:

Goals for Listening

- Musical concepts: syncopation, improvisation, swing rhythm, and characteristic formal structures, such as the 32-bar chorus (four 8-bar phrases with bridge—a a b a), 12-bar blues, riffs, and ostinato (repeated) patterns.
- Common jazz instruments, common ensembles (big band, combo), characteristic tone qualities (vibrato, use of mutes), and unique performance practices (comping, scat singing, walking bass).
- Sounds of individual instruments and instrumental combinations (sections).

In addition, continue developing the ability to recognize and describe the following basic melodic, harmonic, and rhythmic characteristics:

- Repetitive and characteristic patterns, motives, and themes; phrases, phrase groupings (question-answer phrase patterns), and cadences (open and closed).
- Musical lines other than melody (drum patterns, bass lines, comping).
- Personal interpretation and melodic embellishment.
- Rhythmic impulse: the character of the rhythm (a driving beat, a fluid rhythm, a weak or uneven pulse).
- Chord changes and chord progressions: becoming more skillful in recognizing, in sound, the three primary chords (remember that their names—tonic, dominant, subdominant—indicate their relationship to each other).

Listening examples feature various styles of jazz: Dixieland, big band, bebop, cool jazz, modern jazz, and popular jazz ballads.

Jazz began in the bars and nightclubs of poor urban neighborhoods. These bars and clubs were the places where jazz musicians were able to obtain employment.

What Is Jazz?

Jazz has come a long way, however. Today it is international and has a strong following in continental Europe, Scandinavia, Japan, Africa, South America, Canada, and elsewhere. In fact, it is performed and listened to nearly everywhere. It is heard not only in bars and nightclubs but also in the finest hotels, on college campuses, in concert halls, and even in churches. Jazz has become an accepted part of the curriculum in schools and colleges. Courses are devoted to the study of jazz, and music students in many schools can pursue degrees in jazz. The International Association of Jazz Educators was organized to further the study and performance of jazz in our educational system. Jazz ensembles are offered for academic credit in American colleges and universities, and most high schools have stage bands.

Jazz has been to a large extent an art form created by black people and performed by black people. Most important, the major innovations in the history of jazz development were contributed by black artists, including Jelly Roll Morton, Louis Armstrong, Fletcher Henderson, Duke Ellington, Count Basie, Coleman Hawkins, Lester Young, Charlie Parker, Dizzy Gillespie, Miles Davis, the Modern Jazz Quartet, Ornette Coleman, and John Coltrane. However, jazz history also includes many important and successful white artists, such as Benny Goodman, Stan Getz, Gerry Mulligan, Stan Kenton, Bill Evans, and Dave Brubeck. Women who have achieved distinction as jazz musicians include Lil Hardin Armstrong, Mary Lou Williams, Marian McPartland, and Toshiko Akiyoshi. Many women have been influential as composers or arrangers, as leaders of jazz groups, or as writers and teachers.

Of the art forms that have emerged from American culture, jazz is unique. It is an art that blends the traditions and cultural values of the diverse peoples that make up our society. Jazz essentially resulted from combining the songs, dances, and musical instincts and preferences of people of African and European (particularly French and Spanish) heritage.

Today, jazz is part of a large and complex entertainment industry. It began in the early days of radio and recordings and was brought to the attention of the public through these media. Recordings, especially, brought the music of jazz musicians to their colleagues—an invaluable way to share, to learn, to grow, and to influence other musicians and, indeed, the future course of jazz. Jazz musicians make records to sell, to become popular, but not at the expense of the integrity of their art. Jazz polls do exist, jazz pieces occasionally show up on the pop charts, and elements of jazz are evident in virtually all styles of popular music. However, jazz is much more than pop music.

Jazz aspires to do more than entertain, and the great jazz musicians strive for better ways of expression, sometimes in very sophisticated forms and styles. Perhaps for these reasons, jazz has never achieved mass popularity except during the swing era. Most jazz is not considered pop music, commercial music, or music created for the sole purpose of entertaining; rather, for many musicians, it is a genuine form of art music. The great jazz artists have a high level of musicianship, a sense of what jazz is and of its power to communicate feelings, and a desire to share their art with others.

The Jazz Style

The beginning statements of each item below describe common characteristics of jazz, although, as can be seen, exceptions can be made to virtually any of the statements:

- To be jazz, the music **swings**. This is the feel of jazz—the jazz rhythm.
- To be jazz, musicians improvise—for improvisation is at the heart of jazz. However, much jazz is not improvised, and improvisation is not unique to jazz: it exists in classical music, black gospel music, and the music of many foreign cultures.
- To be jazz, the rhythm is syncopated. Although jazz emphasizes syncopated, or off-beat, rhythms, not all jazz has such rhythms. And again, syncopation is also found in other styles of music.
- To be jazz, music is played on certain instruments, such as the saxophone, trumpet, trombone, drums, bass, and piano. These are jazz instruments only when they are played in a jazz style in a jazz context. However, all of them are used to play other types of music, such as band, orchestra, popular, theater, and religious music. And jazz is also played on the flute, tuba, organ, harp, and other instruments that are not common in jazz performance.

Listen to popular songs, hymns, folk songs, marches, or any pieces that do not fall into the category called *jazz*. Do they swing then? Listen to pieces that are identified as jazz, including the pieces included in this chapter. Note the differences and identify the factors that make the jazz music swing.

Swing is a manner of performance, perhaps more a feel than a precise, describable, easily analytical technique. At the risk of being too simplistic, we might say that swing is the product of some combination of the following:

1. Swing rhythm. This music is played rhythmically in a way that creates heightened energy and vitality. In jazz, repeated evenly spaced rhythms are rare. More commonly, swing rhythm is made up of syncopated long-short figures, symbolized in a most elemental way by the patterns below (each number represents a beat):

```
Evenly spaced pattern   1 + 2 + 3 + 4 + 1
Long-short pattern      1 +2 +3 +4 +1
                        >     >   >  >
Syncopated, long-short  1 +2 +3 +4 +1
```

2. *A unique combination of timekeeping and syncopation.* The drummer may keep time with the bass drum and a cymbal while emphasizing off-beat accents with the snare drum or another cymbal. In accompanying a soloist, the bass player often keeps time by playing a note on each beat (this is known as **walking bass**) while the pianist plays syncopated chords at irregular time intervals, providing rhythmic energy and vitality (this is known as **comping**). In big band jazz, this rhythmic energy is also generated by **riffs**. These are short, syncopated patterns usually written for specific groups of instruments. They provide punctuated background material while another section or a soloist is playing the melody or improvising. Occasionally an entire chorus will be made up of riffs without a recognizable melody.

3. *Melodies that are not played as written.* A jazz musician will always interpret a melody to make it swing. The musician may vary the rhythm, slide into or out of pitches, shift accents, bend pitches, add notes, and do whatever else feels right to give a tune the feel of jazz—to make it swing.

4. *Vibrato that is consistent with the jazz style.* A shaking or wobbling of tones— particularly of sustained tones in a melody—is essential to the jazz style. This is frequently a slow, wide vibrato, sometimes a combination of a straight tone followed by vibrato. Compare the clarinet vibrato of Benny Goodman (in Listening Guide 2, p. 32), with that of any classical clarinet soloist. Compare the vibrato of Miles Davis's trumpet playing (in Listening Guide 21, p. 104) with that of trumpet players in bands, orchestras, or brass quintets.

5. *Instruments played in ways unique, or nearly unique, to jazz.* For example, in jazz, the drummer plays a drum set that has a variety of percussion instruments—snare drum, tom-toms, several different cymbals, and bass drum—whereas in a band or orchestra, these instruments, if used, are likely to be played by different musicians. In jazz, the bass player will usually pluck the strings rather than use a bow, as bassists most commonly do in an orchestra. In jazz, the trumpet or trombone player frequently will use a mute to alter the quality of the sound; mutes are less common in bands and orchestras. Also, the instruments are used in jazz in numbers and in combinations different from those found in bands or orchestras.

The development of jazz has brought what may be called standard jazz instruments and instrumentation, but we need to acknowledge that there are many exceptions. We will consider **big band jazz**, which involves from 10 players on up, usually from 15 to 18 players; and **combo jazz**, which involves from 1 to 9 players.

Groups of instruments are known as **sections**: the rhythm section (piano, bass, and drums), the brass section (trumpets and trombones), and the sax section (traditionally two altos, two tenors, and one baritone). A big band usually has three or four trumpets and three or four trombones, on occasion French horns or a tuba, and often a guitar and a featured singer. Probably the most basic instrumental group is the rhythm section: piano, bass, and drums. The rhythm section is basic to both combo and big band jazz and frequently functions as a self-contained jazz combo. In this case, the piano is the primary **lead** or solo instrument, with occasional solos from the bass and drums. The guitar is sometimes included in the rhythm section, although it frequently also functions as a solo instrument. The rhythm section, incidentally, is also common in urban blues, traditional gospel, and popular music.

A common jazz combo adds one or more lead instruments to the rhythm section: trumpet and tenor or alto sax are most common (listen to Listening Guide 20, p. 100, and Listening Guide 23b). Sometimes we find trombone, clarinet, vibraphone (vibes), flute, soprano sax, or baritone sax. In modern jazz, groups often add a percussionist to play a variety of instruments such as bongos, claves, and castanets to add color and vitality to the rhythm.

The conventional piano is often replaced by the electric piano, synthesizer, and **MIDI** technology or a combination of electric and nonelectric (acoustic) keyboard instruments. The electric organ occasionally is used. In fact, the term *keyboards*, is now used (rather than *piano*) to reflect this versatile electronic technology. The acoustic (stand-up or nonelectric) bass has, for the most part, given way to the electric bass (bass guitar). The influence of electrified rock is evident in modern jazz.

To fully appreciate jazz, learn to recognize the sounds of the instruments and to differentiate sections, instruments, and styles.

Improvisation

To improvise music is to compose it at the same time it is performed—making it up as you go along. Improvisation is a fundamental characteristic of jazz and is important in every jazz style. This concept does not imply total freedom; to improvise is not simply to play whatever one feels like playing. In all jazz styles, there is structure upon which creative improvisation is based. In some styles, the structure is clear and controlling. In others, the control or guideline is minimal. A structure might be an eight-bar phrase of a 32-bar chorus; it might be a specific chord progression that underlies a popular tune or a 12-bar blues tune; or it might be a meter that the improviser adheres to. Listen to Listening Guide 2, p. 32) and Listening Guide 23a and b, p. 106).

The ability to swing and the ability to improvise often set the jazz musician apart from other musicians. Many of the best classically trained musicians do not have these skills, and they sometimes say that they envy the jazz musician's ability to improvise. A classically trained musician who does not have jazz skills will play a jazz piece in a square, unswinging way; the "feel" of jazz is lacking.

The Beginnings of Jazz

Jazz—like American society—is the product of many cultures and influences. In some ways, it represents a merging of cultures and musical styles; in other ways, it retains distinct ethnic characteristics.

Roots

In the late nineteenth and early twentieth centuries, Americans, both black and white, sang and danced to "jazzy" music. The roots of jazz were thus in the existing music of Americans of the North and South and can be found in the following types of music:

1. *Popular songs*. These are the syncopated melodies and rhythms of the popular music of the late nineteenth and early twentieth centuries—minstrel songs, cakewalks, vaudeville songs and dances, and the dance music of New York City and other emerging centers of popular music. For the most part, these notated songs had considerable rhythmic vitality. They typically had a syncopated melody and a strongly pulsating accompaniment. The music was written largely in major keys, and based mostly on the tonic, dominant, and subdominant triads. (Refer to the section on early popular music, "Tin Pan Alley," in chap. 7, and listen to Listening Guide 25, p. 122.)

2. *Blues songs*. Blues as such is not jazz. It was originally part of the oral tradition of folk music (see chapter 4), and blues songs express the feelings of the oppressed blacks in the Deep South. They were derived from the shouts and work songs of slaves and their descendants and were originally sung by black men accompanying themselves on guitar (country blues or folk blues; listen to Listening Guide 8, p. 52). When blues singing shifted to cities in the first decade of the twentieth century, these songs often were performed by women singers accompanied by a Dixieland-type jazz ensemble. By the 1920s, blues and jazz became inseparable, always influencing each other. The music and spirit of the blues were compatible with the emerging jazz style. The most famous early jazz-blues singers included Ma Rainey and Bessie Smith, and, later, Jimmy Rushing and "Big Joe" Turner.

3. *Ragtime*. **Ragtime** became a notated form of popular music, originally for solo piano. It developed in and around St. Louis, and its most popular creator and performer was Scott Joplin (1868–1917). Joplin, incidentally, aspired to be a composer of classical music; his opera, *Treemonisha*, was first performed in Atlanta in 1972, more than a half century after his death. Through performances by various traveling musicians and the sale of popular pieces, ragtime arrived in New Orleans and other southern cities. It was then arranged for instruments derived from the popular black brass bands.

4. *Brass bands*. Brass bands of New Orleans and other southern cities were associated with private black lodges, social clubs, and fraternal organizations that employed black musicians to play for dances, parties, parades, and especially funerals. A typical instrumentation included clarinets, trombones, cornets, banjos, bass horns, and drums. The first jazz pieces were arranged for a similar instrumentation, but with one player to a part.

5. *Gospel music*. Early gospel music, particularly that of rural and nonliterate blacks, combined the shouts and moans of black blues with exciting rhythms, high energy, religious fervor, theatrical presentations, and religious texts. This style developed through the nineteenth century and still exists today, and became popular among both blacks and whites.

Merging of Cultures and Styles

The blacks of the Deep South were of African heritage and usually had little opportunity for formal education. Whites and people of mixed blood (such as the Creoles in Louisiana) were educated according to western European traditions. The mingling of people from these two disparate heritages—African and European—was the most pervasive factor that enabled jazz to flourish and contributed significantly to developing the music into a unique art. (Perhaps the minstrel show was the only other unique American art.)

The most famous mingling of cultures seems to have taken place during the mid-nineteenth century in New Orleans. On Sunday evenings, people of different races and backgrounds shared their traditional songs and dances in Congo Square (now known as

Louis Armstrong Park). They created new music, forms, and expressions, some of which became jazz. It happened in New Orleans more than in any other southern city because New Orleans was cosmopolitan and had comparatively liberal social attitudes.

American society in the second half of the nineteenth century and the first half of the twentieth century was becoming more mobile. Transportation was becoming more readily available, enabling urban people to move easily from city to city, rural people to move to cities, and immigrants to arrive from many different countries. It became increasingly easy for music and culture to be interchanged and, likewise, for jazzy music, such as the syncopated, highly rhythmic music described earlier, to become widely accepted.

The music industry (the composing of songs to be sold and, it was hoped, to become popular) was emerging. The style of popular music created in New York City incorporated many elements that were to become part of jazz, particularly syncopation and a strong rhythmic pulse. Musical instruments were inexpensive and easily available, especially through mail-order houses such as Sears, Roebuck.

Chronology of Styles

The history of modern jazz style begins with New Orleans jazz. The desire for musicians to entertain and for the public to be entertained seemed increasingly compatible with music having jazzy characteristics. Jazz music became established in New Orleans when artists began to emerge, particularly in the second decade of the twentieth century.

New Orleans Jazz

New Orleans jazz was performed mostly in a part of the city known as Storyville, which included bars, nightclubs, and brothels that hired jazz musicians for entertainment and to provide dance music. In 1917, Storyville was closed down as part of "urban reform." With that closing, opportunities for aspiring jazz musicians were lost. But jazz musicians have to perform, and they left New Orleans, some traveling on boats up the Mississippi River. Many ultimately settled in Los Angeles, New York, and particularly Chicago. By 1920, most of the outstanding musicians of New Orleans had moved elsewhere, and no recordings were made of New Orleans jazz in New Orleans.

The most notable recording artists to come out of New Orleans were Jelly Roll Morton, piano; Freddie Keppard, cornet; Kid Ory, trombone; King Oliver, cornet; Johnny St. Cyr, banjo; Louis Armstrong, cornet; Lil Hardin, piano; Baby Dodds, drums; Johnny Dodds, clarinet; Nick LaRocca, clarinet; and Sidney Bechet, clarinet. Nick LaRocca, the only white person among those listed here, headed a white jazz group from New Orleans that later became known as the Original Dixieland Jazz Band. This group made the first recording of jazz music in 1917 in New York City. King Oliver hired the best New Orleans musicians for his Creole Jazz Band. Kid Ory, after moving to Chicago, headed the first black jazz group to be recorded, but later recordings of Oliver's Creole Jazz Band are said to be the best documentation of New Orleans combo jazz. Thus, we rely on recordings made in Chicago by these transplanted artists to learn about the first style of jazz.

One of the most successful and most famous of early New Orleans jazz musicians was Jelly Roll Morton. He left New Orleans in 1907 to pursue a career as a jazz pianist, composer, arranger, recording artist, and entertainer. Since virtually all the New Orleans jazz was learned "from the head" (from being worked out among the musicians, not from notated music), Morton's compositions and arrangements paved the way for a more sophisticated, rehearsed jazz that was read from notation and was to be common in the 1930s. Morton, perhaps more than any other musician, could combine solo improvisation and a composed piece without losing the spirit of New Orleans jazz.

The George Williams Brass Band in New Orleans.

New Orleans jazz emerged in Chicago in the 1920s, largely through the music of the transplanted New Orleans musicians. It evolved into the first widely popular jazz style, **Dixieland** (listen to Listening Guide 17, p. 93). It has remained popular to this day.

Chicago Jazz (Dixieland)

The 1920s were exuberant years. This was the time of the flapper, the Charleston, prohibition, the beginnings of network radio and commercial recordings, and the great popular music of George Gershwin, Jerome Kern, Cole Porter, and Irving Berlin. But the exuberance ended with the stock market crash of 1929 and the Great Depression.

New Orleans and Chicago jazz are actually quite similar:

1. Both styles have high energy and rhythmic vitality.
2. Both styles have clarinet, trumpet or cornet, and trombone as solo instruments; there are not many exceptions. Both styles have a rhythm section of piano, bass— either string bass or brass bass (tuba)—and drums. Sometimes there is no bass or no drums; and sometimes there is no piano, but there is a banjo or guitar.

3. Both styles use "head" arrangements—those that are not notated but are worked out in rehearsal or, eventually, played by memory according to traditional Dixieland style.
4. Both styles use group improvisation among the solo instruments. This improvisation follows rather strict conventions.
   a. Musicians create melodic lines that fall within the chords dictated by the melody.
   b. The trumpet plays the lead, the clarinet an obbligato (a higher, decorative part), and the trombone a lower melodic line derived from the main chord tones.
   c. All parts move in independent lines but interact with each other.
5. The role of the rhythm section is timekeeping. Sometimes the performers put equal emphasis on each beat. At other times they may stress the first and third beats or the second and fourth beats. The piano (or banjo or guitar) plays block chords in the same manner; none of them plays lead (the main melodic or solo part).
6. The music has occasional **breaks** (stop time). All musicians stop except for a soloist who improvises for two bars. This usually happens at the end of a phrase.
7. Musicians sometimes use **fills** to provide movement while the rhythm of a pattern or phrase stops. Fills provide embellishment between phrases.

Unquestionably, the most successful and most famous Dixieland musician was Louis Armstrong (listen to Listening Guide 17, p. 93), a giant among the transplanted New Orleans musicians. He had an illustrious career as a trumpet player, singer, and entertainer well into the 1960s. His primary influence was from the recordings he made in Chicago in the 1920s with his combos, the Hot Five and the Hot Seven. They not only educated the public about New Orleans jazz but established a model for Armstrong's greatest contributions to the development of jazz:

1. The possibility of innovative jazz improvisations extended for more than a two-bar break.
2. The possibility of solo, improvised jazz singing, a style known as **scat singing** (this is vocal improvising similar to instrumental improvising).

Stride and Boogie Woogie

Because of the Depression, hiring of jazz groups declined, and people's craving for jazz was in large measure satisfied by hiring solo pianists. Ragtime, a notated popular music (see p. 89), evolved into the improvised, more energetic **stride** piano style. This style, like ragtime, featured a strongly rhythmic, walking (striding) left hand and a syncopated right-hand melody, but it was typically improvised and more upbeat than ragtime. The stride style—the first jazz form to feature solo pianists—inspired the artistry of a series of great pianists: Fats Waller, Earl Hines, Art Tatum, Erroll Garner, and Oscar Peterson.

Boogie woogie was the 12-bar blues form combined with a unique style of piano playing featuring a constantly repeated left-hand ostinato pattern moving through the blues chord progression with energetic, syncopated right-hand patterns that varied with each 12-bar repetition.

Swing and Big Band Jazz

The swing era of the 1930s and early 1940s brought the only style of jazz that became popular with the masses. Swing, in fact, was the popular music of the day, and many jazz tunes were on the Hit Parade (the equivalent of the top 40 charts). As Americans rebounded from the Great Depression, they wanted to be entertained and to dance, and they were willing to pay for it. This was a great time for popular music, jazz, jazz musicians, radio, and the recording industry.

The swing era also emerged from the jazz artists' need to explore, innovate, and apply a higher standard of musicianship and jazz sense than was available to them through the

Louis Armstrong
playing the trumpet
with his ever-present
handkerchief.

"Hotter Than That"

Dixieland

Composed by Lil Hardin Armstrong.

Performed by Louis Armstrong and His Hot Five: Louis Armstrong, cornet and vocal;
Kid Ory, trombone; Johnny Dodds, clarinet; Lil Hardin Armstrong, piano; Johnny St.
Cyr, banjo; and Lonnie Johnson, guitar.

Recorded in Chicago in 1927 — **CD1, Track 34, 3:00**

Goals

Recognize syncopation, breaks, and scat singing.

Identify the Dixieland style.

Identify instruments from their sounds.

Describe group improvisation.

Describe the relationship between improvisation and structure.

—Continued

Guide

Count in a fast four or a moderately slow two.

0:00	Intro	8 bars	Full ensemble; group improvisation
0:09	First chorus	32 bars	Solo improvisation, cornet
			First break, cornet
			Second break, clarinet
0:45	Second chorus	32 bars	Solo improvisation, clarinet
			First break, clarinet
			Second break, vocal
1:21	Third chorus	32 bars	Solo improvisation, vocal (scat singing)
			First break, vocal
			Second break extended; vocal and guitar dialogue
2:14	Vamp	4 bars	Piano
2:18	Fourth chorus	16 bars	Solo improvisation, muted trombone; cornet break
		20 bars	Group improvisation, cornet lead, includes stopped time patterns; guitar break; brief cornet and guitar dialogue, the guitar having the "last word" with the final, unresolved chord

Reflections

Be aware of the group improvisation among the cornet, clarinet, and trombone in the introduction and the final chorus.

Recognize the two-bar breaks and the improvised dialogues between both the voice and guitar and the voice and trumpet.

Describe the vocal improvisation known as scat singing.

relatively confining style of Dixieland. This was essentially the era of big bands and of dancing to jazz. Many of the tunes were Tin Pan Alley–type popular songs arranged for big bands in an accessible style.

In the late 1920s, a number of musicians became interested in creating jazz arrangements (now called **charts**) for larger ensembles. To perform these arrangements successfully, musicians had to read music, play precisely with others, and improvise in the context of notated music. The most important arrangers of early big band jazz pieces were Fletcher Henderson in New York, a leader of "sweet swing"; Don Redman, who played with Henderson's group and later became an influential jazz musician in Kansas City; and Duke Ellington, who became one of the most durable and successful of all jazz composers, arrangers, and big band leaders.

Jazz in the swing era fell into three categories:

1. *Sweet swing*. This is intended for entertainment, dancing, and easy listening. Some people would not call this music jazz, because improvisation and the feel of jazz swing are minimal. Sweet swing groups are dance bands, society bands, or syncopated dance orchestras. They had actually existed since the early decades of the twentieth century. The most prominent sweet swing dance bands include James Reese from Europe in the late 1910s, Paul Whiteman in the 1920s, Guy Lombardo from the 1940s through the 1970s, and Lawrence Welk as recently as the 1980s. These bands, particularly Paul Whiteman's, frequently employed some of the best jazz musicians available.

2. *The jazz of Benny Goodman, the "king of swing."* Goodman formed big bands and combos; they played hot jazz and gentle swing. He is probably the best known of all jazz musicians. He has received the highest honors from his peers and from governments. A Hollywood movie about his life had wide exposure. Books and articles have been written about him. He did more than any other to make jazz respectable and to integrate jazz groups and jazz audiences. He has also performed as a clarinet soloist with major symphony orchestras. His combo jazz foreshadowed the bebop era, providing an opportunity for musicians such as Teddy Wilson, Lionel Hampton, and Charlie Christian to develop their improvisatory skills. Listen to Listening Guide 2, p. 32, and Listening Guide 18, p. 96.

3. *Hot swing or big band jazz*. This jazz served the more serious jazz composer, arranger, and performer. It included more musically sophisticated charts, featured more extended improvised solos, and was more demanding musically than sweet swing. The recording industry was flourishing, but the long-play recordings (LPs) had not yet come into existence. Most compositions and arrangements were limited to three minutes, the duration of one side of a 78 rpm record. This greatly

Benny Goodman's swing band.

restricted the possibility of extended improvisations by the leading jazz artists, except in live performance.

The more sophisticated big band charts were aimed more at listeners than dancers. This music was sometimes called *concert jazz*. Among the best and most durable of the big bands were those of Duke Ellington and Count Basie. Other prominent bands included those of Glenn Miller, Woody Herman, Jimmy Dorsey, Tommy Dorsey, Stan

L istening Guide   *No.* 18

"Taking a Chance on Love"

Swing.

Performed by Benny Goodman and His Orchestra, with Helen Forrest, vocal. Listen to another Benny Goodman piece: Listening Guide No.2, page 32.

Arranged by Fletcher Henderson for a 17-piece band:

    4 trumpets
    3 trombones
    1 clarinet
    3 alto saxes
    2 tenor saxes
    Rhythm section: piano, bass, drums, and guitar

Recorded in 1940 — **CD2, Tracks 1–3, 3:03**

Goals

Identify the parts: introduction and vocal and instrumental choruses.

Recognize contrasting and repeated phrase patterns and identify musical factors that make a phrase different.

Recognize instrumental textures, whether solo lines or in sections (groups of like instruments, such as saxes and trumpets).

Recognize meter, syncopation, and tempo.

Guide

Count in duple meter (a moderately fast four).

0:00	Intro	5 bars	Full ensemble
0:10	Instrumental (a a)	8 bars	Bars 1–4: trumpet section melody, sax section providing "fills"; clarinet lead in bars 5–8; open cadence on eighth bar
0:26		11 bars	Trumpet section melody, sax section "fills"; closed cadence on eighth bar followed by four-bar extension that prepares for the vocal chorus (the eighth bar is the closed cadence and the first bar of the extension—a one-bar overlap, adding only three extra bars)

—Continued

Listening Guide— *Continued*				*No.* 18

0:49	Vocal (a a b a)	a	8 bars	Background "riffs" (short punctuated chords and patterns, similar to "fill"); open cadence
1:05		a	8 bars	Repeat—closed cadence
1:21		b	8 bars	Bridge: muted brass riffs—open cadence
1:38		a	8 bars	Closed cadence
1:54	Instrumental	a	8 bars	Full ensemble in first two bars, followed by clarinet lead
2:11	(a a b a)	a	8 bars	Full ensemble in first two bars, followed by clarinet lead
2:28		b	8 bars	Bridge: tenor sax solo with brass riffs
2:44		a	9 bars	First four bars, full ensemble. Then clarinet lead for two bars ending with the full ensemble and a one-bar tag.

Reflections

Describe the elements that make this music swing.

What do the riffs and fills contribute to this music?

Is this music sweet swing? Why or why not?

Notice that the melody, harmony, and rhythm contain few surprises. Everything is predictable, as in most popular music and traditional jazz.

Listening Guide	*No.* 19

"Mood Indigo"

Big band jazz ballad.

Performed by Duke Ellington and His Orchestra.

Featuring Shorty Baker, trumpet.

From the album *Indigos* (1989).

Recorded in New York in 1957 — **CD2, Track 4, 3:04 (SCD) CD1, Track 16, 3:05**

Goals

Recognize the style of a big band jazz ballad.

Describe the style of the first chorus, with walking bass and muted trumpet.

Describe the style of the second chorus.

Recognize the form of the second chorus: four 8-bar phrases (a a b a); identify the bridge.

—Continued

Duke Ellington at a concert in Paris in 1967.

Guide

Count in a moderately slow four.

Intro: four bars; strong to gentle mood.

First chorus: muted trumpet and walking bass.

Second chorus: full ensemble; a a b a form; last phrase extended to a slow quiet ending.

Reflections

What was your response to "Mood Indigo," its quiet, mellow mood with a gentle beat?

How popular is big band jazz today?

Kenton, the Toshiko Akiyoshi-Lew Tabackin Big Band, Maynard Ferguson, Buddy Rich, and the Tonight Show Band with Doc Severinson.

The recordings of some big bands, notably Glenn Miller, Duke Ellington, and Count Basie, are reissued on compact discs. These bands also continue to perform, although, of course, under new leadership. Their compositions and arrangements are the same as or similar to the originals.

Three major factors—economic and musical—created **bebop** (listen to Listening Guide 20, p. 100):

1. Many jazz musicians wanted to find new ways of playing the same chords, imaginative and unexpected chords to work around, and new interpretations of melodies. However, notated swing arrangements, restricted by the three minutes available on 78-rpm disks, offered little opportunity for serious jazz musicians to engage in creative exploration. Combo jazz, common to bebop, would allow greater opportunities for more substantial and extended jazz improvisation.
2. People partied and danced at night; thus, jazz musicians worked at night. When they were working, they played the style the audience and thus the employer wanted or needed. Too often the required style did not allow experimentation or creative exploration. After-hours **jam sessions** resulted, often lasting all night. It was at these sessions that exploration could take place, and bebop was born.
3. By the 1940s, big band swing music was declining in popularity, and during World War II people were less available for dancing and entertainment. Musicians, likewise, were less available. Gasoline was rationed, restricting travel, and many men had gone to war. The response to these circumstances was in part a return to combo jazz and the creation of the bebop style.

Bebop began in the early 1940s in New York City. Dizzy Gillespie, trumpet; Thelonious Monk, piano; Kenny Clark, drums; and others gathered to explore new musical possibilities and to satisfy their own unfulfilled musical instincts. However, the search for a new style did not solidify until a saxophonist named Charlie Parker arrived in New York from Kansas City. Parker's skillful improvisation and musical instincts led to a clarification and synthesis of the bebop style.

The roots of bebop date back to the 1930s in the solo improvisations of the tenor sax players Coleman Hawkins, Johnny Hodges, and Lester Young; the trumpet player Roy Eldridge; the vibraphone ("vibes") player Lionel Hampton; and the guitarist Charlie Christian. All these artists, through their recordings and live performances, influenced those who became the leaders of bebop jazz. Other important bebop musicians include Max Roach, perhaps the most outstanding bop drummer; Mary Lou Williams, piano; and Bud Powell, piano.

Bebop is a cerebral, intellectual jazz. It is complex, intense, and often very fast. The emphasis is on unusual harmonic, melodic, and rhythmic treatments of a song and on the performer's virtuosity. The song was often a popular song of the day; but, not unusually, all that remained of this song were its title and its underlying chords. The melody of the song was likely to be obscure or not present at all, and improvisations were based on harmonic progressions rather than on melodic patterns.

The 32-bar, a a b a song form was common. The following is a model of what a bebop piece might be like:

1. First chorus
   a   The first eight-bar phrase would begin with the full ensemble, the lead instruments in a unique duet, often in unison.
   a   Second phrase repeats.
   b   Third phrase (the bridge) provides contrast, usually with an improvised solo.
   a   Fourth phrase returns to the original theme.
2. Subsequent choruses
   Following the first chorus, the sax may play a full chorus or more. The trumpet player will take one or more choruses, and the pianist will do likewise. The bass and

Bebop

drummer may share a chorus; the piece will end with a return to the ensemble chorus similar to the beginning.

Bebop is combo jazz. The standard instrumentation consists of one or two solo lead instruments and a rhythm section of piano, bass, and drums. The most common leads are tenor or alto sax, trumpet, and piano; but the lead can also be a trombone, vibraphone (vibes), flute, or guitar, or any other melodic instrument.

Listening Guide   No. 20

"Bloomdido"

Bebop

Composed by Charlie Parker.

Performed by Charlie Parker, alto sax; Dizzy Gillespie, trumpet; Thelonious Monk, piano; Curly Russell, bass; and Buddy Rich, drums.

Recorded in New York, June 6, 1950, and billed as a reunion of "Bird" and "Diz".

CD2, Tracks 5–9, 3:24

Charlie Parker, circa 1947. Courtesy of the Institute of Jazz Studies, Rutgers University.

—Continued

Listening Guide— *Continued*   *No.* 20

Dizzie Gillespie.

Goals

Listen to the virtuosity of these legends of jazz: their ability to get around on their instruments and to move with considerable complexity through basic harmonies. Don't try to recognize familiar chord progressions.

Recognize the styles, roles, and functions of the various musicians: lead, timekeeping, harmonic foundation, comping, and so on.

Describe the tempo and the rhythmic impulse.

Distinguish between full ensemble (relatively equal lines) and one instrument taking the lead.

In full ensemble, describe the primary melody and the interaction of the leads.

Guide

Count in a fast four or a moderate two. (The numbers indicate the number of bars in a phrase.)

| 0:00 | Intro | Piano with drums and ride cymbal |
| 0:09 | First Chorus | Full ensemble; sax and trumpet sometimes in unison, sometime in harmony; walking bass; second phrase essentially the same as the first phrase |

—Continued

0:34	Second Chorus	Charlie Parker, lead; walking bass in fast four; piano comping; drums keeping time and adding kicks and prods (syncopated licks); ride cymbal
1:25	Third Chorus	Dizzy Gillespie, trumpet; same style and function in rhythm section
2:03	Fourth Chorus	Thelonious Monk, piano; much open space (thin texture); complex rhythm (no feeling of being compelled to "land" on each downbeat)
2:30	Fifth Chorus	Buddy Rich, drums
2:55	Sixth Chorus	Ensemble chorus

Reflections

Which elements of music seem prominent in this style?

Describe the musical interaction of the musicians.

In what ways is this entertainment music? In what ways is it art music?

Are Charlie Parker and Dizzy Gillespie as important to American music as, let's say, Garth Brooks or Billy Joel? Why or why not?

Cool, Hard Bop, Funk, and Free

Because the bop of the 1940s and 1950s was complex and sophisticated, it never achieved widespread popularity with the public or even among jazz musicians. Immediately, musicians began to explore alternatives. Many styles and influential artists emerged in the 1950s and the 1960s, a period of diversity in the history of jazz. Four of these important jazz styles are **cool**, **hard bop**, **funk**, and **free**. Again, it is important to realize that very few artists adhere to only one style.

Cool jazz began with Lester Young in the late 1930s and was given impetus by Miles Davis, a bebop trumpet player, in an album called *The Birth of the Cool* (1949). It was an attempt to apply musically sophisticated ideas in a more relaxed, softer, more accessible manner than bebop. Cool jazz is typified by the early music of Miles Davis, and the music of the Modern Jazz Quartet, Dave Brubeck, Gerry Mulligan, Stan Getz, Chet Baker, Lenny Tristano, and Lee Konitz. Listen to Listening Guide 21, p. 104).

Hard bop is perhaps a catchall name for the music of the next generation of bop musicians, who attempted to maintain the principles of bop in a way that would not alienate the listening public. Two of the most popular jazz musicians of this period are Clifford Brown (trumpet) and Sonny Rollins (tenor sax). Other jazz musicians continued to experiment with new styles and techniques. One of the most outstanding was John Coltrane (tenor and soprano sax), whose tone quality and approach to improvisation have influenced countless other jazz musicians.

Funk is the name sometimes given to the style of jazz performers who created a post-bop style that returned to the roots of jazz. These musicians explored a new style of jazz that capitalized on harmonic and rhythmic simplicity, a strong beat, and influences from

John Coltrane.

gospel music, R&B, and, later, soul. Influential artists who represented funky jazz are Horace Silver, Art Blakey, and Ramsey Lewis.

Free jazz was pioneered in the 1950s and 1960s by Ornette Coleman (alto sax and violin), who created a style that is almost pure improvisation with no adherence to predetermined chord structures, meter, or melodic motives. The idea is for the musicians to interact musically with each other, building on what others in the group are doing but free to create according to their musical instincts. A typical free jazz ensemble was Coleman on alto sax, Don Cherry on trumpet, Scott LaFaro or Charlie Haden on bass, and Ed Blackwell or Billy Higgins on drums—no piano.

Like bebop, free jazz was not one of the more popular forms of jazz with the public or among many jazz musicians. Some people were averse to it because it lacked the structures on which jazz improvisation was traditionally based. It did, however, attract avid supporters who respected its level of creativity and its new sounds. Incidentally, Coleman continues to be active in modern jazz with his group, Prime Time.

Gerry Mulligan on baritone sax and Dave Brubeck on piano: cool jazz.

*L*istening Guide   *No.* **21**

Miles Davis.

"Summertime," from *Porgy and Bess*

Cool jazz

Composed by George Gershwin; lyrics by Ira Gershwin (Listen to another Gershwin example: chapter 15, additional listening No. 16).

Performed by Miles Davis.

Recorded in New York City in 1958 — **CD2, Track 10, 1:29**

The music, arranged and conducted by Gil Evans, was written for a large and unusual instrumentation:

> 19 pieces: 4 trumpets, 4 trombones, 3 French horns, 1 tuba, 1 alto sax, 2 flutes, 1 bass clarinet, string bass, drums, and featured soloist Miles Davis, trumpet and flügelhorn

Goals

Recognize characteristics of cool jazz.

Distinguish between interpreting a melody in a jazz style and jazz improvisation.

Identify muted trumpet and other instruments.

Notice the ostinato pattern in the background. It is a series of block chords played mostly by woodwinds, sometimes with flutes predominating. Observe the subtle variations to the usually ascending line.

—Continued

Listening Guide — *Continued*   *No.* 21

Guide

Count this piece in a moderate four; no introduction. It starts with a pickup.

a	8 bars	Ostinato in background; open cadence
a	8 bars	Repeat of first phrase but ends with closed cadence
b	8 bars	Contrasting phrase ends with open cadence on bar 7
a	16 bars	Solo improvisation; open cadence on bar 15
Fade		

Reflections

Describe Davis's inventive interpretation on muted trumpet. To what extent and in how many ways does he deviate from the established melody? Be aware of his use of vibrato, the role of the drums and cymbals, and the bass line. What aspects of this music belong to Gershwin the composer, to Gil Evans the arranger, or to Miles Davis the interpreter?

Describe the energy and the mood of this piece. Describe your reactions.

Listening Guide   *No.* 22

"Little Lulu"

Combo jazz—post-bop.
Performed by Bill Evans, piano; Gary Peacock, bass; and Paul Motian, drums.
Recorded in 1963 — **CD2, Track 11, 3:51**
Bill Evans is one of the most influential jazz musicians of the 1960s and 1970s.

Goals

Describe the nature of the improvising and how the musicians interact musically.
Describe the mood of this jazz.
Describe the role of each musician (for instance, lead, comping, timekeeping). Do the roles change?

Guide

0:00   First chorus

      Phrases 1 and 2   8 + 10 bars   Main theme: two-bar extension in the
                      second phrase

—*Continued*

Phrases 3 and 4	8 + 10 bars	Contrasting but related chords and style
Phrases 5 and 6	8 + 10 bars	Contrasting but related chords and style; returns to main theme in the main key (melody starts an octave higher)

1:26	Second chorus	Bass lead; piano comping; drums interacting musically with bass and piano
2:22	Third chorus	Piano lead; drums keeping time
3:18		Extended phrase. Concluding section involving a series of patterns that delay the final cadence

Reflections

To what extent and in what ways does the bass go beyond timekeeping and harmonic foundation?

Describe the bass playing as related to walking bass; describe the drums as related to timekeeping. How have these musicians gone beyond the traditional roles of the rhythm section?

Particularly in the third chorus (the piano lead), listen for what Evans does with his right hand (treble register) and his left hand (bass register). Describe each style. Describe how Evans extends the final cadence of the piece.

What skills and musical insights are needed for these musicians to perform this music in this way?

"'Round Midnight"—two versions

Popular jazz ballad composed by Thelonius Monk in the early 1950s.
A. Thelonius Monk, piano
B. Herbie Hancock Quartet — **CD2, Tracks 14–15, 9:07 (SCD) CD1, Tracks 17–19, 6:20**

Goals

Articulate similarities and differences between the two versions (e.g., tempo, mood, instrumentation, improvisational style).

Recognize sounds of the various instruments.

Recognize places where soloists adhere or depart from the main melody and describe ways they depart.

—Continued

Listening Guide — *Continued*   *No.* 23

Thelonius Monk: bop pianist, composer, and innovator.

Guide

A. Thelonious Monk, piano

Recorded in 1968.

All phrases are eight bars, counting four beats to the bar at a moderately slow tempo.

0:00	Intro		(eight bars)—highly syncopated. Obscure pulses in bars 1 and 5, but the beat is constant
	Chorus 1		
0:24	Phrase 1	a	The main theme presented with considerable embellishment
0:48	Phrase 2	a	More improvisatory than the first phrase and played in a higher range; ends on tonic with an ascending flourish
1:13	Phrase 3	b	Contrasting phrase (the "bridge"); a steady "boom-chick" bass line
1:37	Phrase 4	a	The main melody repeated but modified; the tune is obscure in the first four bars; phrase ends on tonic
2:02	Chorus 2		Four phrases (a a b a), eight bars each; same structure as above; last two bars set up conclusion by slowing down (ritarding); ends with elaborate, descending flourish

B. Herbie Hancock Quartet

Modern, traditional jazz performed by a combo of jazz artists, each of whom rank among the most influential of recent decades: Herbie Hancock, piano; Wynton Marsalis, trumpet; Ron Carter, bass; and Tony Williams, drums

Recorded in Japan in 1982.

—Continued

Listening Guide — *Continued*   *No.* 23

Guide   (The recording on the Student CD set ends at 2:25)

0:00	Intro		Piano; floating rhythmic impulse; gentle feeling
0:22	Chorus 1	a	Muted trumpet lead with piano embellishments; continued gentle feeling with the floating rhythmic impulse; bass and drums add a stronger sense of rhythm
1:15		a	First two phrases repeated with considerable modification an embellishment-phrase extended
2:07		b	Short transitional passage (bridge); two descending motives, the second at a higher pitch level
2:25		a	Main theme repeated with considerable modification and embellishment; two-bar ride cymbal overlaps final cadence, providing transition to next section
2:57	Transition		Contrasting section of two short passages; first, drums and trumpet are predominant; second, trumpet plays furious improvised passage, quickly decreasing in intensity and dynamics, preparing for the next chorus
3:21	Chorus 2		Piano lead; walking bass; patterns of harmonic or rhythmic changes; double time in middle of chorus; returns to regular time-fade

Reflections

Describe traditional jazz. Describe modern jazz.

Distinguish between the interpretation of a melodic line and improvisation.

Be familiar with the use of the term *chorus* in jazz and popular music (a cohesive group of phrases, a stanza), often four 8-bar phrases in a a b a form: a 32-bar chorus.

Notice ways in which Monk improvises by adding notes to the main melody; filling in spaces, such as the ends of phrases; using a wide range of the keyboard; and creating complex and imaginative harmonies and textures.

Consider the skills needed not only to create a lasting piece of music but to have the skills to be able to create while performing in such an elaborate and effective manner as these artists do on these recordings.

Modern Jazz and Fusion

It can be argued that modern jazz began in the mid-1960s, with Miles Davis, again, as the driving force. But this time it was not just his music that was important, but the people he hired as sidemen. Many have become the biggest names in modern jazz and **fusion**: Bill Evans, Keith Jarrett, Herbie Hancock, Wayne Shorter, Ron Carter, Tony Williams, John McLaughlin, Chick Corea, and Joe Zawinul.

Billie Holiday's unique singing style developed from her own deep feelings and experiences.

Ella Fitzgerald proved that both popular and jazz singing can be merged with good musicianship and taste.

Many fusion artists synthesized the jazz style with pop, classical, or rock styles (this kind of synthesis is sometimes called "crossover"), creating a new jazz genre that is referred to as *fusion jazz*. The most dramatic change in jazz was borrowed from rock: electronic keyboards, electric bass, and rock drumming. Synthesizers, computers, MIDI, and other technological advancements are much in evidence in contemporary jazz. Some writers have argued that fusion was the most popular form of jazz since the swing era. Perhaps the most commercially successful fusion artists were Herbie Hancock (keyboards), Chick Corea (keyboards), and Pat Metheny (guitar).

Fusion, however, is a term that was more widely used in the 1970s and 1980s than in recent years. The styles of jazz today are extremely varied, ranging from the easy-listening electronic jazz of many contemporary musicians to the extremely complex post-bop jazz of many others.

Again, diversity is a major characteristic of this music. Without question, the impact of rock and electronic instruments is significant. But fusion may also mean a synthesis of jazz with other styles: jazz and classical music (third stream—Gunther Schuller, John Lewis), Caribbean and South American music (salsa and Latin jazz—Tito Puente), and other American popular styles such as country (bluegrass and jazz—David Grisman,) and the blues (some B. B. King and some Van Morrison). Among the artists who moved easily between traditional jazz and pop styles were, in the early years, singers such as Billie Holiday, Ella Fitzgerald, Tony Bennett, Frank Sinatra, and Mel Tormé, and, in recent years, George Benson (guitarist and singer).

Toshiko Akiyoshi: contemporary big band leader, composer/arranger, and pianist.

Marian McPartland: contemporary jazz pianist, educator, radio host, and spokesperson for women in jazz.

In some styles of modern jazz, it is sometimes difficult to identify jazz in the traditional sense. The style of jazz, in fact, the definition of jazz, is changing. But traditional jazz is not a thing of the past.

Many great modern jazz artists value the instruments, rhythms, harmonic changes, and forms of traditional jazz. The most prominent current jazz musician who builds directly on the past is the gifted trumpeter Wynton Marsalis (listen to Listening Guide 23b, p. 107). Marsalis, who is also an accomplished classical musician, received two Grammies in 1983, one for jazz and one for his recording of classical trumpet concertos. In 1997 he was awarded the Pulitzer Prize in music for his "Blood on the Fields," which was premiered on January 28, 1997, at Yale University.

Long after the swing era ended, big band sounds were again heard from the groups of Maynard Ferguson, Buddy Rich, and Toshiko Akiyoshi. As mentioned earlier in this chapter, the old bands—Duke Ellington, Count Basie, and Glenn Miller—were revived under new leadership. Marian McPartland has kept the sounds of traditional jazz alive for listeners to her long-running public radio series *Piano Jazz*.

As in any art, some musicians are motivated artistically, others commercially. Some look backward and value history and traditions. Others look forward, valuing experimentation and new forms of expression. Future styles of jazz will almost certainly blend all these influences, for most artists respond to the challenges from various sources of inspiration and creativity. It may be that fusion jazz, as a genre, is a remnant of the past, and that current jazz artists are playing wonderfully different manifestations of contemporary jazz, whatever this may be or may come to be.

Listening Guide

"Minute By Minute"

Modern jazz-fusion.

Performed by Stanley Clarke, bass; Larry Carlton, guitar; Billy Cobham, drums; Deron Johnson, keyboards; and Najee, tenor saxophone.

Recorded in 1994 — **CD2, Track 18, 3:22**

Goals

Compare characteristics of modern jazz with earlier jazz.

Recognize static harmony without traditional harmonic progressions.

Identify triple subdivision of the beat.

Recognize contrasting key areas.

Guide

Moderate, four-beat tempo.

0:00	Section 1	Phrase 1: five bars; starts after drum kick; stepwise pattern on keyboard
0:12		Phrase 2: four bars; tenor sax lead; strong 2 and 4; descending contour leads into main theme, starting on a low tonic
0:21	Section 2	Main theme: sax; full texture
0:32		Guitar lead: bluesy style; lighter texture; sustained background
1:00		Main theme: sax; full texture
1:20		Guitar lead in high range; sustained background
1:49		Main theme: sax; full texture
2:06	Section 3	First part: similar to opening; stepwise pattern; tenor sax added
2:15		Second part: sax lead; strong beat; sustained keyboard chords in background; ends with triple subdivision of the beat heard in the drums
2:39	Section 4	Main theme in four phrases; in higher key than original tonic

Reflections

How is this music jazz? How is it not jazz?

How does it differ from bebop or swing? How is it similar to bebop or swing?

Summary

This chapter on jazz was designed to help you know, appreciate, and respect the literature, heritage, people, and sounds of jazz.

Jazz is a broad and complex topic. One can generalize about a style and immediately find exceptions. For example, Miles Davis was at first a bebop musician, then an influential cool jazz artist, and later a leader in fusion and electronic jazz. Max Roach was presented as one of the best of bop drummers, but he also has performed on many cool jazz recordings. One finds cool jazz, bebop, and other styles all in the same piece. The big band jazz of Stan Kenton, for example, frequently has elements of bebop, cool, and swing in one arrangement. Many of the great artists defy classification because they continue to grow and change.

Additional Listening

Example   *No.* 3

"Corcovado"

Bossa nova—a blend of American jazz and Latin American dance music.
Performed by Stan Getz, tenor sax; Antonio Carlos Jobim, piano and songwriter; Astrud Gilberto, vocal; Gary Burton, vibes; Kenny Burrell, guitar; Gene Cherico, bass; Helcio Milito, drums.
Recorded in New York City in 1964 — **CD2, Tracks 19–20, 2:42**

Goals

Describe the rhythmic impulse and the aesthetic mood.
Identify features that are characteristically Latin rhythms and those that are jazz.
Describe the interaction of the tenor sax and the vocal lines.
Describe the roles and functions of the rhythm section, including guitar.

Guide

First chorus	8 + 8 + 8 + 12 bars	Vocal; sax fill
	14 bars	Instrumental (sax overlaps end of previous phrase)
Second chorus	8 + 10	Vocal; sax fill
	5	Sax phrase and drawn out ritard (last two bars)

Reflections

In what ways is this music jazz? In what ways is it not jazz?
Discuss the popularity of bossa nova. Is it an important genre in American popular music? Jazz? American ethnic music?

xample   *No.* 4

"Don't Let Me Be Lonely Tonight"

Modern jazz—an accomplished pop singer and song writer performing with an all-star modern jazz combo.

Performed by Michael Brecker, tenor sax; Pat Metheny, guitar; Herbie Hancock, piano; Charlie Haden, bass; and Jack DeJohnette, drums—with James Taylor, vocal.

Composed by James Taylor.

From the Michael Brecker album *Nearness of You; the Ballad Book* (2001).

CD2, Track 21, 4:43 (SCD) CD1, Track 20, 4:43

Each of the instrumentalists on this recording are among the most successful and most influential modern jazz artists, just as James Taylor has been among pop artists.

Goals

Listen to the lines of each instrumentalist and describe his contributions to the musical style.

Describe James Taylor's vocal style.

Guide

0:00   Chorus—vocal and piano
0:35   Verse 1
1:08   Verse 2
1:46   Chorus
2:15   Instrumental: tenor sax lead
2:56   Verse 3
3:33   Chorus
4:05   Extension of chorus: leads to final cadence

Reflections

Do pop and jazz mix? Do they mix well in this musical example?

Do the jazz musicians in this example play only in a jazz style? Does the pop singer sing only in a pop style?

American Popular Music

Goals for Listening

- **Identify** genres.
- **Recognize** styles of individuals and groups.
- **Refine** understanding of skills of previously presented concepts.

Summary

Additional Listening

Terms and Concepts

Early American songs

Lyrics

Minstrel shows

The nature of popular music

Styles and genres

Tin Pan Alley

Musicals—stage and film

Radio and recordings

Standards

Country music

African American influences

Contemporary popular music

Charts

This chapter discusses the major contemporary genres of American popular music, their historical backgrounds, the trends and influences that helped shape them, and representative artists who made them an important part of American popular culture. After a discussion of the nature of popular music and its history before the twentieth century, the popular music of the twentieth century is presented in four broad categories:

1. *The music of Tin Pan Alley*: the beginning of modern American popular music and the music industry
2. *Country music*: shifting from a regional folk music to a major part of the music industry
3. *Music having African American influences*: blues, gospel, Motown, and the hip-hop culture
4. *Pop and rock*: from rockabilly and the "British invasion" to a wide array of current sounds and styles

The purpose of these discussions is to help students learn about musical styles with which they may already be familiar, to increase their awareness and understanding of less familiar styles, and, again, to use relatively simple music to sharpen their listening skills, musical vocabulary, and awareness of the elements of music.

Goals for Listening

In this chapter, listening skills are based on skills learned in previous chapters, especially Chapter 6. Thus, rather than responding to new musical concepts, develop those listening skills already experienced.

The purpose of the listening guides is to reveal a breadth of styles (though not a complete overview) and to provide listening experiences in popular music styles with which some readers may not be familiar.

The listening guides provide a small sampling of the many styles of American popular music, including a song from a Broadway musical of the 1930s, Western swing, traditional and contemporary bluegrass, rock and roll of the 1950s, contemporary R&B, pop and rock of the 1980s and 1990s, and the unique sound of Béla Fleck and the Flecktones.

The Definition and Scope of Popular Music

By definition, popular music at any given time is music known by the majority of interested people. Yet many listeners focus on and appreciate a limited number of styles. For example, readers may know the sound and style of Garth Brooks or Faith Hill but know little if anything about Bob Wills or Alison Krauss. To know a name is important, but to recognize and know a person's style requires a higher level of experience and understanding.

One goal of this chapter is to learn the common characteristics that classify a piece of music as popular, as opposed to jazz, classical, or folk music, which may also be popular but among smaller groups or specialized audiences.

A second goal is to perceive and articulate factors that distinguish one popular style from another. What makes a country tune different from a Tin Pan Alley tune? What makes rock different from R&B, or R&B different from blues, or contemporary rock different from classic rock? What makes R&B of the 1950s different from R&B today?

In popular culture, music that is said to be popular has mass appeal. It is cross-cultural; it transcends regional, ethnic, economic, political, and educational boundaries. It is music that is consumed (bought) by the largest number of people and has the widest appeal. It speaks directly to people in ways to which they can respond, both musically and emotionally.

Traditional pop songs typically are easy to listen to. The dominant attributes are the melody and the **lyrics**, and the sound is easily recognizable. These songs are simple and tuneful, singable, repetitive, and based on tonic, dominant, and subdominant chords (or sometimes on fewer chords). The music usually has a strong beat and regular meter, rhythmic patterns, and phrases.

In rock, however, it is the beat—the rhythmic vitality—that is dominant. In live concerts, the artists' persona is influenced by dress (anything from conservative suits to bizarre costumes) and often highly energetic stage movement and stylistic behavior. Up-to-date technology is seen in musical instruments, lighting, sound enhancement, and special effects.

Popular music is vernacular music, not high art. By definition, it is music that appeals to the masses. It is not better or worse than art music—it is simply different in style and function. It is visceral, foot-tapping, emotional, and immediately understandable music, at least to most people.

Much popular music has, or can have, extramusical associations: the personality of the performers; the social activity that is always part of a live concert; a relationship to our social, economic, or political history; and memories of friendship and romance.

Popular music is an integral part of the music industry, which relies on marketing, advertising, and distribution and sales strategies to influence taste, maintain consumer interest, and create and promote hits and star performers. The public is swayed by musical fads, rapidly changing tastes, and manipulation by advertisers and the music industry. As a result, songs will typically not remain popular for a long time; they come and go, frequently in a matter of months. Only a few songs are popular for decades or generations. These songs are called **standards** (listen to Listening Guide 2, p. 32; Listening Guide 18, p. 96; Listening Guide 21, p. 104; Listening Guide 23, p. 106; and Listening Guide 25, p. 122).

Although individual songs may change rapidly as tastes change, the overall characteristics of popular music styles are relatively consistent. For example, a country and western song may be popular for a few months, but the style of country and western can usually be recognized year after year as distinct from rock, swing, or folk. An arrangement of a popular tune for swing band may have been popular only in the 1930s, but the basic character and form of that song may have been consistent and consistently popular ever since.

The popularity of songs is measurable and has been measured for decades: by the number of times a song was played on a jukebox or on the radio (**airplay**) and by the sales figures of LPs, cassettes, and now CDs. Before recordings, popularity was measured by sales of sheet music. Popularity has been reported to the public by *The Hit Parade*, the long-running radio show of the 1930s and 1940s, and by *Billboard* magazine, which still provides weekly **charts** of sales in a wide variety of categories, including contemporary Christian and gospel, country, adult contemporary, Latin, new age, rock, world music, R&B, and rap. Virtually every country or region of the world has its own charts, easily accessed on the Internet.

The shift from printed music to recordings had deep impact on American musical culture. Sheet music, is a printed song usually arranged for voice and piano accompaniment; to learn a song from sheet music, one had to perform it by singing it or by accompanying a singer. Thus the consumer was an active participant in the music.

With recordings, radio, and television, one need only listen to know and appreciate a popular song. Thus instead of making music (performing), the listener is a nonperforming participant. Consumers may listen intently to a song, may frequently memorize the lyrics, and may often learn to sing a song from listening to it. Without performance, however, listening too frequently is passive.

We are in an age of essentially casual, passive listening: to music in the background while we are doing other things, or to music that was created for nonmusical, nonartistic purposes. Background music permeates our environment. One can wonder what impact generations of passive listening will have on our ability to listen actively and intently to music.

Because popular music is ever-changing, we need to consider the roots of American popular music: the events, artists, and styles that have created it. What influences shaped today's popular music?

Pre-Twentieth Century

Popular music did not flourish during the early years of our nation. Although religious music and concert art music were acceptable, moral and religious scruples, some manifested as laws, prohibited "entertainment" music, particularly music for the stage. After the Revolutionary War, many of these strictures were relaxed and entertainment music became commonplace.

The Colonial Period

By the early part of the nineteenth century, more Americans were learning to read music and play the piano, and they could afford to buy sheet music. The earliest popular songs were composed for amateurs to sing and enjoy at home with small groups of family and friends. Songs that colonial Americans enjoyed were mostly imported from Europe and the British Isles and included melodies from European operas fitted with English texts, settings of traditional Scottish and Irish airs, German art songs, and simplified arrangements of vocal solos composed for professional singers. A typical popular song was strophic. It was set in a relatively low vocal range with a simple piano accompaniment. The music was usually in a major key and relied on the three primary chords (I, IV, and V).

The first person known to have written songs for voice and piano in America was Francis Hopkinson, a signer of the Declaration of Independence and the first secretary of the navy. Some examples of early American popular songs follow:

"The Blue Bells of Scotland"—traditional Scottish air

"Auld Lang Syne" and "Coming through the Rye"—traditional
Scottish airs with texts by Robert Burns

"Ave Maria" and "Serenade"—composed by Franz Schubert

"Home Sweet Home"—text by Sir Henry Bishop (which sold 100,000 copies in 1832, its first year, and several million by the end of the nineteenth century)

"The Last Rose of Summer" and "Believe Me if All Those Endearing Young Charms"—traditional Irish tunes with texts by Thomas Moore

During the mid-nineteenth century, American popular music took on a more diverse character. Songs influenced by British music and European opera continued, but others began developing a distinctively American character.

The First "American" Songs

Henry Russell   Henry Russell, an influential songwriter, was born in England, came to America to advance his career as a performer and composer, and concertized widely. His songs and his singing were intended to appeal to many types of people and to elicit emotional responses from large audiences. He had a sense of what type of song would be popular. Although his songs were influenced by European opera, he was able to infuse them with an American spirit that helped shape popular songwriting. He influenced others, notably the greatest of all nineteenth-century composers of American songs, Stephen Foster. Russell's most famous song is "Woodman, Spare That Tree."

Stephen Foster   Stephen Foster was, like Russell, trained and knowledgeable in the art music of his day. Also like Russell, he wanted to "speak to the American people in song." No composer created so many songs that became a shared experience for so many Americans as Stephen Foster. His works included minstrel songs and plantation songs: many were sentimental; others were dramatic. In his later minstrel songs, Foster began offering an image of blacks as human beings who experience pain, sorrow, and love. Many of his songs have become so identified with American culture that they are now a part of the American folk song tradition.

Here are some examples of songs by Stephen Foster:

"Old Folks at Home" (also known as "Swanee River")

"Oh! Susanna"

"My Old Kentucky Home"

"Old Black Joe"

"Jeanie with the Light Brown Hair"

"Come Where My Love Lies Dreaming"

"Beautiful Dreamer"

Sheet music cover for "Jeanie with the Light Brown Hair" (1854).

Another genre that emerged in the mid-nineteenth century is rally and protest songs, songs openly associated with social or political causes such as temperance, abolition (antislavery), women's suffrage, antiwar movements, and political campaigns. The most popular of these songs were in step with the pulse of the people and in tune with their mood. This genre was discussed in chapter 4 as part of the American folk song tradition, and it illustrates the blurring of the line between folk (traditional) and popular (composed) music.

Rally and Protest Songs

Examples of rally songs include:

"John Brown's Body"

"Battle Hymn of the Republic"

"Dixie"

"Rally 'Round the Flag"

"When This Cruel War Is Over"—a song that expressed the emotions of the millions of Americans who bought copies of it in 1863

"Grandfather's Clock"

Inspired by the popularity of the Hutchinson Family Singers in the mid-nineteenth century, rally and protest songs became an integral part of American popular music, particularly the music of Woody Guthrie in the 1930s and 1940s and of his successors in the urban folk song movement of the 1960s: Bob Dylan, Pete Seeger, Joan Baez, and others.

The mainstay of the **minstrel show** was the minstrel song. A product of rural American folk traditions and emerging urban composed music, it may be considered the first distinctively American music genre. Typically, it was lively, syncopated, and often humorous. These songs were originally written by white Americans for white Americans, were sung by white Americans in blackface, and were a caricature of the "Negro" way of life, often portraying black Americans as comical and illiterate. This portrayal had little to do with the realities of black culture, but the songs became an important part of American popular music. Two of the most famous of early minstrel entertainers were "Daddy" Rice, who capitalized on Jim Crow routines; and Dan Emmett, one of the earliest composers of minstrel songs, who wrote "Dixie" and "Old Dan Tucker."

Minstrel Show

By the middle of the nineteenth century, minstrel songs were popular in America and in Europe, partly because of the success of traveling minstrel troupes such as the Virginia Minstrels, with Dan Emmett, formed in New York in 1843; and the Christy Minstrels, also formed in New York in the 1840s. These troupes paved the way for hundreds of successors and imitators. It was a logical step to take the popular minstrel songs and dances performed by troupes and individual entertainers and present them as a sequence of acts onstage: thus the minstrel show was created. Hundreds of shows were produced in the late 1800s in America and Europe.

The music for a minstrel show was drawn from traditional folk material, popular songs of the day, songs from Italian opera, and songs newly composed for the show. These shows also included comic dialogue, dances, acrobats, blackface songs, and instrumental pieces. Since the plot was minimal, the music was incidental and did not necessarily enhance any dramatic action. Ironically, white performers' blackface minstrel shows were so popular that blacks themselves began writing and performing in such shows.

The first black songwriter of note was James Bland, who wrote "In the Evening by the Moonlight," "Carry Me Back to Old Virginny," and "Oh, Dem Golden Slippers." Black minstrel shows began in 1865 in Georgia with the Georgia Minstrels. The style and content were essentially the same as in white minstrel shows.

Twentieth Century

Twentieth-century American popular music includes many genres and styles derived from a merging of European and African musical traditions. It was influenced by a dramatic expansion of the music industry with the advent of recordings, radio, and later television. In this section, we will consider the extent to which an artist was innovative, influenced other artists, and helped shape the future of popular music; but this is difficult to judge after only a short time has elapsed. Sometimes it takes decades to gain sufficient perspective to assess the significance of an artist.

The roots of today's popular music, as noted previously, go back to the second half of the nineteenth century with songs from minstrel shows, followed, in the early part of the twentieth century, by Tin Pan Alley songs, ragtime, blues, and songs from vaudeville, Broadway musicals, and film. Later, hillbilly music expanded from a regional genre to a nationally popular genre that included western swing, bluegrass, and the Nashville sound. Hillbilly became country and western and today is simply country music. Black popular music, including R&B, gospel, soul, and more recently rap or hip-hop, is now enjoyed by both black and white Americans. Rock and roll became rock in its many manifestations and substyles. Currently, crossover music, songs incorporating characteristics of two or more styles, is common.

Tin Pan Alley

The 1890s through the 1950s was the greatest period of songwriting in the history of American popular music: these were the years of the **Tin Pan Alley** tradition. The most productive years were the 1920s and the 1930s. From Tin Pan Alley have come our pop tunes and standards, our most beloved songs—songs for amusement, entertainment, and escape. They include sentimental love songs, syncopated songs and dance tunes, Latin American music, nonsense songs, and show tunes.

Tin Pan Alley symbolizes three aspects of popular music:

1. A street in New York City where virtually every publisher of popular music was located in the early twentieth century. The term *Tin Pan Alley* referred to the sound of the cheap upright pianos that publishers maintained in their salesrooms for customers who wanted to try out a song.
2. The part of the music industry that was devoted to the production, promotion, and sale of popular songs. In the early years, the primary medium of publication was sheet music; thus the industry stimulated the sale of pianos, player pianos, and piano rolls. Beginning in the 1920s, the industry promoted the sale of radios, phonographs, and recordings. Publishers assessed the public taste and proceeded to write and publish more of the same. They maintained their own composers (sometimes called "hacks") who ground out songs daily. Most of these songs were forgotten soon after they were published.
3. The type of song written during these decades (listen to Listening Guide 18, p. 96). Typically, Tin Pan Alley in this sense meant a song in verse-chorus form. The chorus usually consisted of 32 bars with four equal phrases and had the more memorable lyrics and melody. The lyrics of Tin Pan Alley songs ranged from those that had no message to those that expressed strong feelings about contemporary social conditions.

Tin Pan Alley songs were performed in vaudeville, the Ziegfeld Follies, and other revues; in Broadway musicals, films, and nightclubs; on radio and recordings; and by big band jazz and swing bands and their singers. The most durable and popular American songs are the Tin Pan Alley standards, sometimes called *classics*.

Tin Pan Alley, despite its widespread use of hacks, had a way of encouraging genius among America's popular composers, lyricists, and performers. Among the best of the composers who flourished in the Tin Pan Alley tradition were Jerome Kern, Cole Porter, George Gershwin, Irving Berlin, and Richard Rodgers. Among the outstanding performers of this period were Al Jolson, Eddie Cantor, Rudy Vallee, Kate Smith, Paul Whiteman, and Bing Crosby.

Three styles of music, ragtime, blues, and swing (discussed more fully in chaps. 4 and 6), became extremely popular among both black and white Americans. The music industry (Tin Pan Alley) exploited these styles by producing hundreds of songs called *rags* and *blues*, whether or not they really were.

Vaudeville   Vaudeville, a type of variety show, was centered in New York City and replaced the minstrel show in popularity. As in a minstrel show, the entire vaudeville troupe was usually onstage and included a sequence of unrelated acts: singers (not usually in blackface), dancers, comedians, jugglers, child performers, trained animals, and dramatic sketches. Its more sophisticated counterpart on Broadway was the revue. These variety shows were known at different times as follies, scandals, or vanities. The most famous was the Ziegfeld Follies, produced from 1907 through 1932.

Tin Pan Alley songs were an essential element of vaudeville. They included sentimental popular songs, some blackface minstrel songs, and songs in racial or ethnic dialects. Vaudeville represented a new direction in American popular music. It introduced songs that dealt with contemporary city life in what was still a basically rural, agrarian society.

Musicals   The American musical includes songs, staging, and drama. In contrast to minstrel and vaudeville shows, it is a unified piece with dramatic flow: a musical play. Musicals were created by songwriters of genius such as Kern, Gershwin, Porter, and Berlin.

Old hit of the all-black show "Shuffle Along" (1921) was used as the campaign song for presidential candidate Harry S Truman in 1948.

L istening Guide

Irving Berlin rehearsing
with Ethel Merman.

"I Get a Kick out of You"

Tin Pan Alley.

From *Anything Goes*, a Broadway musical.

Composed in 1934 by Cole Porter.

Sung by Ethel Merman in 1934 — **CD2, Tracks 22–23, 3:06**

Goals

Recognize the style of a Tin Pan Alley song.

Identify patterns of contrast and repetition in the standard Tin Pan Alley verse-chorus song form.

Recognize open and closed cadences.

Recognize motives, a tempo (a return to the original tempo), extension, and tag.

—Continued

L i s t e n i n g   G u i d e—*Continued*   *No.* 25

Guide

Count in a slow two.

Section		Length	Description
Intro		2 bars	Instrumental
Verse		20 bars (8 + 12)	Vocal; Ritard in bar 10 of the second phrase, then returns to the original tempo in bar 11 (a tempo); leads into the chorus
Chorus	a	16 bars	Based on an ascending stepwise motive; the title phrase "I Get a Kick Out of You" occurs in the last four bars of each a phrase; closed cadence
	a	16 bars	Closed cadence
	b	16 bars (8 + 8)	Contrasting section (bridge); based on another ascending stepwise motive at another pitch level; open cadence
	a	18 bars	Phrase extended by two bars after closed cadence
	b	16 bars (8 + 8)	Bridge, piano lead; open cadence
	a	20 bars	Ritard in bars 13 and 14, resolves to tonic in bar 15, then continues a tempo for the final six bars.

Reflections

In the verse, do the phrases repeat or contrast? In the chorus, identify the form. Listen for repetition within each phrase.

How important is syncopation in this example?

The best musicals have been produced on Broadway. Although centered in New York, the American musical reached the entire country.

The first important composer of Broadway musicals was George M. Cohan, who was also the lyricist for his productions. His *Little Johnnie Jones* was produced in 1904 and included the song "Give My Regards to Broadway." Cohan, of Irish heritage, used popular, patriotic airs such as "Yankee Doodle" and "Dixie." His own patriotic song "You're a Grand Old Flag" is from his production *George Washington, Jr.* (1906).

The best Tin Pan Alley composers wrote Broadway musicals: George Gershwin wrote *Girl Crazy, Strike Up the Band, Lady Be Good* (which included "Fascinating Rhythm" and "The Man I Love"), and *Porgy and Bess* (which included "Summertime") (see Listening Guide 21, p. 104); Cole Porter wrote *Anything Goes*, Jerome Kern wrote *Roberta* and *Showboat* (which included "Ol' Man River"); Irving Berlin wrote *Annie Get Your Gun* (which included "There's No Business Like Show Business"); and Richard Rodgers wrote *Oklahoma* and *Carousel* (the latter included "If I Loved You").

The tradition of the Broadway musical continues in the music and lyrics of, among many others, Stephen Sondheim, who wrote *West Side Story, Gypsy, A Funny Thing*

Happened on the Way to the Forum, Company, A Little Night Music, and *Sweeney Todd;* and Andrew Lloyd Webber, who wrote *Jesus Christ Superstar, Evita, Cats,* and *Phantom of the Opera.*

Film   *The Jazz Singer,* the first commercial movie with a synchronized sound track, was made in 1927. In the decade that followed, composers, arrangers, singers, dancers, and producers headed for Hollywood. The early movie musicals used large orchestras, lavish sets and costumes, large casts, and expensive stars. They provided marvelous opportunities for talented artists.

These movies were entertaining spectacles. They presented an unreal world of glittering sophistication, the carefree world of show people, exotic travel, and the make-believe world of childhood. They offered escape from the hardships of the Great Depression and depicted things that were not available to most Americans. People who were deprived of luxury wanted to be entertained by seeing excess. Moviegoers were aware of the luxurious lifestyles of the rich and famous and of the extravagant incomes of movie stars. They didn't seem to mind; no one protested this imbalance in our society. Seeing these unreal experiences and situations must somehow have made their lives a bit more bearable.

Many songs from these movies became very popular. Evidently, they took people's minds off their troubles. The lyrics do not convey how people lived as much as their reactions to the way they lived. Tin Pan Alley composers became important creators of film music, and many of their most successful songs came from films. Also, many popular singers had successful careers in film. These include Al Jolson, Bing Crosby, Doris Day, Frank Sinatra, and, more recently, Barbra Streisand.

Radio and Recordings   Two media—network radio and the production and national marketing, advertising, and sales of recordings—changed the face of the music industry. They created hit songs, determined what songs earned a profit for the creators and producers, and developed a way to report hits—the *Lucky Strike Hit Parade* and later the charts of *Billboard* magazine and other polls of the industry (see "Publishing" in chap. 16). To a large extent, the media determined who would be the stars of popular song, what songs Americans would listen to, and, in effect, what their tastes in popular music would be. Tin Pan Alley stars, such as Rudy Vallee, Bing Crosby, and Kate Smith, achieved great success as radio artists.

The first radio station was established in Pittsburgh in 1920, the first commercial sponsorship came in 1922, and the first radio network came in 1926. By 1929, 40 percent of American families owned a radio. Radio thus became a powerful medium for selling popular music. Network radio in the 1920s exposed people in the rural South and southwest to the urban music of the northeast. In time, this influence caused a shift in taste from British-influenced folk songs and ballads to commercial hillbilly music. In Atlanta, WSB radio was established in 1922 and broadcast hillbilly music: singers, fiddlers, and string bands. In Chicago, WLS established the National Barn Dance, and WSM in Nashville started the Grand Ole Opry.

In the 1920s, the commercial record companies recognized the financial benefits of field recordings of the folk songs and dances of various immigrant groups, the blues of black singers, and white rural folk songs, ballads, and dances (see chap. 4). These companies made money by selling the recordings back to these specialized audiences, but the companies also preserved a diverse folk repertoire, created an invaluable resource for American culture, and transformed many traditional folksingers into professional recording artists.

The most popular jazz bands or swing bands achieved national exposure from touring, particularly from network radio broadcasts from hotel ballrooms, dance halls, and nightclubs. This made them a prime target for Tin Pan Alley song pluggers. Publishers marketed (plugged) their songs through the big swing bands, particularly those who featured vocalists, such as Ella Fitzgerald, Frank Sinatra, Peggy Lee, and the Andrews Sisters, whose acceptance of a song would virtually guarantee its commercial success.

With modern advances in the manufacture of recording equipment, particularly microphones, audio engineers have been able to easily balance the sound of a solo singer with the sound of a big band or a full theater or studio orchestra.

A Transition The period of Tin Pan Alley in the history of American popular music ended in the 1950s, when three things happened. First, rock and roll, a dramatically new style of popular music, emerged. Second, the presentation of a song became as important as the music, as was vividly demonstrated by Elvis Presley. Third, the center of songwriting, publishing, and recording shifted to Nashville, which ultimately made country music a significant part of mainstream popular music.

In time, singers felt hampered by the inflexible pulse of swing. They valued the intimate personal lyrics of their songs and wanted the freedom to add their own interpretations and feelings. This crooning, melodramatic, personal style was not conducive to dance music; it lost its rhythmic vitality and spark; and this led to a decline in the popularity of Tin Pan Alley songs in the 1950s. The "down home" country and western songs of Hank Williams, Roy Acuff, Bob Wills, Kitty Wells, and Bill Monroe and the vibrant rock and roll of Fats Domino, Little Richard, Chuck Berry, Buddy Holly, and Elvis Presley rose to take the place of Tin Pan Alley songs.

Country Music

Chapter 4 presents music derived from oral tradition, which includes fiddle tunes, string band music, and country singing with a nasal twang. This is the folk music of the rural South. In this chapter, *country music* refers to songwriting, recording, and the making of "stars" in a popular style which is closely related to this southern folk music. It is a regional music made national. The music includes hillbilly music, string band music, and other old-time country songs; western swing, honky tonk, and cowboy songs; bluegrass; and the "Nashville sound," the beginning of modern, commercial country music. Bluegrass, perhaps, is the only contemporary medium in which traditional southern rural folk music can survive in our modern urban society, although a few current country artists seem to value the old sound.

Hillbilly Originally, **hillbilly** was used to describe in a negative way the "culturally and musically inferior" songs of poor, white, rural, uneducated southerners. This music was a product of the rural South—a regional music for a regional audience. However, in the second quarter of the twentieth century, hillbilly records were sold widely, and hillbilly music was broadcast from Atlanta, Chicago, Nashville, and many other cities. The popularity of hillbilly music as measured by record sales may have represented an image of an older and simpler America, an alternative to jazz and the popular dance music of the 1920s, and a yearning for the good old songs of the nineteenth century. Hillbilly music was often projected as wholesome, down-to-earth, family-style entertainment.

Hillbilly songs are variants of British ballads, camp meetings songs and hymns, and popular, sentimental songs of the late nineteenth century. They represent a merging of rural and urban influences and a conflict between maintaining rugged simplicity and a desire to be accepted by middle-class, urban America. The songs were simple and direct, reflecting the values, aspirations, and fears of the rural, Protestant South. Hillbilly singing projected sincerity, deep human emotions, and real situations related to love, death, and religion. The singers preserved their regional accents and dialect, the familiar twang and nasal vocal quality, and the slides and ornamentation of much southern mountain music.

The 1920s saw a tremendous national effort by record companies to record music not only by blues, jazz, gospel, folk, Tin Pan Alley, and vaudeville artists but also by hillbilly performers. Radio created additional demand for performers. The first hillbilly recording artists were Uncle Dave Macon, the Carter Family, and Jimmy Rodgers.

Western Swing and Cowboy Songs   Western music is an extension of hillbilly. Southern singers, along with many others, headed west in search of greater opportunity, taking with them their religion and their songs. The gulf widened between hillbilly and its folk roots. Western hillbilly dealt with loneliness and infidelity rather than religion, sentiment, and nostalgia. Some western music was performed on the piano in small-town saloons and was called *honky-tonk*.

By the 1930s, the movie industry began making westerns that romanticized the Wild West and produced a vast quantity of cowboy songs. Gene Autry, Tex Ritter, and Roy Rogers were the most famous of the singing cowboys. Their most famous songs, such as "Tumbling Tumbleweed," "Cool Water," "The Last Roundup," "Back in the Saddle Again," "The Yellow Rose of Texas," "Deep in the Heart of Texas," "Don't Fence Me In," and "I'm an Old Cowhand" were newly composed, many by Tin Pan Alley composers.

A type of western music that used a larger instrumental ensemble including saxes, brass, and a standard jazz rhythm section of piano, bass, and drums is **western swing**. The most influential exponent of western swing was Bob Wills, who, with his Texas Playboys, flourished in Tulsa from 1934 to 1942 (Listening Guide 26, see below). By 1938, Wills was using 14 musicians and virtually a swing band instrumentation plus fiddle and Hawaiian steel guitar. He popularized his music through radio broadcasts, recordings, dances, and personal appearances throughout the Southwest.

Listening Guide   *No.* 26

"New San Antonio Rose"
Western swing
Performed by Bob Wills and His Texas Playboys (1940) — **CD2, Track 24, 2:32**
The word *new* in the title differentiates the vocal from Wills's earlier instrumental version.
Adapted from the fiddle tune "Spanish Two Step."

Goals

Identify solo instruments and sections of instruments.
Recognize motives as a means of identifying phrase structure and form. Identify the phrase structure.
Recognize open and closed cadences, question-answer phrases, and modulation.
Recognize the sounds of western swing.
Listen for repetitive patterns of harmonic change: for example, I—IV—V—I.

—Continued

Guide

Count in a moderately fast two.

Intro			Four bars, instrumental
First chorus			Instrumental, with muted trumpets prominent
	a	8 bars	Ascending-descending motive at the beginning
	a	8 bars	First theme repeated
	b	8 bars	Second theme with a descending-ascending motive at the beginning
	b	10 bars	Modulation in last two bars provides transition to the vocal chorus
Second chorus			Vocal. Four phrases, each 8 + 8, paired in question-answer relationships (open-closed cadence patterns)
	a	16 bars	First question-answer phrase group; new key
	b	16 bars	Second motive
	c	16 bars	Second new theme suddenly in a second new key; modulates in last bar
	a	16 bars	Return to the original motive in the tonic key of this chorus
Third chorus			Instrumental
	c	16 bars	The second new key; trumpets in parallel motion giving a hint of a mariachi sound (see chap. 8); modulates in last bar
	a a	18 bars	Sax section prominent (8 + 10); in tonic key of second chorus; concludes with two-bar tag

Reflections

Does this music sound like hillbilly? Jazz? Pop music? Cowboy music? Folk music? Mariachi?

Does western swing have contemporary counterparts?

Does music that incorporates elements of several different styles add to or detract from the listening experience?

What effect do the several modulations have?

What do the little shouts ("a-ha") contribute to the music?

The Nashville Sound   In 1925, radio station WSM in Nashville started a hillbilly program that would eventually become the Grand Ole Opry. In 1938, Roy Acuff was engaged as a regular performer, achieving national success. He was in part responsible for Opry's new prominence—it attracted national interest. All the great country artists have appeared on Grand Ole Opry, some as regulars for years and even decades; they include Bill Monroe, Ernest Tubb, Eddy Arnold, Hank Williams, Kitty Wells, Patsy Cline, Loretta Lynn, Dolly Parton, Ricky Skaggs, and Randy Travis.

The record companies in New York were aware of this nationalization of country music. Many opened studios in Nashville to be close to the stars of country music. They began producing records and attracting songwriters. Chet Atkins, a talented and successful guitarist, singer, and songwriter, was employed as RCA's recording director in Nashville and was a prime force in the innovations that took place in response to the popularity of rock and roll in the 1950s. These innovations, collectively, became known as the **Nashville sound**, which was most influential from 1957 to 1971.

The longtime director of the Country Music Foundation, William Ivey, offers these insights on the nature and influences of the Nashville sound:

1. It was an era in which country music responded to the pressures and demands of the marketplace. It would create a product that would have the widest possible appeal, become a part of the larger popular music spectrum, yet preserve as much as possible the traditional attributes of country music.
2. It was an era in which the music changed, partly because of commercial forces at work but also because of the interests, talents, and instincts of the record producers during this period. They were more inclined toward popular music than the "primitive ruralisms" of hillbilly music, the style that is now called *hard country*.
3. It was an era of a distinctive musical style that was influenced by the following factors:
   a. Studio musicians who functioned as "teams" and who worked together regularly moved from studio to studio. Their primary skills were technical competence (the "chops") and the ability to understand and deliver on demand exactly what was required. They improvised background music and fills, and sometimes their creative licks contributed significantly to the popularity of a song.
   b. The instrumentation became standard: as many as six guitars of different types, backup singers, small or even large string sections that included violins and cellos, and horn sections. Sometimes the background music was laid down on separate tracks after the main core of musicians had finished.
   c. Improvisatory head arrangements with a special style of notation were used to create the backup music on the spot during a recording session. Although arrangements of country tunes became more elaborate, sophisticated, and urban, the sound was sparse, staying out of the way of the lyrics and the singer.

With the Nashville sound, the roots of country music in the southern folk tradition were becoming increasingly obscure. It was hillbilly made popular by adding pop sophistication to country performance style. Nashville now symbolizes the full-scale commercialization of country music. To this day, it reigns as the recording capital of the industry.

Bluegrass   In hillbilly music, a typical song accompaniment might have included guitar, banjo, and fiddle. With its commercialization and the addition of the Hawaiian steel guitar and electronic instruments, **bluegrass** continued in the style of the old-time songs and dances. The purpose was not to become regional and culturally isolated again but to make the transition from a rural folk music to a part of the national popular culture. This

Bill Monroe and his Bluegrass Boys at the Nightstage in Boston, Massachusetts.

is mountain music that originally was the music of Appalachian ethnic groups and is now an internationally popular style of country music. Bluegrass includes story songs, part singing, fiddle tunes, and religious music, and it was taken to cities, parks, nightclubs, college campuses, and bluegrass festivals. The typical instrumentation of a bluegrass group includes acoustic guitar, fiddle, mandolin, bass fiddle, and five-string banjo—no electric guitars, no drums, no keyboards.

The pioneer of the style that would be known as bluegrass was Bill Monroe, who in 1945 headed a group called the Bluegrass Boys. Lester Flatt and Earl Scruggs split away from Monroe in 1948 and formed a bluegrass group called the Foggy Mountain Boys. Many other groups soon followed as the popularity of bluegrass spread. Like ragtime and blues (styles that became extremely popular), bluegrass was exploited by the industry in order to sell more records: "bluegrass" was added to titles or descriptions whether or not the music was really consistent with the style or instrumentation created by bluegrass pioneers.

The audience for bluegrass is knowledgeable and vocal. It knows the bluegrass style and is suspicious of groups attempting to broaden that style. A group that adds piano or drums may be seen as "selling out" to the commercial interests or simply relinquishing its identification with bluegrass. This creates a dilemma: how can artists create within the perhaps rigid conventions of a style and at the same time develop an individual style to set themselves apart from other artists in the marketplace?

For example, David Grisman is a successful contemporary artist who has fused his affinity for jazz with bluegrass. He combines his ability as a mandolin player and his interest in acoustic sounds (such as that of mandolin, guitar, violin, and bass), creating bluegrass music in a jazz style. But is it bluegrass music? Alison Brown is a guitarist who also combines bluegrass with her interests and abilities in jazz. On the other hand, Alison Krauss is recognized as a top bluegrass fiddler and vocalist and is highly respected within the bluegrass community, but she carefully steps out of bounds. First, she is a young woman, the first female bluegrass star in a genre traditionally dominated by male performers. She grew up in the university town of Champaign, Illinois, which is definitely not

L istening Guide   *No.* 27

"Backtrackin'"

Traditional bluegrass
Performed by Nashville Bluegrass Band.
From the album *Waitin' For the Hard Times to Go* (1993).
Banjo, mandolin, fiddle, guitar, bass, vocals — **CD2, Track 25, 2:58 (SCD) CD1, Track 21, 2:58**

Traditional bluegrass uses all acoustic sounds, no drums, no keyboards, and, as in this example, a vocal trio (lead, tenor, and baritone). Bluegrass became famous in the late 1940s with the music of the Bluegrass Boys (Bill Monroe) and the Foggy Mountain Boys (Lester Flatt and Earl Scruggs). Originally it was a form of hillbilly music—Appalachian mountain music. It has since become widely popular in both country and urban settings and clearly an important part of American popular culture.

Goals

Recognize a style of music without keyboards, drums, or electronic sounds.
Describe the vocal quality and inflections of the singers.
Recognize antecedent-consequent phrase groups.
Recognize the distinctive sounds of the mandolin, banjo, and fiddle.

Guide

In a moderate 4

Intro	$4\frac{1}{2}$ bars	Starts with a pickup
Verse 1	8 + 8 bars	
Chorus	8 bars	
Banjo	8 bars	
Mandolin	$4\frac{1}{2}$ bars	
Verse 2	8 + 8 bars	
Chorus	8 bars	
Fiddle	4 bars	
Chorus	4 bars extended to final cadence	

Reflections

What does the sliding into and out of pitches by the singers in the Nashville Bluegrass Band contribute to the bluegrass style?

How does the pronunciation of words affect the style?

How does this music differ from other forms and styles of contemporary country?

Considering background, training, and experience of singers, what does it take to produce the various sounds within each genre: folk, pop, rock, jazz, musical theater, opera, and so on. For example, can a jazz singer easily learn the bluegrass style? Why or why not?

a natural environment for a bluegrass musician. On her third album for Rounder Records (*I've Got That Old Feeling*, 1990), she challenged bluegrass conventions by adding piano and drums and downplaying the banjo. But the album was very successful commercially and gave her, and bluegrass, wide exposure. Broadening an audience base while promoting a traditional style are two aims that are difficult to achieve simultaneously.

Contemporary Country Sounds   It appears that hillbilly, made more accessible to a larger audience through the Nashville Sound, has moved farther away from its roots. Recent crossover styles, commonly known as pop country and country rock, are dominating the market. Major artists who have gone beyond the bounds of traditional country music include Willie Nelson, Kenny Rogers, Emmylou Harris, Dolly Parton, Mary-Chapin Carpenter, Barbara Mandrell, k d lang, Alabama, and many others.

Is this new music commercialized country ("watered-down" hillbilly), or is it an emerging new style American popular music that will be loved by many consumers of popular music? As with all music, the best songs will last.

How do artists decide on a musical style and a professional persona? These decisions are typically driven by the marketplace. Successful artists develop and maintain loyal audiences for their live concerts and, more important, their recordings. For example, how does Alison Krauss develop a wider audience for herself and for bluegrass without alienating the bluegrass traditionalists? How does she stay in touch with bluegrass traditions and also infuse her music with nontraditional elements? How does she promote bluegrass when others feel that this is an unwelcome intrusion of commerce into the bluegrass culture? The line between tradition and crossover is unclear; country artists are found at all parts along this continuum.

Hank Williams.

Barbara Mandrell.

Randy Travis.

Any genre has its innovators, its commercial exploiters, and its traditionalists. Contemporary country music has practitioners who have stayed within the traditions of Roy Acuff, Hank Williams, Bill Monroe, Kitty Wells, Patsy Cline, and Loretta Lynn. Performers of this neotraditional, hard country style include Ricky Skaggs, George Jones, and George Strait. Randy Travis, Reba McIntyre, and Garth Brooks have been very successful country singers who remain traditional to some extent and, because of their popularity, are among those who have, at times, appeared on pop and country lists. These artists are not hanging on to a dying genre that no longer sells but are promoting the enduring appeal of country music among an increasingly large segment of our population.

African American Influences

Black music, in one sense, is music performed by black Americans and is intended primarily for black audiences. It includes gospel, R&B, and soul. All these styles and the artists who created them have made important contributions to the development of American popular music.

Seldom, however, does music fit neatly into categories and definitions. Any music conceived to "rise on the charts" must have a wide enough appeal to sell a sufficient number of records to be declared a hit—a status intensely desired by artists of popular music. Thus, some black music is intentionally watered down, commercialized so those unfamiliar with the style would be more likely to appreciate it. This is particularly true of gospel music, the Motown sound (a style of black music produced in Detroit in the 1960s), and rap.

(a)

(b)

Rhythm and blues, as well as rock and roll, generate enthusiastic audience responses, especially when the performers are (a) James Brown; (b) Tina Turner; and (c) Stevie Wonder.

(c)

Gospel   Modern black gospel music (see chap. 5) represents the urbanization of the spirituals and hymns sung in rural churches and at camp meetings. It is the sacred counterpart of the blues. The leading proponent of modern black gospel was Thomas A. Dorsey, a blues pianist, promoter, organizer, and manager. The superstar of traditional black gospel was Mahalia Jackson, who died in 1972 (listen to Listening Guide 15, p. 78). Her popularity began after she joined forces with Dorsey in the early 1940s.

Rhythm and Blues   Country blues (see chap. 4) is perhaps typified by an old black man from the South singing blues songs while accompanying himself on a guitar. Urban or classic blues was originally sung by women, such as Ma Rainey and Bessie Smith, with instrumental accompaniment by a jazz ensemble.

Traditional **rhythm and blues (R&B)** was blues singing with a boogie-woogie–style accompaniment by piano and electric guitar. It resulted when blacks migrated from the rural South to cities, primarily Memphis and Chicago. Rhythm and blues, which flourished during the 1940s and early 1950s, was black music intended for black audiences, then called *race music*. *Billboard* published R&B charts from 1949 through 1969.

Country blues singers who could adapt to city music and electrified sound became part of the R&B tradition. The most notable of these were Lightn'n Hopkins, John Lee Hooker, Howlin' Wolf, T-Bone Walker, and Muddy Waters. These were older blues men, some from the Mississippi Delta, who did not find fame until they moved to Memphis or Chicago. Walker used electric guitar as early as 1935, developed the single-string technique of guitar playing, and took the blues to the West Coast, where he became very popular.

The most famous traditional R&B artist is B. B. King, also a bluesman from the Mississippi Delta who moved to Memphis (listen to Listening Guide 11, p. 59). His success was due in part to his popularity among British rock musicians of the 1960s.

Other R&B musicians of the 1950s were Fats Domino, Little Richard, and Chuck Berry. Their music was taken up by white teenage audiences who liked its freedom, expressiveness, and sensuality. In the mid-1990s, the concept of R&B expanded to include any black popular music incorporating elements of traditional gospel, soul, or R&B itself.

The Motown Sound   Berry Gordy was a songwriter from Detroit who founded his own record production company, Motown Records, in the early 1960s. At first, he drew talent exclusively from the black population of Detroit. He had an instinct for making black music widely popular with both black and white listeners. He focused on arrangements in a style derived more from black gospel than from blues or jazz. He exerted firm control over the recordings and produced a consistent style known as the **Motown sound**.

Motown recordings, with their studio-controlled sounds, climbed to the top of R&B charts and the white pop charts. Usually, the recording artists were singing groups with featured soloists: Gladys Knight and the Pips, Diana Ross and the Supremes, Smokey Robinson and the Miracles, and Martha and the Vandellas. One Motown superstar of recent decades is Stevie Wonder, and a star group since the 1990s is Boyz II Men.

Success brought increasing commercialization to the Motown sound. Blacks began to feel that the music, which had a heavily diluted pop sound, was too commercial. The artists began to perform more for white audiences, and the backup instrumentation began to look and sound more like a symphony orchestra. The Motown sound, or black pop, had moved away from the black music and the black audiences that had been its original source of recognition and success.

Soul   Soul was an extension of R&B and in fact was popularized by former R&B singers. In 1969, *Billboard* magazine changed the name of its R&B chart to *soul*, meaning black popular music. Soul came to symbolize any black music of the 1970s no matter how pure or how commercial. The pure sound, intended only for black audiences, had singing styles derived from blues, jazz, and black gospel.

Soul became black music for the black audiences that Motown no longer served. Among blacks, it represented a communication and sharing of strong emotions and a wide spectrum of experiences. It was the music of the ghettos and of militants within the black power movement; it could be identified with and was a product of the black experience in the United States. It was the music of northern-born former "Motown blacks" and of southern-born former "Memphis blacks." It was the music of Ray Charles, Otis Redding, Aretha Franklin, Ike and Tina Turner, Sam Cooke, and James Brown.

However, soul now symbolizes many forms of black popular music, including traditional R&B (B. B. King) and R&B pop music performed by black artists (such as Whitney Houston, Toni Braxton, Babyface, and Michael Jackson).

Rap   Rap, which is well known, grew from the streets of New York City. It is one part of hip-hop culture which includes inner-city manifestations of four arts: street poetry, rap, graffiti, and break dancing. Rap was a black, male-dominated genre, but before long Hispanics were enjoying its beat and empathizing with its poetry. Hispanics developed rap groups, as did women and whites. Now, like all previous forms of black popular music—the blues, R&B, gospel, and soul—rap represents an ethnic music that entered the mainstream of American popular music.

The rap style evolved from disco, incorporated a stronger beat, and was used as background for break dancing. Because rap is repetitive, it took advantage of electronic technology, particularly drum machines, prerecorded tracks, and rhythms and sounds derived from scraping turntable needles across vinyl records. The styles that emerged in the 1980s included rap-pop and gangsta rap.

As rap evolved, the "singer" recited socially aware street poetry that ranged from light, entertaining lyrics intended to increase public awareness of social concerns to lyrics that extolled bigotry, black supremacy, and violence. Typically, the poetry described the harsh realities of American street life for urban blacks: drugs, poverty, racial injustice, gang violence, AIDS, battered women, and child abuse. Today, rap is very big business and is still dominated by African American performing groups.

Rock

World War II pretty much stopped the dancing craze of the 1930s. By the early 1950s, popular music, particularly among white Americans, consisted of sentimental ballads and trivial novelty songs. The black popular music was jazz, blues, and R&B. Country and western was just emerging as a national popular music market.

Rock and Roll   Rock, originally called **rock and roll**, began in the mid-1950s. It was essentially an underground antiestablishment protest music. Yet it was a commercial product that was soon to become a powerhouse of the recording industry. The older generation (the "establishment" of the 1950s) believed that rock and roll was a fad and would not contribute anything substantial to our musical culture. A significant fact contributing to this feeling was that rock had grown out of an American youth culture that rejected traditional attitudes and values. Rock was more than music. It had a kinship with folk art in its spontaneous and immediate communication. It was art unseparated from life. The music and lyrics reflected a segment of the culture, politics, morality, and taste of society.

From the beginning, rock performers and their audiences were interracial and international. Rock was an umbrella for young people (the teenyboppers) that provided common symbols, language, and dress codes for white and black people alike. Rock

L istening Guide   *No.* **28**

Little Richard.

"Good Golly, Miss Molly"

Rock and roll.

Performed by Little Richard.

Recorded in 1958 — **CD2, Track 26, 1:37**

Little Richard is one of the most influential of early rock musicians.

This is a 12-bar blues. The text, in typical blues form, is a a b (second line repeats the first; third line is different).

Goals

Recognize the 12-bar blues form.

Recognize breaks, riffs, and boogie-woogie patterns.

Guide

The chord progression of each phrase of this 12-bar blues is the same:

I — — — IV — I — V IV I —

Chorus

1   Piano: boogie-woogie pattern

2   Vocal chorus

3   Vocal chorus

4   First four bars: "break" or "stop time" (rhythmic activity in accompaniment stops—a common jazz technique. Notice the extra two beats)

    Last eight bars: the second and third lines of the text

5   Chorus with big band jazz accompaniment, riffs, and tag: 11 bars and extension in free rhythm

—Continued

L i s t e n i n g   G u i d e — *Continued*   *No.* **28**

Reflections

What is the main function of the piano part in this piece?

Notice, as in previous pieces, the frequent repetition of phrases that give the piece conciseness, cohesion, and identity.

Describe any relationship of this music to jazz. To bluegrass. What musical characteristics make this music different?

How is this music different from current popular music? How have tastes changed since the late 1950s?

appealed to urban and rural people; to wealthy, middle-class, and poor people; and especially to the rebellious young people. Rock was music all young people could dance to.

Before rock, most radio stations, catering to white audiences, did not play songs performed or written by blacks. Concerts typically were still segregated. However, this was the time of landmark civil rights legislation (in 1954) and of intense national awareness of racial issues, particularly segregation and integration.

Rock was an amalgamation of several styles and influences, especially R&B and country and western—black and white traditions. White Americans discovered that they enjoyed listening and dancing to R&B. White artists began recording R&B songs previously recorded by blacks and found that these sold considerably better, though they lost the earthy quality of the originals. These versions were refined, watered down, and more acceptable to white consumers than the original R&B arrangements.

Since many R&B artists were from the South and a number of country artists had rubbed elbows with southern blacks, it was no surprise that country performers were attracted to rock and roll. The resulting form has often been called **rockabilly**.

Rock and roll cannot be traced to a single song or a single artist. Significant contributions were made by Bill Haley and the Comets, Chuck Berry, Little Richard (listen to Listening Guide 28, p. 136), and Elvis Presley, who recorded hits in the 1950s. "Rock Around the Clock" was the first rock and roll song to climb to the top of the pop charts, and it came to symbolize the powerful attraction of early rock and roll. Through television as well as recordings and personal appearances, Elvis Presley became a superstar. He was an explosive performer who elicited a frenzied response from his audiences, but eventually retreated into a more conventional, conservative style that appealed to a wider market.

The Establishment   Mainstream white popular music (conservative, Tin Pan Alley–type music) was controlled by several major recording companies, such as Decca, Columbia, and RCA. These labels were the establishment. However, all the early rock and roll hits were produced by much smaller independent labels, and the popularity of their songs made the establishment sit up and take notice.

At first, this new teenage music was discredited by the establishment. When this strategy did not succeed in redirecting the public's taste, the major labels countered with more watered-down versions of R&B, sung (covered) by white pop stars such as Pat

Boone and the older crooners such as Bing Crosby, Frank Sinatra, and Perry Como. The big labels then "manufactured" teenage idols: Fabian, Frankie Avalon, Ricky Nelson, Bobby Vinton, Bobby Rydell, and others. Their music was white, urban, and only remotely related to R&B. It dealt almost solely with teenage romance. The music of these teenage idols was given considerable exposure on the *Ed Sullivan Show* and, most importantly, on Dick Clark's *American Bandstand*, a show that unquestionably was a powerful force in taming rock and roll and making it acceptable to the establishment.

The establishment won out. Rock and roll diminished in popularity at the end of the 1950s and did not resurge until February 8, 1964, when the Beatles appeared on the *Ed Sullivan Show*. The "British invasion" had begun.

The British Invasion   Liverpool, England, a seaport city with a large population of working-class people, supported hundreds of local musical groups. Sailors who had been to America brought home R&B and rock and roll records. This music influenced these local musicians and sustained the popularity of rock and roll in England after it had waned in the states. Local favorites were the Everly Brothers, Buddy Holly, Chuck Berry, and Little Richard. The most durable and influential groups coming from England were the Beatles, the Rolling Stones, the Who, and Pink Floyd.

In 1967, the Beatles' album *Sgt. Pepper's Lonely Hearts Club Band* was the first one with music clearly and completely in the new rock style to climb to the top of the pop charts. The album became known to virtually everyone interested in popular music. For many, this album was their first exposure to a style of popular music now simply called *rock*. It

The Beatles.

The Rolling Stones.

became more than dance music. It was music for listening, and it was respected as "legit-imate music" by many educated musicians. This album signaled a new age in American popular music.

The music of the Beatles and other British groups appealed mostly to urban white people. It did not become very popular among black and country and western audiences. Thus, although it gave new life to popular music, it did not recapture the cross-cultural aspect of early rock and roll.

Modern Rock   Modern styles of rock (styles of the 1970s, 1980s, and 1990s) result from advanced electronic technology, including sound amplification, studio manipulation of sound, synthesizers, MIDI applications, sampling, studio mixing, a wide range of instruments, and flexible and varied forms. Performances now have an audio and a visual impact. Performers stress unique, often bizarre, dress and onstage behavior. Bizarre presentations were particularly popular in the 1980s among heavy metal bands such as Mötley Crüe, Kiss, and Alice Cooper.

Rock opened a time when popular culture would be studied by scholars, authors, and writers of theses and dissertations. It also began to expand, incorporating a diversity of styles that included folk rock, art rock, southern rock, acid rock, punk rock, new wave, alternative music, jazz rock, industrial rock, gospel rock, pop rock, metal, heavy metal, and alternative heavy metal, among other substyles that came and went in the continuously evolving and fascinating world of American popular music.

As stated earlier in this text, categories can be useful if they are not adhered to rigidly, that is, if they acknowledge the tendency for styles to change, for artists to change, perhaps even from album to album, and for more than one style to be embodied in a song or an album. This last characteristic is called *crossover*; a crossover artist can have hits on more than one chart and may have multifaceted talents and interests that defy classification.

Listening Guide

"Bad Rain"

Rock

Performed by the Allman Brothers Band.

From the album *Shades of Two Worlds* (1991) — **CD2, Tracks 27–29, 5:31**

The Allman Brothers Band was formed in 1969. Greg Allman, Dickey Betts, and Butch Trucks, on this album, were part of the original band. The group sometimes blended progressive rock and R&B; at times it was clearly a blues band and at other times clearly a country rock group. In the 1970s, however, the band was influential in shaping a southern, blues-based style of country rock.

Goals

Describe the rhythmic style, guitar style, vocal quality, and overall musical style.

Compare your response to the first goal with other styles of popular music and with styles of other rock artists.

Describe elements of contrast and repetition and other aspects of formal structure in this example.

Guide

The tempo is a moderately fast four. The meter is duple, in four. The rhythm is regular. With a few exceptions, the phrase structure is regular.

0:00	Intro	Instrumental, started by a drum kick; lead guitar prominent, two phrases, eight bars each; establishes the main melodic motive, heard in the first chorus, of a descending minor third ("Bad Rain")
0:23	Chorus 1	Vocal; five phrases, each one repeated—a a b b a a c c a a (b and c are closely related)
2:20	Chorus 2	Extended lead guitar solo, rock style
3:50	Chorus 3	Four phrases, eight bars each—c c a a (as related to the first chorus); four-bar extension to fourth chorus
4:41	Chorus 4	Guitar lead; four phrases, eight bars each—fourth phrase fades

Reflections

Share a style, an artist, or a song that you would have chosen as representative of rock and that has enjoyed sustained public acceptance over a period of years. In what ways (if at all) was your choice influential in shaping current popular musical styles?

In what ways is this example by the Allman Brothers Band representative of recent popular styles? In what ways is it not?

Popular music in 2001 includes the artists mentioned below; do not be surprised if one of your own favorites is not mentioned, or if you ask "Who's that?" Today, contemporary pop includes Garth Brooks, Britney Spears, Elton John, Billy Joel, Sting, Ricky Martin, Christina Aguilera, Faith Hill, Madonna, Mariah Carey, Vince Gill, Toni Braxton, and groups such as Destiny's Child, *NSYNC, Boys-II-Men, and Backstreet Boys.

At any time, it would be hard to predict which artists will be popular in future years. Yet, some artists have significant lasting qualities, such as Tony Bennett who won a Grammy in 1998 at age 72 and is still performing in 2001; Frank Sinatra, who won a Grammy in 1996 at age 81—he died in 1999; and Barbra Streisand, who, like Sinatra, enjoyed a successful career in music and in film over many years.

Rock, as always, is very diverse and includes the well-known Alanis Morissette, Tracy Chapman, Eric Clapton, and Elton John (soft rock or pop rock); Aerosmith and Metallica (metal and hard rock); Tori Amos, The Smashing Pumpkins, and R.E.M. (alternative pop or rock); and folk rock singers Bob Dylan, Joni Mitchell, and Joan Baez, the Indigo Girls, Kate and Annie McGarrigle, and Bruce Springsteen in some of his recent songs.

Today, rhythm and blues and soul are genres that have taken on new meanings, compared with the R&B of Muddy Waters, Howlin' Wolf, and B. B. King, whose music is sometimes called *urban blues* (discussed in chap. 4), or with the soul music of James Brown, Sam Cooke, Ray Charles, and Aretha Franklin. Today, R&B, gospel, and rap are labels describing various forms of contemporary black popular music, and soul refers to the spirit or feeling of any of this music. Contemporary R&B styles tend to have black gospel roots, with considerable melodic embellishment and improvisatory lines; they represent a different style of black popular music than the R&B of Muddy Waters and B. B. King.

One need only look at the current Grammy or *Billboard* categories to sense the considerable overlap of styles and labels. For example, Grammys are awarded to outstanding blues recordings and to outstanding R&B recordings, which more than likely do not contain blues songs.

Rap and hip-hop seem to be used interchangeably, whereas originally (from the late 1970s and early 1980s), hip-hop referred to the culture that generated the musical style called rap (see the discussion of the roots of rap presented earlier in this chapter). Rap, like the popular music of many ethnicities, has entered the mainstream of American music. The edge has been softened, most songs are less abrasive, and the good rap songs generate wide appeal. Many elements of early rap—the driving rhythm, chanted lyrics, on occasion the scratching turntable sounds, high energy, and active (sometimes choreographed) stage movements—have become part of contemporary popular culture.

Gospel and Christian music are current genres of commercial, popular music that are intended for both inspiration and entertainment but not normally for worship. Increasingly, however, many churches are including music in their religious services that is in the style of secular, commercial pop and rock groups. Electric guitars and keyboards are evident in many large and small churches. Taped music provides professional accompaniments, even large orchestras, for solo music and choir music. Gospel has escalated in popularity in recent decades.

Until recently, gospel music tended to refer to music from the African American tradition (such as black gospel), and contemporary Christian and Christian rock referred to music derived from the southern gospel and white American traditions.

The Gospel Music Association, which sponsors the annual Dove Awards that are devoted to Christian music and its artists, has traditionally been oriented to white American people and styles. However, the 1990s saw a merging of styles and traditions in

Early Twenty-First Century Music

Listening Guide   No. 30

"When Can I See You"

Contemporary R&B-pop.

Performed by Babyface, vocal and acoustic guitar.

From the album *For the Cool in You* (1993) — **CD2, Track 30, 3:49**

Kenneth "Babyface" Edmonds has emerged as one of the most powerful forces in American popular music, achieving success as a performer, songwriter, and producer, and earning many awards in each area. He has won 10 Grammys since 1993, including 4 for Producer of the Year. He has received many similar honors: American Music Awards, NAACP Image Awards, Soul Train Music Awards, Billboard Awards, and BMI (Broadcast Music) Awards. Babyface has written award-winning songs or produced award-winning recordings for Whitney Houston, Madonna, Brandy, Boyz II Men, Toni Braxton, Eric Clapton, and Stevie Wonder.

Babyface wrote "When Can I See You," creating a mood that is soft, romantic, and soulful—perhaps sad. In this recording, he plays acoustic guitar.

Goals

Describe the rhythmic impulse (the degree of rhythmic energy).

Identify the musical form.

Describe the vocal style (such as degree of melodic embellishment, voice quality, and any unique performance characteristics).

Guide

In a moderate four. A quiet mood. Vamps are instrumental; verses are vocal with instrumental accompaniment. Verses and choruses musically are similar and have similar texts.

0:00	Intro (vamp)	The characteristic, underlying bass drum rhythm
		> >>
		(1 — 2 — 3 — 4 —) repeats throughout the song
0:12	Verse 1	Ends with "When can I see you," a musically unfinished feeling—an unanswered question
0:49	Chorus	Begins with "When can I see you again" and ends with a musically unfinished feeling
1:20	Verse 2	Ends with "When can I see you," a musically unfinished feeling
1:57	Chorus	Ends on tonic at beginning of vamp
2:28	Vamp-Verse 3	Vocal fill added; ends on tonic, followed immediately by second part of verse
2:51	Chorus	Ends on tonic at beginning of vamp
3:22	Vamp	Vocal fills to end

—Continued

Listening Guide — *Continued*   *No.* **30**

Reflections

Describe the aesthetic qualities of this song.

Is Babyface's voice well suited to the mood? The lyrics?

How does the instrumentation support or detract from the mood of the song?

What makes this song effective? Not so effective?

What does the recurring bass drum motive contribute to the song?

Christian, popular music. Now, music from both white and black Americans is included on the same Christian music charts, on the same albums, and in the selection of Dove Awards. Doves include the usual Song, Songwriter, Artist, Group, Male Vocalist, and Female Vocalist of the Year awards. But other classifications now include Rap/Hip-Hop, Alternative/Modern Rock, Metal/Hard Rock, Pop/Contemporary, Southern Gospel, Contemporary Gospel, Country, and Traditional Gospel. These classifications (labels) are not substantially different from the Grammys or the American Music Awards.

New age music combines elements of jazz, classical, popular, or rock styles to create a mellow, soothing, "back-to-nature" mood. Much of it is processed sound (electronically produced) and occasionally combined with acoustic instruments such as piano, guitar, or harp. It often lacks a strong beat, a clearly definable melody or tune, dissonance, or any musical attributes that could detract from its intention of making its listeners feel good, enjoy the mood, and respect aspects of nature. Listen to Listening Guide 31, p. 154). In

Amnesty International concert.

Willie Nelson.

early years in record stores, (1970s) new age recordings could be found in the jazz bins. In the 1990s, new age albums usually have their own bins.

World music, international, and ethnic styles have become important in American popular culture: the long-lasting reggae and salsa styles of the Caribbean (listen to Listening Guide 32, p. 158) and Afro-pop and other "world beat" styles from southern Africa (listen to p. 199). Much credit for interest in African popular music must be given to Paul Simon and his album and video *Graceland*. Other rock musicians leading these efforts include Mickey Hart, longtime drummer of The Grateful Dead, and British rock musician Peter Gabriel. Global genres and styles are discussed further in chapters 8 and 9 as part of world and ethnic music.

Summary

This study of American popular music has focused on three aspects: (1) its musical development, (2) its social implications, and (3) its economic impact. We are all affected in one way or another by our relationship to popular music.

Popular music has developed in clear stages, and this growth has been recorded in the literature of music. For these reasons, one can approach the study of vernacular music

(music other than art music) from a scholarly perspective. Many universities offer programs and degrees in the study of popular culture.

We have examined the roots of important styles and trends that have contributed to current popular music. We have attempted in this chapter to explore styles, influences, and artists that represent the beginning and other important stages of various popular styles in music, from the minstrel song to Tin Pan Alley, country and western, several manifestations of black popular music, and rock and other contemporary styles.

The tastes of the masses often change rapidly, causing popular music styles to change. One cannot study popular music without knowing something of the impact of mass media and advertising on taste and about the music industry and how it functions. These influences are covered more thoroughly in chapter 16.

 x a m p l e *No. 5*

Additional Listening

"Hoe-Down"

The original orchestral piece from a ballet (example A) and a bluegrass-pop-jazz version (example B) — **CD2, Tracks 31–32, 8:00**

A. "Hoe-Down," from *Rodeo: Four Dance Episodes* (IV)
Composed by Aaron Copland.
Performed by the New York Philharmonic; Leonard Bernstein, conductor.

Rodeo, a classic of the American dance repertory, was choreographed by Agnes de Mille; it was first presented in 1942 at the Metropolitan Opera House. The four episodes are "Buckaroo Holiday," "Corral Nocturnes," "Saturday Night Waltz," and "Hoe-Down."

B. "Hoe-Down"
Classical, jazz, and bluegrass.
Performed by Béla Fleck and the Flecktones.
From the album *Outbound* (2000).
Instrumentation: electric and acoustic banjos, bass, stereo tenor bass, tenor sax, synth-axe drumitor, tabla, bassoon (through harmonizer), penny whistle, and string quartet.

Béla Fleck is a virtuoso banjo picker. His interests are diverse—bluegrass, bebop, classical, and more. While attending New York City's High School for Music and Art, he began arranging bebop for banjo. According to Sandra Brennan of *All Music Guide*, Fleck was influenced by Charlie Parker, John Coltrane, and Chick Corea (jazz), Earl Scruggs (bluegrass), and Allman Brothers, Aretha Franklin, and the Byrds (popular music).

—Continued

E x a m p l e   *No.* 5 *— Continued*

Béla Fleck has been recording since 1979 and continues today. One of his strengths is to gather outstanding artists for his sessions, artists as diverse as Ricky Scaggs (fiddle and vocal), Yo Yo Ma (cello), Edgar Meyer (bass), David Grisman (mandolin), Jerry Douglas (dobro), Mark O'Connor (fiddle), and Evelyn Glennie (marimba). Fleck's latest CD (2001) includes settings of classical pieces by Scarlatti, Chopin, Tchaikovsky, Bach, Beethoven, Brahms, and others.

Goals

Identify images created by this music, and describe musical elements that help to create those images.

Describe various moods evident in these examples.

Which musical element seems to be most important—melody, harmony, rhythm, or timbre? Is your choice the same for each example?

Guide

A. (Aaron Copland)

Section 1

0:00	Opening fanfare	
0:16	Extended vamp	Mostly piano and strings
0:34	Theme	In the manner of a fiddle tune; in a b a b b a form; extended

Section 2

1:26	Theme 1	Stated first in the trumpet
1:34	Theme 2	Stated by oboe, then solo violin
1:41	Theme 1	Trumpet and violins
1:48	Theme 3	Returns to the energy and style of section 1; ends with energetic, syncopated passage

Section 1

2:07   Extended vamp, this time at a dramatically slower tempo. A passage starting with trombone gets slower in tempo and lower in pitch. The vamp ends with a quiet passage that suggests for a moment the beginning of a quiet section, but shifts abruptly to an energetic return of the first "fiddle tune."

2:32   Return to first theme of section 1 in an exuberant mood and a powerful ending.

B. (Béla Fleck)

0:00	Intro	
0:16	Section 1	a, a
0:31		b

—Continued

E x a m p l e   *No.* 5 — *Continued*

0:39		a
0:46		b, b (repeat at higher pitch)
1:02		a
1:17	Section 2	c
1:24		d, d
1:40		c
1:47	Section 3	Miscellaneous sounds, rhythms, and textures—jazz influence
2:18		Jazz influence
2:27		New material—related to hoe-down fiddle tune
2:37		Passage in thin texture with little emphasis on melody
2:52		Mandolin lead: instruments added—builds in intensity and energy
3:21		Jazz-blues-bluegrass influences
3:35	Section 1	a, a
3:51		b, b
4:06		a
4:13	Closing section (coda)	

Reflections

What surprises you most about each example?

How did you react to each example? Which one did you enjoy the most? Why?

he classical music that is part of American culture has its roots in the history and traditions of western European civilization. Its development proceeded through distinct yet overlapping historical periods, each period reflecting characteristics growing out of, yet different from, that which preceded it. These changes emerged, at least in part, from cultural and technological developments, from shifting progressive and conservative attitudes on the part of composers, and from composers' desires to experiment—to go beyond existing musical practices.

Alternating patterns of contrasting musical aesthetics and styles evolved over long periods of time. Among other attitudes and musical characteristics, some creators of music emphasized personal feelings, imagery, and romantic notions about music, in contrast to others who took a more objective, intellectual, classical approach, emphasizing form and structure, balance, and craftsmanship.

These cumulative changes are sufficiently identifiable to be treated as specific periods of development in the history of Western music which scholars have labeled medieval (A.D. 200–1450), Renaissance (1450–1600), baroque (1600–1750), classic (1750–1820), romantic (1820–1900), and modern (1900 to the present). These dates must be considered approximate, allowing for the overlap of musical styles, composers, and influences.

Chapters 10 through 15 trace this development from the beginning of the Christian era to the present with chapters 14 and 15 focusing on twentieth-century European and American classical music. Chapter 16 concludes Part IV with an examination of the values and functions of music in contemporary American society.

Each chapter includes information about women in classical music within the cultural context of the time, drawing attention to significant composers and their music. Throughout modern history, women have been active as performers and composers, but, because of certain social customs that were based on gender distinctions, they often participated in music as amateurs rather than professionals. As performers, they were mainly singers or keyboardists.

The first well-known woman composer was Hildegard of Bingen, a nun and theologian in twelfth-century central Europe. The first woman to publish her music and to consider herself a professional composer was Maddalena Casulana in sixteenth-century Italy. Francesca Caccini, in the early seventeenth century, became the highest paid musician in the court of the Medici and was one of the first woman performers to tour.

During the seventeenth and eighteenth centuries, women's role in classical music expanded to include teaching and performing at court and in public concerts. The nineteenth and early twentieth centuries saw an even greater expansion of opportunities for women. Women composed in every genre of music, including symphony and opera; they increasingly had their music published, though sometimes using a man's name; they performed throughout Europe; they studied in the newly established music conservatories and subsequently taught in these conservatories; and they became scholars of music and wrote about music.

When women were paid for their musical artistry and creativity, however, they were not compensated equally with men. They still were denied many opportunities for performance, such as positions in symphony and opera orchestras. Perhaps more importantly, historians largely ignored their creative accomplishments.

Only in the past few decades has a vast quantity of research uncovered considerable information about women in Western classical music. Many of their works have now been performed, published, and recorded. Improvements in the status of women in music, however, must be considered relative to previous conditions and opportunities. For example, many of these works have become known as a result of initiatives by women in establishing their own performing, recording, and publishing outlets. One learns music and assesses its quality as a result of considerable study and contemplation over time. Widespread availability with abundant opportunities to hear and study this music is necessary to the process.

Music to 1600

Goals for Listening

- **Describe** melodic shape (contour) and rhythm of chant.
- **Understand the** relationship of music and words.
- **Recognize** flexible pulse and rhythm.
- **Describe** phrase structure.
- **Recognize and describe** monophonic and polyphonic textures.
- **Identify** motive.
- **Recognize** imitation.
- **Describe** ornamentation.

Summary

Additional Listening

Terms and Concepts

Western classical music

Cultural context

Church influences

Historical periods

Chant

Text settings: Syllabic and melismatic

Cantus firmus

Notation

Polyphony

Renaissance

Music genres

Reformation

Master composers

*U*nderstanding and describing western European classical music requires additional vocabulary and discussion of musical concepts—a supplement to chapters 2 and 3. Terms useful in music from this tradition will be found as they are needed throughout chapters 10 through15 and in the glossary.

Goals for Listening

To understand and discuss western European classical music, you will need to increase your understanding of musical concepts presented in previous chapters and to understand additional vocabulary included below and in following chapters:

In chapter 3, **texture** described the relative thinness or thickness of sound—whether a few notes or lines of music at one time creating thin texture, or many notes or lines creating a full, thick sound. In another sense, texture refers to the organization of these lines:

- **Monophony**. A single, melodic line without any other horizontal or vertical sounds is described as **monophony** (a monophonic texture). Chant and other unaccompanied solo singing fall into this category.
- **Polyphony**. Music with more than one melody sounding at the same time and having equal emphasis but not necessarily starting and stopping at the same time is called **polyphony** (a polyphonic texture). Any familiar song performed as a round, such as "Row, Row, Row Your Boat," is polyphonic. A word commonly used to describe this compositional technique is *counterpoint* (music having a contrapuntal texture).
- **Homophony**. When one melody is predominant (in the foreground) and is supported by a harmonic or chordal accompaniment (in the background), the music is **homophonic**. Almost all our popular music, folk music, and recent religious music fall into this category.

Much music incorporates combinations of textures. Music that has a polyphonic texture may also incorporate homophonic texture. This is a matter of which texture predominates.

To begin exploring the sounds of Western classical music, chapter 10 includes three examples of chant, a polyphonic choral setting of one part of the Mass, an Anglican anthem, a madrigal, lute music, and a transcription of a choral motet for brass choir.

The Beginnings of Western Music (until c. A.D. 1450)

Western European and American classical music and much of American vernacular music are part of a musical tradition that can be traced to the theoretical writings and teachings of ancient Greek scholars. This period extends from the time of Pythagoras in about 500 B.C. to Ptolemy, around A.D. 200, and includes Aristotle and Plato.

Western music was influenced by Greek music theory, not Greek practices—that is, by doctrines and descriptions rather than Greek music itself. The Greek scholars wrote about the nature of music, its place in the universe and in society, and its materials and principles of composition. They examined its effects on people and particularly tried to define the relationships between music and mathematics, morality, poetry, education, and character or personality. The Greek writers began our vocabulary for discussing and describing music. In terms of music itself, however, the history of Western practice is traced from the beginning of the Christian era.

Whereas the theory of Western music was derived from the Greek philosophers, the religious ritual (liturgy) of the Roman Catholic Church and its music were borrowed and adapted from the Jewish synagogue services: the singing of hymns and psalms, prayers, the position of the cantor (the chief solo singer), and responsorial, or antiphonal, singing. Additionally, as the church spread into Africa, parts of Asia, and Europe, its music absorbed elements from these diverse areas.

The Roman Catholic Church dominated the history of Western music for its first 1400 years. This time is frequently divided into the medieval period, or Middle Ages (up to the early fifteenth century), and the Renaissance (from about 1450 to 1600). Music of the Middle Ages was mainly vocal. Instrumental genres, including those for keyboard instruments, were not fully developed until around the sixteenth century.

Historical information about secular music, the prevalent folk and entertainment music of an era, dates from around the twelfth century. Secular music was not notated until the late Middle Ages. It was often related to dancing, and so it was more metric and had a stronger rhythmic feeling than sacred music. It also included instruments for accompanying songs and dances. This music was often performed in the context of other forms of entertainment, such as acting, storytelling, poetry, juggling, acrobatics, and dancing. Secular music and drama were occasionally added to the church liturgy. By the thirteenth

Crucifixion of St. Andrew, from an Antiphonary. German, Regensberg, late 13th–early 14th century, tempera and gold leaf on vellum.

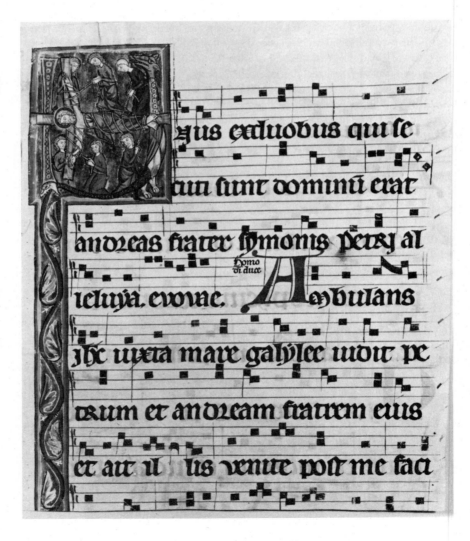

century, such insertions developed into what are now known as liturgical dramas, and these eventually became entities in themselves that were performed outside the church. The two most common liturgical dramas, dating from the twelfth century (and available on modern recordings), are *The Play of Daniel* and *The Play of Herod*. These dramas used instruments such as flutes, trumpets, and percussion.

The liturgy of the early Western churches was varied, as local churches at first were relatively independent. The main musical style of religious music was the **chant**. A chant is a type of song found in many cultures and traditions. Chants range from the intoning of a two-note melody to elaborate, melismatic melodies. In the Roman Catholic Church, chants were sung in Latin.

From the fifth to the seventh centuries, the music of the church developed boy choirs, established schools for training boys and men as church musicians, and revised its liturgy and music.

The most significant musical reform came under the papacy of Pope Gregory I at the end of the sixth century. Gregory established an order for the liturgy, assigning particular items to the various services throughout the church year. An outgrowth of this reform was the beginning of a uniform repertoire of chant for use by churches in all countries. Pope Gregory became associated with reforms that became standard practice for centuries and the music was so highly regarded that this repertoire became known as **Gregorian chant**.

Gregorian chants are the earliest examples of Western classical music. These relatively short pieces were used in the liturgy of the Roman Catholic Church, with various regions developing their own distinct liturgies and repertoires. By the eighth century, however, regional variations either disappeared or were absorbed into the single uniform practice established by the church leaders.

Gregorian Chant

A chant was sung in Latin by a priest or a cantor, by the men and boys of the choir, or by the congregation. Originally, these chants were performed without instruments, although by the thirteenth century instrumental accompaniment was sometimes used. In recent years, much of the Catholic liturgy has been presented in the vernacular (the spoken language of the people) rather than in Latin, and set to music in accessible contemporary styles.

A chant (Listening Guide 46) is monophonic in texture, of relatively short duration, and sung in an unhurried manner. Its rhythm is fluid, reflecting the natural inflection of the mainly unmetered text. Its accents are compatible with the accents of the text, that is, without a regular accent and without a strong metric feeling. Originally, these chants were not notated. Manuscripts containing notated chants date from the ninth century, and many were done in beautiful calligraphy. The composers of Gregorian chants—mostly priests, monks, and nuns—are unidentified in these manuscripts.

The text can be treated in a **syllabic** manner, with one note to each syllable of text; in a florid, melismatic manner with several and sometimes many notes to a single syllable; or frequently in a combination of these two treatments. The shape of a chant melody is fairly flat, is mostly stepwise, and encompasses a small range. Figure 10.2, page 219, shows the typically flat contour (conjunct melody) and the relationship of notes to text. Recognize both the melismatic and the more syllabic portions of the chant.

The scale patterns of Gregorian chants are derived from a system of church modes (scales) that preceded the major-minor tonal system. The church modes give the chants their oriental, mystical quality. This modal quality is also found in much American traditional folk music and in recent jazz and popular music. The modal system formed the basis of Western music for over a thousand years.

L istening Guide

"Antiphon for Easter Sunday and Kyrie XI"

Gregorian Chant—Two Examples

A. Antiphon for Easter Sunday in Praise of Mary
   Performed by the Choir of the Vienna Hofburgkapelle.
B. "Kyrie XI, A (Modo I)"
   Performed by the Benedictine Monks of Santo Domingo de Silos.

CD3, Tracks 25–56, 1:59

Gregorian chants function as an integral part of the liturgy of the Roman Catholic Church. They are an aid to worship, many having specific purposes in the ritual of the mass.

Goals

Identify the musical characteristics of the chant, particularly its melodic shape, texture, and rhythm.

Recognize monophonic texture.

Recognize the relationship of music to words, noticing especially the phrasing and accents and whether the treatment of the words is melismatic or syllabic.

Guide

A. Antiphon for Easter Sunday in Praise of Mary

Latin	*Regina caeli laetare, alleluia.* *Quia quem meruisti portare, alleluia.* *Resurrexit, sicut dixit alleluia;* *Ora pro nobis Deum, alleluia.*
Translation	*Rejoice, Queen of the Heavens, Alleluia; He whom you were worthy of bearing, Alleluia; has risen as He promised, Alleluia; pray to God for us, Alleluia.*

B. Kyrie XI, A (Modo I)

Greek	*Kyrie eleison.*	Lord, have mercy upon us.
	Kyrie eleison.	
	Christe eleison.	Christ, have mercy upon us.
	Kyrie eleison.	Lord, have mercy upon us.
	Kyrie eleison.	

Reflections

Notice the flexible pulse. The music is nonmetric because it flows with the natural inflection of the text.

Although the chant is sung by a group of men rather than a soloist, the texture is monophonic in that the one melodic line exists by itself without accompaniment or supportive harmony.

Notice the frequency with which syllables of text are treated melismatically. Typically, how long are the melismas?

istening Guide

"Benedicta Es"

A chant performed by The Tallis Scholars, Peter Phillips, director.
CD3, Track 27, 2:11 (SCD) CD2, Track 9, 2:12

This chant is not actually a part of the Gregorian repertoire and is not a specific part of the Catholic Liturgy. It is known as a sequence—an addition to the Liturgy—and is usually inserted after the Alleluia. However, it has all the musical characteristics of chant as presented in this chapter.

Goals

Recognize monophonic texture, a flexible rhythm with no sense of meter, and an essentially stepwise melodic contour with a very small range.

Describe the syllabic setting evident in this example.

Recognize aurally the phrase structure as outlined in the guide (see figure 10.1).

Guide

The six verses are in pairs. The music changes every other verse, so the form could be described as a a b b c c; an amen concludes the chant. Much unity results from the fact that only the first phrase of each verse changes; subsequent lines are the same as those in the first verse. The first four verses have three lines of text; the fifth and sixth verses have four lines. Follow the chart that depicts the melodic contour and phrase relationships.

> *Benedicta es, caelorum Regina,*
>   *et mundi totius Domina,*
>   *et aegris medicina.*
> *Tu praeclara maris stella vocaris,*
>   *quae solem justitiae paris,*
>   *a quo illuminaris.*
> *Te Deus Pater, ut Dei Mater*
>   *fieres, et ipse frater*
>   *cujus eras filia.*
> *Sanctificavit, Sanctam servavit,*
>   *et mittens sic salutavit:*
>   *Ave plena gratia.*
> *Per illud Ave prolatum*
>   *et tuum responsum gratum*
>   *est ex te Verbum incarnatum,*
>   *quo salvantur omnia.*
> *Nunc Mater exora Natum*
>   *ut nostrum tollat reatum,*
>   *et regnum det nobis paratum*
>   *in caelesti gloria.*
> *Amen.*

—Continued

Listening Guide—*Continued*   *No.* 47

Figure 10.1
"Benedicta es"

Benedictus es, caelorum Regina,	a
et mundi totius Domina,	b
et aegris medicina.	c
Tu praeclara maris stella vocaris,	a
quae solem justitiae paris,	b
a quo illuminaris.	c
Te Deus Pater, ut Dei Mater	d
fieres, et ipse frater	b
cujus eras filia.	c
Sanctificavit, Sanctam servavit,	d
et mittens sic salutavit:	b
Ave plena gratia.	c
Per illud Ave prolatum	e
et tuum responsum gratum	e
est ex te Verbum incarnatum,	b
quo salvantur omnia.	c
Nunc Mater exora Natum	e
ut nostrum tollat reatum,	e
et regnum det nobis paratum	b
in caelesti gloria.	c
Amen.	A—men

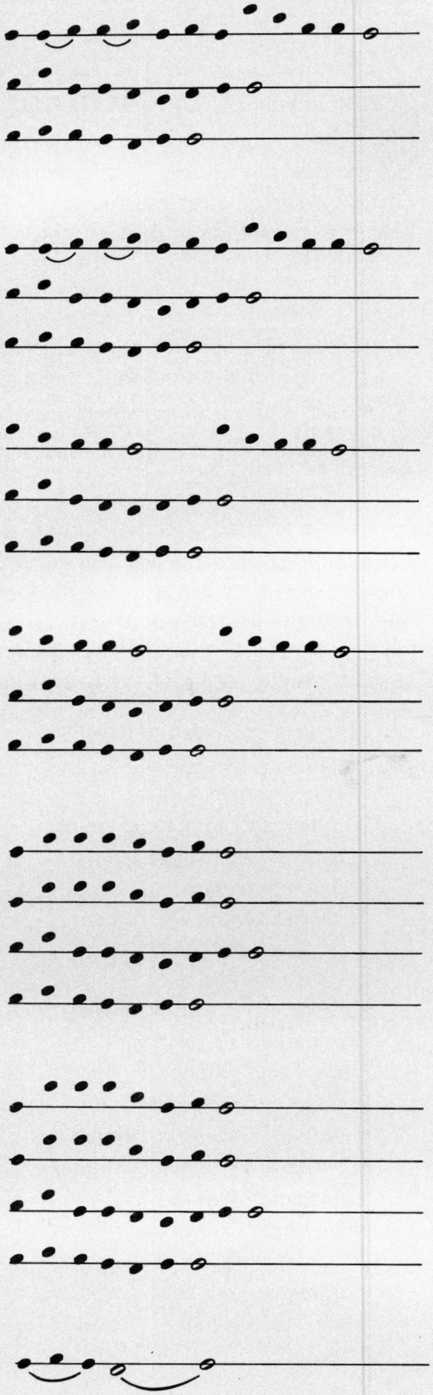

—Continued

Reflections

What is a syllabic setting? A melismatic setting? Describe the setting of this chant.

Notice the slurs in the first phrase, the only place in the chant that more than one note of music equals one syllable of text, other than the Amen.

Does this music convey feeling, mood, and emotion?

Notice the duration of pitches. Notes are equal in length with the exception of a longer note at the end of each phrase.

Chant was functional music. It was an aid to worship rather than music that people would passively listen to. The several thousand chants make up a significant body of literature in Western music. Many have been used as bases for other types of musical compositions, such as the **polyphonic** settings of the mass and sacred motets prevalent during the sixteenth century.

Notation

Notation—a system of visual symbols—was developed to reinforce the singer's memory of a chant melody learned from oral tradition. Notation was also developed to specify pitches so that melodies for chants would be uniform throughout the far-flung Roman Catholic Church. In figure 10.2, an example of medieval square notation can be compared with its counterpart in modern notation.

A system of notating music was also devised to convey several melodic lines of music for others to perform. This system specifies both pitch and rhythmic patterns in order to achieve accurate performances of increasingly complex music. Therefore, singers were taught to read this notation.

It is obvious that notation was a great aid in the teaching of polyphonic music. By the thirteenth century, music in three parts was common, and the person who created a piece of music (the composer) was no longer always anonymous but began to be acknowledged in the notated manuscripts. An important region for the development of notation was northern France, and the first known composers of notated polyphony were Léonin and Perotin.

Figure **10.2**   Medieval square notation and modern notation.

Cathedral of
Notre Dame.

Polyphonic Music

The ninth through the thirteenth centuries saw fundamental changes in Western music. Composition was becoming structured, adhering to certain principles and techniques. Chant was not only an entity in itself but was becoming a basis of other compositions. By the eleventh century, musicians had added a second melodic line to a chant, creating vertical sounds (harmony) and polyphonic texture. These melodies either moved with the same rhythm or, more commonly, had contrasting rhythms and a contrasting sense of movement (one melody moving faster than the other). Polyphony became a common technique in creating music.

The various melodic lines of Renaissance polyphonic music (see the next section) were considered equal in importance. In this music (unlike a melody with accompaniment), no line was dominant. Each line was a singable melody, rhythmically independent from the other lines. In figure 10.3, notice that each voice enters separately in a rising contour and that the words *absalon fili mi* are not sung at the same time. It was common for composers to write in imitative **counterpoint**: that is, each voice entered separately but imitated the voice that had started the previous phrase. This technique was usually worked out so that each voice would begin with the same melodic and rhythmic pattern, perhaps on a different pitch, and then soon deviate from the pattern. Because the melodic lines were moving independently, the strong beats would fall at different times. The music was metered, but the rhythmic independence among the lines minimized the metric feeling, with a resulting gentle, flowing rhythm. The example of polyphony in figure 10.3 is also written imitatively. Notice the identical contour of each entrance of *absalon fili mi*.

Polyphony may give unity to a piece but also may make it sound more complex and challenging than a homophonic song with a single-line melody supported by an accompaniment. The multiple independent lines and overlapping imitative parts also tend to

Figure 10.3

Excerpt from a Josquin motet demonstrating rhythmic independence.

Listening Guide   *No.* 48

"Gloria," from *Missa Benedicta Es*

A polyphonic setting of the second part of the Ordinary of the Mass composed by Giovanni Pierluigi da Palestrina (c. 1525–1594).

Performed by The Tallis Scholars, Peter Phillips, director.

This mass is based on the chant "Benedictus es" (see Listening Guide No. 47).

CD3, Track 28, 3:37 (SCD) CD2, Track 10, 2:47

Goals

Follow the respective voice parts—soprano, alto, and bass—and the cantus firmus.

Recognize polyphonic texture and points of imitation.

Describe the vocal-choral quality, with particular regard to the use of vibrato.

—Continued

Guide

The music begins with the liturgical chant "Gloria in excelsis Deo." The polyphonic setting can be counted in a slow two or a moderately fast four.

Part 1

0:00	Chant	"Gloria in excelsis Deo"
	Bar 1	First theme begins in the alto: "Et in terra pax . . ."
0:21	Bar 7	Points of imitation among tenors and basses
	Bar 11	Now six-part polyphonic texture
0:53	Bar 21	"Laudamus te . . .": New but similar motives follow. Much imitation is evident, although some imitation is modified. In this extended section, polyphonic interplay, mostly in six-part texture, continues until the final cadence

Part 2

2:47	A brief excerpt	"Qui tollis peccata mundi miserere nobis" is included to illustrate the remarkable contrast with part 1 in both style and mood

Reflections

Imitation of a motive might be modified through small changes in pitch or rhythm, but the basic idea of the motive is evident. A goal is to recognize points of imitation, that is, points where imitated motives or melodies begin.

Notice that this piece combines restrained dignity with a highly expressive, uplifting quality. It exhibits cerebral polyphonic control yet a tender, human spirituality. To what extent can these moods be conveyed despite a polyphonic texture in which the words, for the most part, cannot be understood? In what ways can music communicate without text?

Describe the vocal quality and how it contributes to the spiritual mood. How do you respond to this music?

obscure the text, a problem particularly disadvantageous to the liturgy. Renaissance choral polyphony may be challenging, but those who know the music consider it beautiful and noble, ranking it among the most inspired choral music in Western literature.

By the end of the sixteenth century, composers of both sacred and secular choral music were paying more attention to vertical sounds: harmonies or chords. In fact, much choral music, especially secular music, placed sufficient emphasis on its harmonic aspects to be considered homophonic rather than polyphonic. This is in contrast to thirteenth- or fourteenth-century works, which had independent lines and in which vertical sonorities were quite incidental and of little concern.

The Renaissance in Europe saw a magnificent flourishing of knowledge and productivity in the arts and letters. This was the age of Michelangelo and Leonardo da Vinci, Raphael and El Greco, Luther and Shakespeare, and many other of the world's great artists and writers. This was also the golden age of polyphonic choral music created by the first significant group of great composers, a group that included Josquin des Prez, Giovanni Pierluigi da Palestrina, and Giovanni Gabrieli.

The Renaissance (1450–1600)

The Renaissance was an age of humanism, optimism, and reform. Artists and scholars expanded their interests into secular society, and patronage of the arts began to shift from the church to the courts. Developments that were important in shaping Western culture occurred during the Renaissance. The invention of gunpowder and the compass changed the course of history. The art of printing books, perfected by Gutenberg in the fifteenth century, soon led to the dissemination of printed music and books about music.

Choral music is intended for more than one singer to a part—for example, a choir of sopranos, altos, tenors, and basses (SATB). Choral music is of course vocal, but the specific term usually refers to solo pieces or ensemble works in which there is one singer to each part. Three choral genres that became established by the end of the Renaissance were the mass, the motet, and the madrigal.

Choral and Vocal Music

The Basilica of St. Mark's interior, Venice.

Mass   The part of the liturgy that has produced the most important sacred music literature is the **mass**, particularly the music from the Ordinary of the High Mass.

In the Low Mass, the priest intones or recites the prayers; the congregation remains silent. In the High Mass, the service is recited and sung by the choir either in Gregorian chant or in a combination of chant and polyphonic choral settings.

The High Mass consists of the Proper, which varies according to the season of the church year or the particular commemoration, and the Ordinary, which does not vary.

The music of the Ordinary is often sung by the choir. Its five parts are the *Kyrie, Gloria, Credo, Sanctus,* and *Agnus Dei.* The polyphonic settings of these sections of the mass have produced much of the great choral literature in Western music, some of it intended not for liturgical use but for concert performance. This music has been sung in churches and concert halls by Catholic, Protestant, and secular choirs, sometimes with the Latin text preserved but other times with it translated into the vernacular.

The first important polyphonic setting of the mass was the *Messe de Nostre Dame,* composed by a Frenchman, Guillaume de Machaut, in the mid-fourteenth century. The significance of this work was its unity. Previously, little concern had been given to the relationships among style, mode, or thematic idea from one part of the Ordinary to another. Machaut, however, regarded his mass as a complete composition.

Two other important composers of masses are a Franco-Belgian who worked many years in Italy, Josquin des Prez (c. 1450–1521), whose best-known mass is *Missa L'homme armé,* and the Italian Giovanni Pierluigi da Palestrina (c. 1525–1594), whose most influential work is the *Missa Papae Marcelli.* Josquin and Palestrina rank among the greatest of the early composers.

Polyphonic settings of the mass have been composed consistently since the late Middle Ages, but this form was most prevalent through the sixteenth century, particularly in Italy.

Motet   The **motet** is a sacred polyphonic composition, usually sung in Latin without accompaniment (a cappella). It is a choral genre intended to be sung by choirs of trained singers, rather than by congregations. During the Renaissance, a motet usually had from four to six independent melodies, in contrast to the more common three-part melodies of thirteenth-century motets.

The thirteenth-century polyphonic motets were composed anonymously in France and England, frequently in three voices with a different text in each voice—either in Latin or in the vernacular. One voice, usually the tenor, was based wholly or partly on a chant. It would be slow, whereas the other composed melodies would be more rhythmically active. The chant that was used as the basis for polyphonic composition—either a motet or a section of the mass—was known as the **cantus firmus**, or fixed melody. Because the cantus firmus had no liturgical function, it was frequently sung in the vernacular or played on an instrument. The Kyrie by Dufay is based on one of the most popular songs used in polyphonic composition. The original melody is presented first. Its shape in the polyphonic texture can be observed by following the arrows.

The popularity of the motet spread throughout western Europe. The cantus firmus continued to be borrowed not only from the chant repertoire but also from popular songs of the day. Composers freely borrowed melodies, texts, or fragments of either from existing sources. Motets usually were not intended to be sung as part of the liturgy, but became a common repertoire for trained choirs in church services and concert settings and are still performed in those settings today.

Renaissance choral music culminated in the great **polychoral motets**—motets for multiple choirs—of Giovanni Gabrieli. Although polychoral music was established before

Gabrieli, he was able to exploit it most effectively in his work for St. Mark's Cathedral in Venice. St. Mark's was built in such a way that Gabrieli, who was the choirmaster and a noted composer, could have two or more independent choirs placed to allow music to be sung antiphonally, that is, with two or more choirs singing in alternation or one in response to the other. St. Mark's had two great organs, and Gabrieli was interested in writing sacred choral music that included not only organ but a variety of wind and string instruments; thus, he composed motets and other choral pieces for several choirs with numerous independent melodic lines. These works also featured **homorhythmic** sections in which the text was sung by all voices at once, making the words more understandable.

Gabrieli's use of instrumentalists performing lines that were independent of the voices and his use of multiple choirs contrasting with each other and with the instruments became basic principles of the baroque style that emerged at the turn of the seventeenth century (see chapter 11). Gabrieli's music and the natural acoustics of St. Mark's must have provided a thrilling and exalting musical experience.

Madrigal　　The Renaissance **madrigal** (Listening Guide 49) typically is in four or five parts with one singer to a part; thus it is considered vocal chamber music. A madrigal is a secular composition, reflecting the growing independence of the arts from the church. In the vernacular, the poetic text is about love, a pastoral theme, or some other secular topic. The music, usually more metrical and lively than a motet, combines elements of ancient modal scales with the harmonies of modern major tonalities and combines polyphonic and homophonic textures.

Madrigals, which flourished in Italy and England, were sung at court festivities, social gatherings, and meetings of learned societies. Because the madrigal did not have to adhere to the strictures of the church, composers were more free to experiment with bold harmony, pictorial and expressive writing, or even the baroque notion of a solo part contrasting with a harmonic bass line or with a chordal background.

Listening Guide

No. **49**

"April Is in My Mistress' Face" and "Il est bel et bon"

Vocal Chamber Music (madrigal, chanson)

A. "April Is in My Mistress' Face"
   Madrigal composed in 1594 by Thomas Morley (1557–1602). Performed by Deller Consort.

B. "Il est bel et bon."
   French Chanson composed in 1534 by Pierre Passereau (flourished 1509–1547). Performed by The King's Singers.
   From the album *Madrigal/Mystery Tour* (1984) — **CD3, Tracks 29–30, 2:47**

Goals

Be aware of the shifting of polyphonic and homophonic textures.
Identify the metric organization.

—Continued

Recognize the equal emphasis given to each vocal part (SATB).

Recognize imitation and modified imitation.

Guide

A. ("April Is in My Mistress' Face")

Morley was an English composer known primarily for madrigals (secular choral compositions of the Renaissance). He was known also for writing the first book that taught music in English.

"April Is in My Mistress' Face" is a madrigal for four voices. Although the voices move polyphonically, even imitatively, they come together more frequently in homophonic texture than they typically would in the sacred polyphonic music of the same period.

The text follows.

> *April is in my mistress' face,*
> *And July in her eyes hath place,*
> *Within her bosom is September,*
> *But in her heart a cold December.*

Count at a moderately slow tempo. All phrases are described by a number of beats or by a number of patterns (groups of beats), rather than a number of bars, such as an eight-bar phrase. A number of patterns begin with pickups; they count with patterns that follow the pickups.

Phrase 1: Three patterns	18 beats grouped in patterns of 5, 6, and 7 beats; Sopranos and altos start, then tenors and basses join
Phrase 2: One 12-beat phrase	modified imitation; entrances in order: soprano and alto, bass, tenor
Phrase 3: Three patterns	16 beats grouped in patterns of 4, 4, and 8 beats
Phrase 4: One 14-beat pattern	imitation; entrances in order: soprano, tenor, bass, soprano and alto, bass
Phrase 5: One 15-beat pattern	Modified repetition of phrase 4; imitation; entrances in order: alto, tenor, soprano, bass, soprano and alto, bass; ends with ritard; hold on last beat

B. "Il est bel et bon" ("My husband's fine and good")

Passereau composed mainly French chansons. The melodies for many chansons, including this one, were taken from currently popular tunes.

The singers include two countertenors (high tenors), one tenor, two baritones, and one bass.

—*Continued*

The piece is lively. Count in a moderately fast two. Instrumental parts include flutes and percussion. The texture is polyphonic throughout.

0:00	Drum intro
0:02	Theme 1: instrumental
0:10	Theme 1: vocal
0:18	Theme 2: vocal
0:24	Theme 1: vocal
0:31	Theme 3: vocal
0:46	Theme 4: vocal
0:54	"Petite coquette, qu'est-ce ci?" ("Little coquette, that's what it is?")
1:01	Theme 1: vocal
1:09	Instrumental

Reflections

Differentiate between texture in which several melodic lines are equal in emphasis (polyphony) and a single, dominant line that is supported by a secondary chordal texture or accompaniment (homophony).

Compare the mood and style (musical characteristics) of these pieces with the mood and style of the piece by Palestrina (Listening Guide 48). In particular, describe the degree of rhythmic vitality and the dominance of one texture over another.

What makes music sound sacred? What makes it sound secular?

Instrumental Music

Instrumental music—music for drums and other percussion instruments, lyres, and various kinds of flutes—must have existed throughout prehistory, that is, before recorded history. By the twelfth century, it had an important part in many liturgical dramas. The development of printing facilitated the spread of secular, instrumental music. During the medieval and Renaissance era, instrumental music typically was more metric, livelier, and less polyphonic than sacred liturgical music, and it was probably created not for its own sake but for its important role in accompanying singing and dancing.

The harp, lyre, psaltery, and viele were instruments in common use in the Middle Ages. The viele, a bowed instrument, was a forerunner of the viol, which itself was a forerunner of the violin. Instruments common in the Renaissance were recorders, viols, shawms, krummhorns, cornetts, and lutes. The most common keyboard instruments were the harpsichord and the clavichord. The organ as we know it today became popular during the sixteenth century.

For the most part, Renaissance instrumental music modeled itself after the vocal style, and it was common to have an instrument either double or substitute for a vocal part. Music was sometimes written for a **consort** of similar instruments, such as soprano, alto, tenor, and bass recorders or a group of viols of various ranges.

In the sixteenth century, instrumental music had developed to the point that composers wrote pieces specifically for instruments, and the first instrumental genres evolved: the ricercar and the canzona. Although the stylistic distinction between these genres is blurred, the ricercar was generally written for keyboards or an instrumental

Singers with lute and
viola da gamba (bass viol).

Listening Guide

"The Frog Galliard"

Composed by John Dowland (1563–1626).

Performed by Jakob Lindberg, lutenist.

Recorded in 1995 — **CD3, Track 31, 2:02 (SCD) CD2, Track 12, 2:02**

John Dowland was an English composer who wrote almost 90 lute songs and many other pieces that include the lute.

"The Frog Galliard" was taken from Thomas Morley's "First Booke of Consort Lessons" (1599, rev. 1611). This galliard is derived from Dowland's song "Now, O Now I Needs Must Part."

Jakob Lindberg was born in Sweden, developed his first serious interest in music from the Beatles (according to Lindberg's own liner notes accompanying this recording), and studied lute at the Royal Academy of Music in London.

Goals

Identify (1) the original theme, (2) phrases in which this theme is repeated, (3) the several contrasting phrases, and (4) those phrases having an antecedent-consequent relationship.

—Continued

Follow the bass line and determine how consistent it is from phrase to phrase.

Describe the relationship of melodic contour to phrase structure.

Describe techniques of ornamentation evident in this music.

Describe the aesthetic mood of this music.

Guide

Triple meter at a moderate tempo. Essentially diatonic. Eight phrases of eight bars each, grouped in four phrase groups.

0:00	Phrases 1–2	Antecedent phrase; descending motive with melodic line rising in pitch then returning down to the cadence; open cadence at end of first phrase; consequent phrase similar to the first but ends on closed cadence
0:30	Phrases 3–4	Antecedent-consequent pattern; variation of previous material
0:59	Phrase 5	In new key; new melodic motive with same style and texture
1:15	Phrase 6	Almost an exact repeat of the first two phrases
1:30	Phrases 7–8	Seventh phrase derived from the fifth phrase; ritard and descending line to final cadence

Reflections

Compare these plucked sounds with those of modern and more familiar-sounding instruments, such as the guitar or banjo.

Discuss the technique of variation in music.

Which parts of this music would be considered relatively simple and which parts relatively complex?

ensemble and was modeled after the polyphonic motet; the less sober canzona was similar to the madrigal or the French chanson. It usually was entertaining, fast moving, metric, and contrapuntal in a light and easy manner.

The Reformation

In 1517, Martin Luther began a reform that was to separate the Christian church into two major divisions: Catholic and Protestant. This reform had a dramatic impact on the history of music. In the Calvinist version of this reform, congregations sang texts, particularly psalms, that adhered rigidly to the Bible. Psalm singing involved rhymed metrical translations of psalm texts that were published in psalters (hymnbooks; see chap. 5). Among the best-known and most widely used psalters were the *French Psalter* (1562), the *Scottish Psalter* (1564), and the *Ainsworth Psalter* (1612). Editions of these books became important sources of hymn singing in American churches, beginning with the *Ainsworth Psalter*, which was brought to New England by the Pilgrims in 1620.

In 1534, the Church of England separated from the Roman Catholic Church, paving the way for even more church music to be sung in the vernacular. The anthem, sung in English, became the Anglican counterpart of the Latin motet.

*L*istening Guide   *No.* 51

"If Ye Love Me"

Anthem composed by Thomas Tallis (c. 1510–1586) for the Anglican liturgy.

Performed by The Tallis Scholars, Peter Phillips, director — **CD3, Track 32, 1:58 (SCD) CD2, Track 13, 2:00**

Anglican music is a product of the Reformation (see page 229).

Goals

Describe the vocal quality and interaction of voices (vocal textures).

Recognize shifting textures (homophony; polyphony).

Recognize clear cadences using common chord progressions (not common in Tallis's time).

Guide

A cappella. Pure, unadorned vocal quality. Flowing, gentle quality. A mix of homophonic and polyphonic textures.

If ye love me, keep my commandments,	Homophonic setting; chordal
And I will pray the Father,	Polyphonic setting; points of imitation; no clear cadence
And He shall give you another comforter,	Polyphonic setting; points of imitation; a clear V—I cadence
That He may abide with you forever,	Polyphonic setting; points of imitation; Open cadence on V
E'en the spirit of truth.	Polyphonic setting; points of imitation; closed cadence (V—I)
	Last two phrases repeated; open and closed cadences; ritard at end

Reflections

What is the primary function of this music? In what other ways can it appropriately be used?

Describe your aesthetic reactions to this music and the reasons for those reactions.

Is Renaissance choral music better sung in Latin?

Of course, the Roman Catholic Church countered with its own reforms (the Counter Reformation). Palestrina's music is considered especially important in that it established a model for making liturgical music more worshipful, more dignified, and easier to understand.

Composers   One of the earliest known composers is Hildegard of Bingen, a nun, theologian, mystic, poet, writer on medical and scientific matters, and composer of 77 religious songs, numerous chants, and a lengthy music drama. Although she lived in central Europe at a time when women were forbidden to teach or to hold authority over men, many of her song texts were focused on women, inspiring them to exercise power in a material world.

By the end of the Renaissance, numerous composers, some well known and widely performed today, were very successful and influential in the development of Western classical music. Three of the greatest are discussed below. Others include Guillaume Dufay, Orlando di Lasso, Thomas Tallis, Don Carlo Gesualdo, Tómas Luis de Victoria, Thomas Morley, William Byrd, and John Dowland.

Josquin des Prez (c. 1440–1521)   Josquin was born in the border region between France and what is now Belgium. He became a successful court musician and composer, particularly in Italy. Much of his music was published in printed collections; it includes 18 masses, 100 motets, and 70 secular songs with French texts (chansons).

The mass, with its restricted nature, offered few opportunities for experimentation; thus Josquin used the motet to create his most innovative and influential works. In his motets, he was able to use a wider range of texts and to develop a new compositional style with flowing melodies, rich harmonies, and less restricted rhythms. He was able to convey through this music a more humanistic attitude—an attitude of the Renaissance—that provided expressive power and a more vivid and clear text.

His mark of genius was his ability to combine the intricacies of polyphonic composition with emotional expression. In so doing, he was able to transcend the limits of the musical language of his time. Josquin's role in history makes him one of the great composers of the Renaissance.

Giovanni Pierluigi da Palestrina (c. 1525–1594)   Palestrina was born near Rome, and his entire professional life was spent as a choirmaster and composer in Rome. He spent the last 24 years of his life at St. Peter's. His music is primarily sacred and includes 102 masses, 450 motets and other liturgical compositions, and 56 spiritual madrigals with Italian texts.

Palestrina's music is characterized by its purity (detached from secular influences) and its appropriateness to the formal ritual of the Roman Catholic liturgy. It serves as the model of the best in sixteenth-century imitative counterpoint, capturing the essence of the conservative elements of the Counter Reformation. Palestrina set out to show through his music that polyphony is not necessarily incompatible with a reverent spirit or with an understanding of the text.

Palestrina's contrapuntal texture is not overly elaborate; his melodies are diatonic, mostly stepwise, and easily singable. A large number of his sacred polyphonic pieces are for four voices, each given equal importance. Cadences (ends of phrases) overlap because of the polyphonic textures. Palestrina incorporates much chordal, homorhythmic writing with clearly perceivable chord progressions. These sections end with strong, full cadences that generate tonic-dominant relationships and clear tonal centers. This signals a shift away from modal writing and foreshadows the emerging major-minor tonal system that would become fully established in the seventeenth century.

Giovanni Gabrieli (c. 1557–1612)   Giovanni Gabrieli was the organist and choirmaster at St. Mark's Cathedral in Venice from 1585 until his death. He was also an exemplary composer of sacred works for multiple choirs and for combinations of voices and wind and string instruments.

Performances by multiple choirs positioned in different areas of a church were not begun by Gabrieli and did not begin in Venice, but they flourished in Venice because of the design of St. Mark's and the receptiveness of the people to the grandiose music of multiple choirs with contrasting instrumental sonorities. Gabrieli's music for multiple choirs used the antiphonal dialogue technique (echo) and chordal homorhythmic writing contrasted with rich contrapuntal textures.

Gabrieli's role in history, like that of Josquin before him, places him at the border between two historical eras. He was a master of the older polyphonic Renaissance style, yet his use of contrasting sonorities foreshadowed essential qualities of the baroque era to follow.

Summary

Although the beginning of Western music can be traced to ancient civilizations, for our purposes we have started with the beginning of Christianity and the liturgy of the Roman Catholic Church. Gregorian chant, in common use in the church since about A.D. 500, represents the first body of music literature in Western civilization, a literature on which much later music was to be based.

Adding a second line and then a third or more lines to Gregorian chant created polyphonic texture. By the sixteenth century, the texture stabilized at four or five parts, and most polyphonic compositions were created independently of a chant. The development of notation facilitated this kind of composition. Notation allowed composers to communicate more complex music so that others could perform it. By 1600, the invention of printing greatly facilitated the dissemination and preservation of music. Printing also greatly expanded the communication of information and ideas about music.

The Renaissance saw the first professional composers and performers—people who create and make music for their livelihood—of classical music. The initial employers were the churches; later, the aristocracy became important employers of musicians. Creators of music became known for their talent and their contributions, the most outstanding becoming our first master composers.

The main genres after Gregorian chant were choral settings of the mass, the Renaissance motet, and Italian and English madrigals. Instrumental music was used mainly to accompany dancing and folk and popular songs. When instrumental music did exist as a separate entity, it was patterned after choral music. No distinct instrumental genres had yet emerged.

This period of Western music, dominated by the influence of the Roman Catholic Church, culminated in the golden age of choral music—the music of Josquin, Palestrina, and Gabrieli.

The Protestant Reformation opened up new directions in sacred music: Music in Protestant churches was now sung in the vernacular in hymn style by the congregation rather than chanted in Latin form by the priest or sung by the choir as in the Roman Catholic Church. The Reformation also began a rich heritage of Protestant polyphonic choral music, much of it based on hymn or chorale melodies, in much the same way that earlier polyphonic music was based on Gregorian chants.

Additional Listening

E x a m p l e *No.* 10

"Jubilate Deo"

Renaissance motet originally composed for voices—here performed by brass instruments.

Motet in eight voices composed by Giovanni Gabrieli (c. 1557–1612).

Performed by the Canadian Brass and the Berlin Philharmonic Brass.

CD3, Track 33, 3:35

This motet, originally a choral piece for eight voices, was published in 1613 in Venice. It is not a polychoral motet (a piece for two or more separate choirs—see page 224), but a piece for eight separate parts. Listeners, however, will perceive the effect of polychoral writing in the contrasting sounds of instruments, such as trumpets and horns and upper and lower brass instruments.

This is a transcription. It is common to transcribe pieces so that they can be performed in a medium (such as brass instruments here) different from the original (voices). The notes are identical to the original, so only the timbre and the spirit have changed. The brass quality and the spirited performance change the mood from the typically more somber, slower sacred motet to the almost dancelike character of this instrumental version.

Goals

Recognize motives and points of imitation.

Describe the varying textures.

Describe the rhythmic characteristics and metric organization.

Recognize the syncopated motives.

Identify the sounds of the trumpets, horns, trombones, and tubas.

Recognize the sectional organization of this motet.

Guide

Count in duple meter, two beats to the bar, at a moderate tempo.

Part 1

0:00	Bar 1	First motive stated by the trumpet; immediately imitated by the second trumpet; ascending scale; descending leap
	Bar 3	Descending, stepwise motive in a quick dotted rhythm
	Bar 5	Fast ascending motive; tuba enters
0:11	Bar 9	Quiet second theme with a syncopated motive begins in the horns. It ends with a series of loud separated chords preparing the return of another quiet, syncopated motive in the horns. The last passage of this part begins with a three-note motive featuring a descending skip followed by very clipped dotted notes. A strong cadence ends the first part

—Continued

E x a m p l e *No.* **10** — *Continued*

Part 2

1:07   Soft four-note stepwise motive, beginning with a pickup, appears in quick repetitions. This is followed by a soft syncopated passage, repeated at a higher pitch level. This is extended in full texture without syncopation to a cadence.

Part 3

1:45   This part starts with the melody in the horns, in a thin texture. It continues with material derived from previous motives. This extended passage concludes on a strong cadence, followed immediately by a soft passage with slower rhythmic movement.

Part 4

2:43   The first of two alternating passages enters with a loud descending pattern: five bars in a fast triple meter, counted in one, with no cadence. This is answered by a four-beat passage at a slightly faster pulse, highlighted by repetitions of a descending two-note motive, ending on a strong cadence. After two alternations of these passages, the motet ends on a strong IV — I cadence.

Reflections

In what ways is this piece polyphonic, homophonic, or both?

Compare and contrast this motet with the previous polyphonic pieces.

Typically, motets are sacred polyphonic choral compositions. Describe your reaction to this instrumental version.

E x a m p l e *No.* **11**

"O Euchari In Leta Via"

Chant in a new age setting

Composed by Hildegard von Bingen (1098–1179).

Contemporary arrangement by Richard Souther.

From the album *Vision* (1994) — **CD3, Track 34, 3:39 (SCD) CD2, Track 14, 3:40**

Hildegard von Bingen was born and raised in Germany. She became a Benedictine nun and later an abbess in the Benedictine community at Saint Disibode. She was a social activist, poet, preacher, teacher, and a prophet who called for reform. She cultivated the spiritual and the cultural life of her community and became famous throughout the land.

—*Continued*

E x a m p l e *No.* **11** — *Continued*

Hildegard established a monastery in Rupertsburg and, later, another monastery in Eibingen. For centuries, her work as a composer was not known, but her work was preserved in her monastery. The nuns of Eibingen rediscovered her work, which led to it now being respected and appreciated once again.

This example is not a Gregorian chant or a formal part of the liturgy. It is a monophonic song.

Goals

Describe the musical characteristics of the chant.

Describe the vocal quality of the singer.

What instrumental timbres are present?

Is the chant primarily syllabic or primarily melismatic?

Guide

0:00	Unaccompanied chant; ends with vamp setting up chant with instrumental accompaniment
0:20	Chant with instruments
0:38	Contrasting setting
1:05	Second contrasting setting—comes to complete stop
1:41	Third contrasting setting—no percussion—ends with vamp reintroducing opening chant
2:35	Return of opening chant; heard three times; music ends quietly.

Reflections

What sounds unusual about this chant?

Is the scale on which this chant is based tonal, modal, pentatonic, or gapped?

How does the instrumental setting and the "beat" contribute to or detract from the music?

In the opening chant, notice any harmonic characteristics (chords or simultaneous sounds) caused by electronic reverberation.

Identify types of facilities in which this music might be effectively performed using natural acoustics.

Music of the Baroque (1600–1750)

Goals for Listening

- **Develop an understanding of** monophonic, polyphonic, and homophonic texture.
- **Develop an understanding of** relationship of text and music.
- **Develop an understanding of** melismatic and syllabic settings of text.
- **Develop an understanding of** phrase structure.
- **Develop an understanding of** ornamentation.
- **Develop an understanding of** antecedent and consequent phrases.
- **Develop an understanding of** motives.
- **Develop an understanding of** points of imitation.
- **Develop an understanding of** basso continuo.

Summary

Additional Listening

Terms and Concepts

Patronage
Textures
Polyphony
Fugue
Major and minor tonality
Continuo
Word painting
Instruments
Concerto and concerto grosso
Overture
Dance suite
Sonata and trio sonata
Chamber music
Keyboard works
Cantata and oratorio
Chorale
Aria and recitative
Opera
Composers
  Bach
  Handel

*T*he baroque era, a time of absolute monarchies, flourished in regions that are now Italy, France, Germany, and England. The era was marked by pomp and splendor, a dynamic and dramatic spirit, and emotional expressions full of color and movement. It was romantic and grandiose, an age of innovation and adventure. This era saw major contributions in science, philosophy, and the arts from such men as Galileo, Newton, Descartes, Spinoza, Milton, Rubens, and Rembrandt.

The aristocratic courts, in addition to the churches, were patrons of the arts. The rulers of the royal courts were wealthy monarchs who built magnificent palaces and maintained court composers and musicians for orchestras, chapel choirs, and opera companies. Although folk and entertainment music and music for churches continued, secular classical music was abundant, performed mostly for the courts and the upper class.

In addition, some city governments now joined churches and courts as centers of music and culture and as employers of musicians. Musicians were needed to meet the demand for church music, for entertainment at the courts, and for festivals, ceremonies, and other public occasions in the cities. The audiences were interested in and enthusiastic about the music of local composers—the contemporary composers.

The Catholics were rebounding from the effects of the Reformation, but the Protestant church nevertheless became firmly established and added significantly to the repertoire of Western music. There was a significant shift in emphasis away from Renaissance polyphonic pieces, sung in Latin and based on Gregorian chants or other known melodies, to various compositional forms based on the Lutheran chorale:

- Lutheran **chorale** melodies sung by the congregation in unison and in the vernacular. These were analogous to modern hymn tunes.
- Polyphonic settings of chorale melodies performed by a choir, with the text in the vernacular.
- By the end of the seventeenth century, chorale harmonizations in a simple, chordal, homophonic, strophic, hymnlike style for congregational singing.

Listen to Listening Guide 54

Goals for Listening

Continue to develop your understanding and use of musical vocabulary: texture, melismatic and syllabic setting of text, phrase structure, ornamention or melodic embellishment, antecedent and consequent phrases (open and closed cadences), melodic and rhythmic motives, and polyphonic texture. Additional vocabulary will be presented as needed, including fugue, points of imitation, and basso continuo, and choral genres, such as chorales, cantatas, and oratorios.

Musical Characteristics

New techniques of composition, new musical forms, the development of opera and the orchestra, and the establishment of the major-minor tonal system are hallmarks of the baroque period. It now was common for composers to write music with specific tone colors and instruments in mind. Judging from the music composed during the late baroque period (the first half of the eighteenth century), instrumentalists became more proficient than ever before, placing greater emphasis on technical skill and virtuosity. Furthermore, organists and other keyboard performers added to the notated music by improvising harmonies or embellishing a melodic line according to certain prescribed practices.

Many genres and forms, particularly for instruments and keyboards, emerged that remain in common use today. Many instruments and musical sounds that we know and feel comfortable with today came into common use during the baroque period.

Texture

One of the first major developments in the baroque period was the emphasis on harmonic or chordal writing (homophonic texture), with one predominant melody and subordinate lines or an accompaniment (harmonic background). This was a change from the older style of composition that emphasized the combination of two or more equal melodic lines (polyphonic texture).

Composers still wrote polyphonic music, but many now created music with homophonic texture, an essential ingredient in the development of opera. By the late baroque, it was common to use polyphonic textures in instrumental and keyboard music as well as sacred choral works.

Major-Minor Tonal System

Another important development was the major-minor tonal system. The basis of composition shifted from the system of church modes (modality) to the major-minor tonal system (tonality)—the system of scales and keys that produces the sounds with which most of us are familiar. This is the system of the tonic, (the chord of rest) and the dominant, (the chord of movement).

We can hear the tonic, the stable home tone or tonal center of a key; and we can hear modulation, a change of tonality from a key of stability (the tonic) to a key of contrast or instability (frequently but not always the dominant). The tonal system allows for diatonic writing (notes in the key) and additional color and modulation through chromatic or altered tones (notes outside the key). Much baroque music is diatonic.

Continuo

The **continuo** had a significant role in baroque performance practice. It typically involved two instruments: a keyboard (organ or harpsichord) and a bass instrument (a cello or similar instrument). The keyboard player would fill in or improvise harmonies based on chord symbols and a bass line. The player of the bass line (usually a cellist) would play a simple, continuous, notated bass line that emphasized the principal notes of the harmonies or chords (a concept similar to the walking bass in jazz).

The keyboard improvisation is sometimes known as "realizing" harmonies (bringing them into reality as a jazz pianist or guitarist does). By harmonically supporting one or more instrumental or vocal melodic lines, the continuo provided a harmonic basis for the new homophonic tonal (rather than modal) music.

A form of musical shorthand (chord symbols) was devised to assist the keyboard player. The notes of the chords were not written out; rather, numbers were placed below the notes of the bass line, identifying the chord tones so that the keyboardist could realize the harmonies. The shorthand was called **figured bass**. Such improvisation expanded in scope, becoming a high art and a coveted skill among keyboard performers in the late baroque period. (See figure 11.1 for an example of a continuo with figured bass.)

Word Painting

Word painting began during the Renaissance as composers realized that music could convey the moods and meanings of a text, expressing a wide range of ideas and feelings. Triumph or resurrection, for example, might be described musically in a very different manner from death or crucifixion. During the baroque period, the interest in word painting became more pronounced and the technique became more sophisticated. Composers went to great lengths to depict not only specific images but also the emotions of a text, to mirror the text in the music as literally as possible.

Other Musical Characteristics

Baroque music is music of contrasts: voices and instruments; loud and soft; changes of key (modulations); section A and section B as in a da capo aria a; small group of instruments and a large group within the same piece. Rhythm is regular, metric, and often

Figure 11.1

Figured bass. J. S. Bach, Cantata no. 140, from "Wachet auf."

energetic. A steady pulse is often maintained in the bass. Baroque pieces were sometimes derived from popular and court dances, and this practice increased the tendency toward a dynamic baroque rhythm. Yet, the strong metric feeling is in contrast to the free rhythm of the recitative and the free rhythm common in improvised passages, especially in keyboard works.

Melody is often perceived as a continuous expansion of an idea, without short, regular phrases. Dynamics (levels of loudness) are contrasting and abrupt, achieved by adding or taking away instruments or voices rather than by gradually changing the loudness of the music. This technique is known as *terraced dynamics*.

Instruments

For the first time in Western music, instruments became equal in importance to the voice, for composers and for listeners. Orchestras were made up of instruments similar to those of today, but there was no standard set of instruments or instrumentation. Also, the baroque orchestra was not as large or as varied as the modern symphony orchestra, and the instruments generally were smaller and quieter than their modern counterparts. The primary instruments were the violin family plus trumpets, oboes, and flutes.

The lute was a popular plucked instrument, and the primary keyboard instruments were the harpsichord and the organ. The fortepiano, the forerunner of the modern piano, had been invented but was not well enough developed to be widely used during the baroque period.

Musical Forms and Genres

New musical forms or genres that developed in the baroque period ranged from keyboard works and chamber music to multimovement orchestral pieces, large choral works, and operas. Older forms, of course, continued. Renaissance polyphony and imitative counterpoint were adapted to baroque instrumental music in such forms as the ricercar and fantasia. These one-movement pieces (without sections) eventually led to the fugue (see page 242). The sectional canzona form led to the baroque sonata.

Orchestral Works

The two orchestral forms that reached their peak in the late baroque period were the **concerto** and the concerto grosso. The concerto involved one solo instrument with orchestra; the concerto grosso had a small group of soloists, usually two or three. The element of contrast between the soloist or soloists and the orchestra was germane to these as well as other baroque forms. Both concerto forms were in three movements—fast, slow, fast—with the slow movement in a contrasting key.

Another widely used genre was the French **overture**. It was originally intended to create a festive atmosphere as an opening to an opera, but it later became an independent instrumental genre. The French overture was in two parts: the first in a slow, majestic, homophonic style and the second in a faster yet serious polyphonic style. It often ended with a reference to at least the rhythm of the opening section.

The **dance suite** was sometimes written for orchestra, sometimes for keyboards. It is a set of contrasting dances combined to form a single multimovement work. The main dances are the allemande, courante, sarabande, and gigue, but most dance suites have a flexible format that can include additional or substituted dances and perhaps movements other than dance forms.

Listening Guide

Concerto Grosso, op. 6, no. 8 ("Christmas Concerto") (IV, V, VI; excerpt)

Composed by Arcangelo Corelli (1653–1713).

Performed by Kammerorchester Carl Philipp Emanuel Bach; Hartmut Haenchen, conductor — **CD4, Tracks 1–3, 1:52**

Goals

Describe a baroque instrumental style.

Identify the various meters, phrase structures, textures, and points of contrast and repetition.

Identify diatonic melody and harmony in each movement.

Compare the styles of the three movements.

Guide

IV		Triple meter; in a fast three or a moderately slow one; dance-like; crisp, rhythmic drive; diatonic in a major key; small string orchestra	
0:00	Phrase group 1	8 bars; open cadence	
		8 bars; open cadence	
0:16	Phrase group 2	8 bars; open cadence	
		12 bars with 4-bar extension; closed cadence	
0:37	Phrase group 3	Repeat of second phrase group	
V		A duple meter in a moderately fast two; starts with a pickup on the second beat; an aggressive, stylized dance	
0:59	A	24 bars	
		a	4 bars
		a	4 bars
		b	16 bars: ascending then descending motives with last 4 bars repeated
1:22	A	24 bars: first section repeated with ornamentation	
1:46	B	22 bars (11 + 11): contrasting style; ascending sequence in second half	
2:08	A	21 bars: first section repeated but modified after the first statement; ends with cadence on bar 20 followed by a 1-bar extension and a ritard; moves directly to the sixth movement	
VI		"Pastorale" (excerpt): in a slow two, with each beat subdivided in three (a 6/8 meter); the mood is quiet and pleasant	
2:31		10 bars (5 + 5): second half; same mood but different pitch area (around the dominant)	

—Continued

2:53   13 bars (5 + 8): first half melody in lower strings in the tonic key; second half melody in high strings with a descending sequence in two-bar patterns; ends in key of the dominant

3:22   8 bars (2 + 2 + 4): two bars on dominant; two bars on tonic; four bars, descending contour to key of the dominant

3:39   Quiet and sustained; fades in fifth bar

Reflections

Notice the sudden changes in dynamics and thus the absence of gradual crescendos and decrescendos.

To what extent is this music homophonic? polyphonic?

Chamber Music

The typical forms for a small number of instruments are the church **sonata** and the chamber sonata, both written for various combinations of instruments. Such sonatas typically included either one solo instrument with continuo (solo sonata, three performers) or two solo instruments with continuo (**trio sonata**, four performers).

These compositions usually had contrasting sections or movements, frequently in dance forms. The church sonata is usually a four-movement work in a slow-fast-slow-fast pattern. The chamber sonata is the ensemble form of the dance suite, although composers frequently incorporated additional dances or movements other than dances, such as a prelude or an aria.

Keyboard Works

Important single-movement keyboard compositions of the baroque were toccatas, preludes, fantasias, and fugues; they were written for either the harpsichord or clavichord (forerunners of the piano) or the organ. The toccata and prelude were improvisatory in character, sometimes having a contrapuntal middle section and sometimes paired with a fugal composition in a performance. The fantasia was a larger, more complex work that might present a series of contrapuntal variations on a single theme.

Fugue is a compositional technique that may be used within any composition, but it often describes the structure of an entire piece (listen to Listening Guide 53). A fugue is an imitative contrapuntal form built on one or two themes. The theme is stated alone and then restated, usually in two or three other voices, now accompanied by intricate contrapuntal lines in voices that previously had stated the theme. This material continues in contrapuntal interplay, including restatements of the original theme, material based on motives of the original theme, and new but closely related themes. The fugue represents the highest form of baroque polyphonic music.

Other keyboard works should be mentioned: the chorale prelude, an organ work based on a chorale tune that serves as a theme for a set of variations; the passacaglia and chaconne, both of which use a repeated bass line (ground bass, or *basso ostinato*) as the basis of the composition; and the dance suite, discussed previously as an orchestral genre.

A man playing the harpsichord.

Listening Guide

No. 53

Fugue in C Minor, no. 2 from the *Well-Tempered Clavier*, Book 1

Performed by Kristin Wachenfeld, harpsichord.

Composed by Johann Sebastian Bach (1685–1750).

Refer to a unique version of this fugue: Additional listening no. 12.

CD4, Track 4, 1:36 (SCD) CD2, Track 15, 1:36

Goals

Recognize the five-note motive, polyphonic texture, and entering voices.

Recognize contrasting patterns and motives.

Guide

Count in a slow four. The subject (theme) is based on a 5-note motive that opens the fugue. The music starts with a two-note pickup on the second half of the first beat; thus the first beat of music falls just after the downbeat (the motive begins: "and-a-two"). The letters A, B, and C identify the approximate initial entrances of each voice, as depicted in the chart below. The first statement of the subject (A) is in the middle voice (compared with the pitch areas to follow), the second entrance is in the high voice (B), and the third is in the low (C).

(1)— 2— 3— 4— 5— 6— 7—8—
  A   B   C

After the entrances are made, the subject is developed in a variety of ways, including varying the subsequent entrances of the motive and making the setting more chromatic and unstable. Ritards lead to the final cadence.

—Continued

Reflections

Listen for the five-note motive throughout the piece as Bach has developed the fugue. Follow the "voices," even when listening to instrumental music.

Be aware of the sound of the minor tonality and the shift of the last chord from the expected minor sound to major, offering a surprise chord quality in the context of the previous minor tonality.

This fugue comprises complex, contrapuntal interplay according to principles common to many fugues from the baroque era.

Discuss the emotional and intellectual qualities of a fugue.

Choral Music

The two major choral forms of the baroque period were the **cantata** and the **oratorio**. These were both dramatic forms; but the oratorio was of much larger proportions than the cantata, was usually longer and more complex, and was intended for concert performance whereas the cantata was intended for a worship service. Both usually were sacred works, and the cantata became an integral part of the German Lutheran Church service. Secular oratorios and cantatas did exist, however. One of the best-known secular cantatas is J. S. Bach's "Coffee Cantata."

Cantata no. 140, "Wachet auf . . ." ("Sleepers, Awake!") (I, VII)

Church cantata composed in 1731 by Johann Sebastian Bach (1685–1750).
Performed by Blanche Moyse Chorale and the Orchestra of St. Luke's.
The chorale tune, "Wachet auf," was composed by Philipp Nicolai (1556–1608).

CD4, Tracks 5–6, 4:48

The seven parts of this cantata are:

   I. Instrumental introduction and polyphonic setting of the chorale tune
  II. Recitative—tenor
 III. Duet—soprano and baritone
 IV. Chorus—based on the chorale tune
  V. Recitative—baritone
 VI. Duet—soprano and baritone
VII. Final chorus—stately chorale setting

For this listening guide, only part I, a polyphonic setting of the chorale tune "Wachet auf" (figure 11.2), and part VII, the chorale setting, (figure 11.3) are included.

—*Continued*

The cantata was written for four-part choir: soprano, alto, tenor, and bass. The instrumentation specified was horn, two oboes, *taille* (alto oboe), *violino* piccolo (small violin), two violins, viola, and continuo (cello, bassoon, and organ).

Goals

Recognize the hymnlike setting of a Lutheran chorale.

Recognize a homophonic piece based on a chorale tune. Be able to identify the chorale melody and describe its relationship to the other voices.

Recognize a polyphonic chorus based on a chorale tune. Be able to identify the chorale melody and describe its relationship to the other voices.

Guide

Part VII Final chorus of the cantata "Wachet auf"—a chorale setting; written in a hymnlike style with all voice parts moving in virtually the same rhythm (fig. 11.3). Most of the parts that do move against the primary rhythm are in the bass voice. The form is a a b. Count in a moderately slow four (a slash denotes a break in the forward energy, either a pause within the phrase or a phrase ending). The chorale is repeated.

Chorale:	Section A	1---2---3--/-4---5---6--/-7---8---/	(three phrases)
	Section A	1---2---3--/-4---5---6--/-7----8--/	(three phrases)
	Section B	-1---2--/-3---4--/-5--/-6---7---8---9--/	(four partial phrases)

Part 1 Opening chorus: an instrumental introduction and a polyphonic setting of the first two sections of the chorale "Wachet auf": part VII, section A (above). It is in triple meter, counted in a moderate three.

0:00 The instrumental introduction begins with repeated dotted rhythms in an alternating, question-answer dialogue in the upper strings and oboes, followed by ascending scalar melodic patterns in the oboe and violin. The continuo provides the harmonic basis and rhythmic impulse. The letter designations refer to the chorale form indicated above.

0:28 Phrase 1: The voices begin on the final cadence of the introduction. The chorale tune is heard in the soprano voice and horn in a simple, slow rhythm. Phrases are separated by instrumental material, and each phrase is always surrounded by faster-moving, intricate, independent lines with much imitation, usually in short melodic fragments.

0:49 Phrase 2

1:14 Phrase 3

2:00 Phrase 1

2:21 Phrase 2

2:46 Phrase 3—fade

—Continued

Figure 11.2

Polyphonic setting of a chorale melody. J. S. Bach, Cantata no. 140, from "Wachet auf."

—*Continued*

Listening Guide — *Continued* *No.* 54

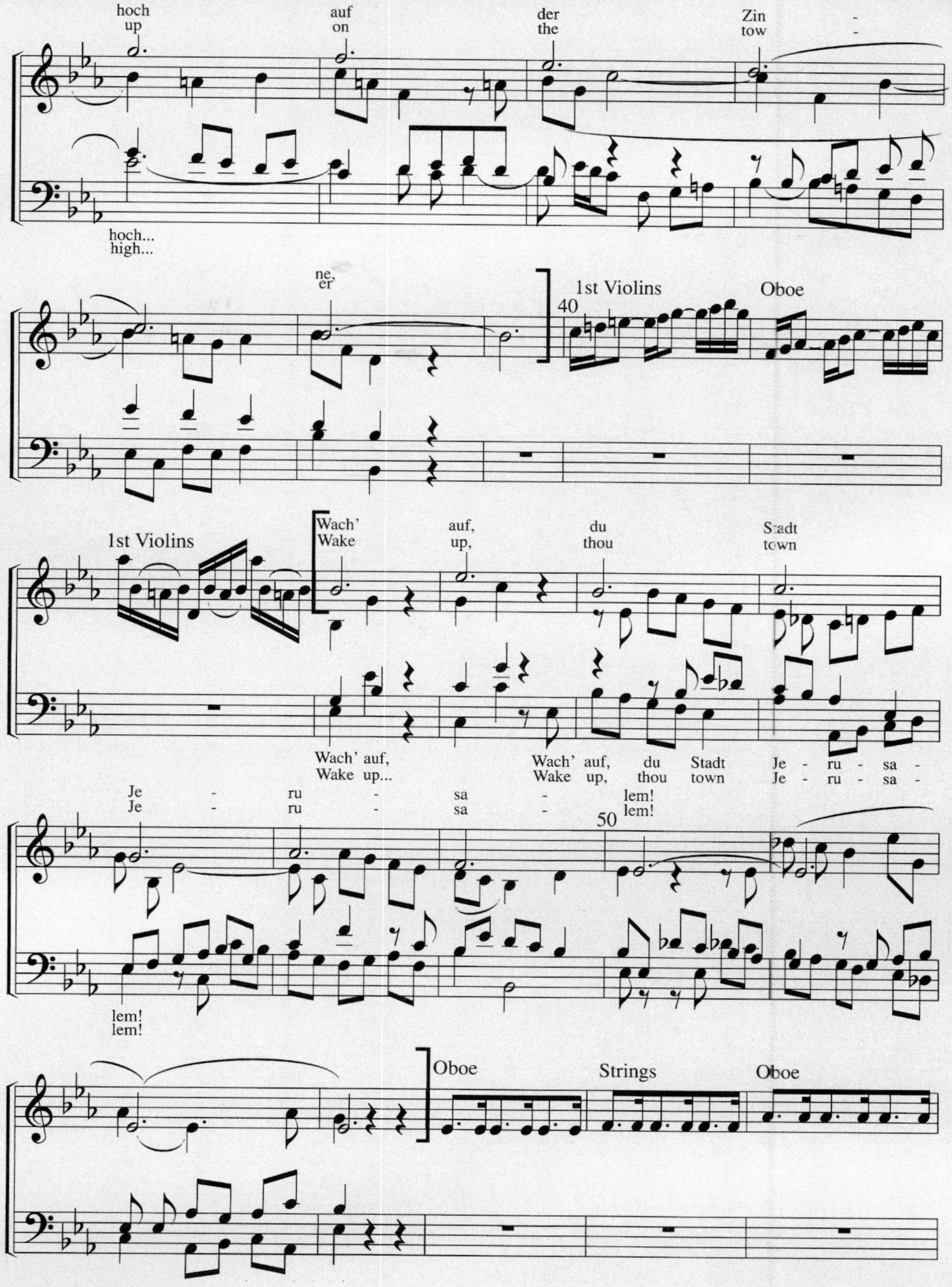

Figure 11.2
(Continued)

—*Continued*

Figure 11.3

Homophony. J. S. Bach, Cantata no. 140, from "Wachet auf."

—*Continued*

Figure 11.3
(Continued)

—Continued

Reflections

Be aware of outer voices (sopranos and basses) and inner voices (altos and tenors). Notice the moving parts in which other voices move for a beat or two in faster rhythm over the notes of the soprano melody.

Identify recurring motives, imitation, and contrasting sounds. Be aware of the various layers of sounds, that is, the various lines, whether vocal or instrumental.

The polyphonic chorus is based on the chorale tune. It is the most elaborate and complex of all the movements of this cantata. Notice that the tune is in a slower rhythm than the other parts, and its phrases are separated.

Cantatas and oratorios included vocal solos (arias and recitatives), solo ensembles and choruses, and instrumental accompaniment. The **aria** typically was more songlike, melodic, and metric than the recitative. The **recitative** had a more important part in oratorios than in cantatas. It was an important technique in opera, describing the action in a way that all could understand. It was sung in free rhythm, declaiming words in a natural inflection with a minimal accompaniment of simple chords. Soloists often introduce their arias by means of the recitative. A narrator as a dramatic character was sometimes included, particularly in the oratorio. The solo ensemble was a small group of solo voices.

The choruses (sung by a choir) were often contrapuntal, even fugal. The accompaniment for the cantata was often an organ, occasionally with a small group of other instruments. An organ and often an orchestra accompanied the oratorio.

Opera

The development of **opera**, around 1600, resulted from several factors:

• Renewed interest among scholars in the famous Greek tragedies and a desire among a small group of scholars in Italy to set dramatic works to music with costumes and staging.

The Santa Fe Opera in the 1986 production of Monteverdi's *L'incoronazione di Poppea.*

The Santa Fe Opera Theatre.

- Heightened interest generally in drama and theatrical elements in music.
- Tendency in the early baroque period for composers to use music to depict the meanings of words and the emotions of the text.
- Shift from polyphonic to homophonic texture (an accompanied melody) that presented words in an understandable manner (an expressive solo singing style).
- Creation of the aria and recitative which carried the dramatic action forward and developed the plot. Arias also provided a way to display vocal virtuosity.

The first operas were produced around 1600 in Italy. The most important and durable early operas were *Orfeo* by the Italian composer Claudio Monteverdi, produced

Listening Guide   No. 55

Le Sommeil d'Ulisse (excerpt)

I. Prelude

II. Recitatif

III. Air de Mer

Three parts of a French cantata for voice, strings, and continuo composed around 1710 by Elisabeth-Claude Jacquet de la Guerre (c. 1666–1729).

Performed by John Ostendorf, baritone, and the Bronx Chamber Ensemble: Johannes Somary, conductor — **CD4, Tracks 7–9, 2:52**

These miniature movements represent many compositional practices of the baroque era.

—Continued

Listening Guide — *Continued*   *No.* 55

Goals

Compare and contrast recitatives and arias.

Recognize homophonic texture and contrasting textures (full orchestra or small ensemble).

Describe *basso continuo*.

Recognize dotted rhythms.

Guide

0:00	1. Prelude (instrumental)
	In a moderately fast four. After a strong descending opening motive, a second passage starting in the third bar has a stepwise ascending contour, then descends. The full orchestra contrasts with the sound of a few instruments. The melody is supported harmonically by the bassoon and the harpsichord.
0:23	The contrasting lighter section features dotted rhythms and short, echolike question-answer fragments. A ritard leads to the final cadence.
1:07	2. Recitatif (vocal, with continuo)
	A flexible pulse accommodates the rhythm of the text. Very thin-textured accompaniment.
1:43	3. Air de Mer (Song of the Sea) (vocal, with continuo)
	In a strong triple meter. Crisp, dotted rhythms prevail in the *basso continuo*. A ritard leads to the final cadence.

Reflections

Listen for diatonic, conjunct melodies; series of chord progressions; and broken chords in the harpsichord accompaniment during the recitative.

The French cantata was lively, dramatic chamber entertainment. Its plots, often mythological, were usually sketchy, but its music was elegant, compact, and refined.

in 1608; and *Dido and Aeneas* by the English composer Henry Purcell, produced in 1689. In the late baroque, the great German composer Handel wrote operas in the Italian style that were produced in England. Also, England saw the beginnings of ballad opera, the genre that satirized Italian opera. Ballad operas included popular tunes or ballads and enjoyed tremendous popularity both in Europe and later in the Americas.

Composers

The most important composer of the early baroque was Claudio Monteverdi (1567–1643), known originally for his madrigals, in the old-fashioned or Renaissance polyphonic style, and later for madrigals foreshadowing many important features that would become commonplace in the baroque period. He was especially known for operas composed in the new baroque style. In addition to *Orfeo,* he wrote *The Return of*

Ulysses and *The Coronation of Poppea*. All three are still performed today by university and professional opera companies for stage productions and for recordings.

Between Monteverdi and the giants of the late baroque era, Johann Sebastian Bach and George Frideric Handel, are the following composers:

- Buxtehude, Dieterich (1637–1701), Prelude in D
- Francesca Caccini (1587–1641) was from an influential musical family. She composed and published both sacred and secular music and stage works. Her opera *La Liberazione di Ruggiero* was the first composed by a woman and the first Italian opera performed outside Italy.
- Arcangelo Corelli (1653–1713) was a violin virtuoso known for his development of modern violin techniques, his trio sonatas, and his contribution to the concerto grosso form (see Listening Guide 52, p. 241).
- François Couperin (1668–1733) was an important French composer of harpsichord music and chamber music and the author of an authoritative method book on playing the harpsichord.
- Elisabeth-Claude Jacquet de la Guerre (1666–1729) was an immensely successful French composer and harpsichordist who is well known today, particularly for her harpsichord works and cantatas (see p. 251).
- Isabella Leonarda (1620–1704) was the most prolific woman composer of the seventeenth century. All her works—of which there are more than two hundred—were composed for use in church.
- Jean Baptiste Lully (1632–1687) was important in the development of French opera.
- Henry Purcell (1659–1695) was England's foremost native composer of the seventeenth century. His success was founded on numerous anthems and other religious works, trio sonatas, and his most famous opera, *Dido and Aeneas*.
- Antonio Vivaldi (1678–1741) was probably the most celebrated of all Italian composers. He wrote operas, oratorios, and church music, but his fame rests on his concerto grossos and solo concertos, of which he composed more than four hundred.
- Barbara Strozzi (1619–1664) was a Venetian composer and singer who published her own compositions: eight volumes that contain more than a hundred vocal works, mostly secular pieces for solo voice and continuo.
- Georg Philipp Telemann (1681–1767) was a prolific German composer of church music (including masses, motets, oratorios, and more than a thousand cantatas); operas; keyboard pieces; and instrumental music (concertos, sonatas, overtures, and chamber music).

The most famous baroque composers, ranking among the greatest creators of Western classical music, are Bach and Handel.

Bach, a member of an illustrious German musical family, lived and worked entirely in Germany. The first part of his professional career was mainly in Weimar where he was court organist and chamber musician to the Duke of Weimar and composed his most significant organ music. Bach then went to Cöthen where he was chapelmaster and director of chamber music for the Prince of Anhalt and composed important chamber and orchestral music. He ended his career in Leipzig, where he was cantor of Saint Thomas's church and school and composed his monumental choral works.

Bach was a master of baroque forms and genres, realizing their fullest potential. His organ music continues to be among the best of organ literature. His tonal counterpoint in choral music, chord progressions in chorale harmonizations, and fugues for keyboard

Johann Sebastian Bach (1685–1750)

Master of Leipzig. This artist's impression shows the Bach family at morning prayers, with Bach himself playing the clavichord. He is accompanied by one of his sons on the violin.

instruments have been and continue to be studied, perhaps more than those of any other composer. Among Bach's most important attributes was his phenomenal grasp of the technique of composition, particularly in his mastery of the grand art of polyphony and the newer art of tonal harmony.

Among his most important works are *Mass in B Minor, St. Matthew Passion*, and church cantatas, of which he composed more than three hundred; numerous chorale preludes, toccatas, fugues, and other works for organ or harpsichord; *The Art of Fugue, Goldberg Variations*, and *The Well-Tempered Clavier* for keyboard instruments; six suites for unaccompanied cello; and six Brandenburg Concertos for various soloists and orchestra. Bach's music was not performed much after he died, until it was rediscovered in the early nineteenth century. Today, his music is played in churches and concert halls throughout the world.

George Frideric Handel (1685–1759)

Handel was a native of Germany who mastered the Italian musical style, particularly in opera, and achieved his most notable successes during the nearly 50 years he spent in England. Unlike Bach, Handel was internationally famous during his lifetime. Initially, he was known as a composer and producer of Italian operas in England, but his most lasting fame was as a composer of oratorios. His best-known work is, of course, *Messiah*.

Handel is also well known for his instrumental music in virtually all the usual baroque forms, notably concerto grossos; harpsichord suites; organ concertos; and two orchestral pieces (now widely recorded), *Water Music* and *Music for the Royal Fireworks*. Handel composed for a wide audience and became a master in the grand style of the late baroque.

Listening Guide   No. 56

The Musik for the Royal Fireworks (II, IV)

Composed by George Frideric Handel in 1749.

Performed by the Academy of Ancient Music (Christopher Hogwood).

The movements of this piece:

I. Ouverture

II. Bourrée

III. La Paix

IV. La Réjouissance

V. Menuet I and II — **CD4, Tracks 10–11, 2:32**

Handel composed this work to accompany a fireworks display in celebration of the end of the war of the Austrian succession, which came to an end in 1748. It was scored, as can be heard, for large numbers of brass, wind, and percussion instruments—not many strings. In fact, the original ensemble may have been more like a band than an orchestra.

Goals

Is Bourée stately? If so, what makes it so? If not, how else would you describe the mood?

Is La Réjouissance majestic? If so, what makes it so? If not, how else would you describe the mood?

Describe the instrumentation. How does it change throughout each movement?

Guide

II. Bourrée: duple meter at a moderate tempo; stately

0:00	a	10 + 10 bars
0:25	b	16 bars
0:45	b	16 bars
1:06	a	10 + 10 bars
1:32	b	16 bars
1:53	b	16 bars—ritard at end

IV. La Réjouissance; duple meter; moderate tempo; brass, winds, and percussion dominate the sound

0:00	a	16 bars
0:19	a	16 bars
0:38	b	20 bars
1:02	b	20 bars
1:26	a	16 bars
1:44	b	20 bars—ritard at end

—Continued

L i s t e n i n g   G u i d e — *Continued*   *No.* 56

Reflections

Imagine the performance context for this music—concert hall? church? arena? salon?

Is this piece a work of art (as in *art music*)? Why or why not?

Compare this music with the other examples in this chapter. Which pieces did you like and why?

Summary

Sacred polyphonic choral music dominated Western music through the late Middle Ages and the Renaissance. The baroque period itself was divided in emphasis fairly equally between choral and instrumental music, and between sacred and secular music.

The major-minor tonal system, homophonic texture, and orchestral writing became standard practice during the baroque period. Instruments as we know them today became common during this period, laying the foundation for the symphony orchestra and classical chamber ensembles, such as the string quartet, that became standard during the classical era.

The baroque period also gave us the beginnings of opera, incorporating the aria and the recitative with their ability to carry the dramatic action forward. This period brought a proliferation of keyboard works for harpsichord and organ, the fugue as the primary polyphonic compositional technique, the oratorio and cantata as important choral genres, and the concerto as an important instrumental genre.

The baroque era produced many composers who are well known today: Corelli, Vivaldi, Monteverdi, Couperin, Lully, Telemann, and Purcell. Influential women composers included Francesca Caccini, Elisabeth-Claude Jacquet de la Guerre, and Isabella Leonarda. But the giants were Johann Sebastian Bach and George Frideric Handel.

Additional Listening

E x a m p l e   *No.* 12

Fugue no. 2 in C Minor (see Listening Guide no. 53, this chapter)

A Bach fugue written for keyboard—sung by a vocal jazz octet

Composed by Johann Sebastian Bach.

Arranged by Ward Swingle.

Performed by the Swingle Singers—with bass and drums.

From the album *Jazz Sebastian Bach* (1963) — **CD4, Track 12, 1:16**

Goals

Identify the main theme (the subject of the fugue). Follow the entrances of each melody and notice many fragments of the subject as they are passed from voice to voice.

—Continued

E x a m p l e　*No.* 12 — *Continued*

Recognize any different thematic material.

Describe the roles of the bass and of the drums.

Guide

In a fairly fast four or a moderately slow two.

0:00	Statement of the subject: altos
0:05	Second entrance of the subject: sopranos
0:14	Third entrance of the subject: tenors
0:33	Fourth entrance of the subject: altos
0:44	Fifth entrance of the subject: sopranos
0:58	Sixth entrance of the subject: tenors and basses
1:05	Seventh entrance of the subject leads to quiet ending—final major chord (having been in a minor key)

Reflections

Is this music classical or jazz? Is it art or entertainment?

Is this music respectful or disrespectful of the music of Johann Sebastian Bach and of art music in general? Give reasons for your answers.

Was this arrangement musically satisfying? Could any of Bach's music be arranged in a jazz style? Could any classical keyboard music be arranged in a jazz style?

CHAPTER

12

Music of the Classic Period (1750–1820)

Goals for Listening

- **Describe** instrumental timbres.
- **Describe** vocal style and technique (opera).
- **Recognize** variations of themes and motives.
- **Identify** contrasting moods.
- **Recognize** tonal centers (keys) and modulations.
- **Identify** stability and instability.
- **Identify** tension and release.
- **Identify** contrast and repetition.

Summary

Additional Listening

Terms and Concepts

Sonata form

Theme and variations

Minuet and trio

Rondo

Sonata, symphony, and concerto

Symphony orchestra

Cadenza

Chamber music: String quartet

Opera

Staccato and legato

Range of expression

The sounds of classical music created in the late eighteenth century as well as the nineteenth century are familiar to twentieth-century Americans who listen to classical music or who have experienced it as part of their formal education. Many of the pieces and many of the composers are household words. This music is widely performed today by school, community, and professional musical organizations; it is heard on any classical music radio station; and recordings of it are frequently purchased by American consumers. Those who know anything at all about classical music know something about Mozart, Haydn, and Beethoven or some of their works, such as Beethoven's Fifth Symphony, his "Moonlight" Sonata, Haydn's "Surprise" Symphony, and Mozart's *The Magic Flute* or *The Marriage of Figaro*.

We can refer to the classic period of the late eighteenth century as the beginning of the modern era. Developments of this time that formed the groundwork for musical practices of the next 150 to 200 years were the sonata, symphony, and string quartet; the instrumentation of the modern symphony orchestra; and public concerts available to everyone. The classic period was centered in the courts and communities of Austria and Germany. This was a sophisticated, aristocratic society. The courts valued artistic and social status and demanded the very best in entertainment. But this period also saw an increase in community concert halls and opera houses as music became more available to common people through public performances. The church's influence on the direction of Western music declined. Although Catholic and Protestant church music continued to be created, the classic period saw a rise in instrumental music.

In this chapter you will continue to explore Western classical music. As you learn to identify and recognize themes, modulations, stability, and repetition, these terms will be helpful in understanding classical music: *Goals for Listening*

Dynamics. In music, dynamics refers to the loudness level: *forte* (loud), *piano* (soft), *mezzo piano* (medium soft), *crescendo* (gradually get louder), and *decrescendo* (gradually get softer).

Form. Forms that are generic, that is, common in many musical styles, include two-part, or **binary** (a b), and three-part, or **ternary** (a b a), forms. An a a b a form is ternary because of its return to the a theme. Among the common forms found in western European classical music are the sonata form, the minuet and trio, the rondo, and the theme and variations.

Scales. In Western music, if most of the tones of a piece are derived from a single **scale**, it is said to be **diatonic**. Frequently, notes are added that are not part of the scale to add interest and color. If many nonscale tones are added, it may obscure the tonality and create a tonally unstable feeling. This music is said to be **chromatic**.

Tempo. To describe **tempos** or changes of tempo, musicians use terms such as *allegro* (fast), *andante* (moderate tempo), *largo* (slow), *accelerando* (get faster), *ritardando* (ritard: get slower), and *rubato* (a flexible pulse; interpreting music in a highly expressive manner).

Whereas the baroque period was a time of opulent splendor, ornamentation, decoration, and emotional expression, the classic period reflected the Age of Reason: emotional restraint, balance, clarity, symmetry, clear and precise formal structure, and simplicity. *Musical Characteristics*

In classical music, melody predominates and all other factors are subordinate to it. Thus to the composer of the classic era, homophonic texture was much more important than contrapuntal or polyphonic writing. Melodies were typically lyrical, with smooth, stepwise contours; phrases ended with obvious tonic-dominant cadences; diatonic melodies prevailed, and to a large extent they reflected the underlying harmonies. Rhythm was for the most part uncomplicated and predictable.

Music was tonal, in a major or minor key, for harmonic practices were a logical extension and refinement of the tonal system established during the baroque period. Tonality was clear. Chords progressions used the most common, most basic harmonies, which to a large extent are easily recognizable. The chords revolved around what had come to be common practice in the use of the primary tonic, subdominant, and dominant chords, with the continued use of dissonances, such as the dominant seventh chord, that demanded resolution.

Modulations to new keys were common, and key relationships took on new significance—relationships of keys from one phrase group to the next, one section to the next, and even one movement of an extended work to the next. New keys represented instability that was resolved only when the tonal center returned to the original tonic. This interest resulted in a strong preference for the a b a structure, with a in the tonic key, b in a contrasting key, and a—a return to the tonic key. The concept of unity and variety, of contrast and return, was valued in classical music and was applied most commonly in the forms developed during the classic period.

Instruments

The classic period was an age of instrumental music. The families of instruments of modern orchestras and bands became standard: strings, woodwinds, brass, and percussion. The baroque continuo and figured bass were no longer needed, as all parts were now written out. The pianoforte (a forerunner of the piano) displaced the harpsichord in popularity and was now used as a solo instrument or as an equal member in chamber ensembles. The instrumentation of the modern orchestra, the string quartet, and other chamber ensembles also became standard during this period:

An artist's impression of Haydn leading a rehearsal of a string quartet.

- The orchestra included the string section, consisting of first and second violins, violas, cellos, and double basses; winds in pairs (flutes, clarinets, oboes, bassoons, trumpets, horns, and sometimes trombones); and timpani, the only widely used percussion instrument.
- Chamber ensembles included a wide variety of string, wind, and piano combinations, commonly ranging from three to eight musicians (trios to octets). Among these ensembles were the following:

    String quartet: two violins, one viola, one cello.

    Piano trio: violin, cello, and piano.

    Piano quintet: string quartet plus piano.

The genres of the classic period grew out of those of the baroque period. These genres changed and stabilized sufficiently in terminology and concept that they became models of formal structure on which much music would be based for the next 150 years. Again, however, descriptions apply to common practice; there are many exceptions to each generalization.

Genres

The primary instrumental genres of the classic era are multimovement works, usually with three or four movements: the **sonata** for one or two instruments, the **symphony** and **concerto** for orchestra, and **chamber music** (the string quartet and other small chamber music groups).

Instrumental Genres

Chamber music is distinguished from orchestral music in that in chamber music each part is played on only one instrument. In orchestral music, more than one instrument may play the same part. For example, 6 double basses might be playing the bass part, or 12 violins might be playing the violin part.

Typical multimovement works have the following arrangement and structure:

I Fast: sonata form.

II Slow: a broad a b a form is common, sometimes theme and variations form.

Emerson String Quartet.

III Dance: usually a minuet and trio or, later, a scherzo and trio; omitted in most three-movement sonatas, particularly the concerto.

IV Fast: usually a rondo, sometimes sonata form.

The sonata genre is a work for one or two instruments. Solo piano sonatas are the most common. Sonatas for two instruments are usually written for an orchestral instrument and piano; of these, violin sonatas are the most common. It is not accurate to describe them as works for solo instrument with piano accompaniment because the piano is usually as important as the solo instrument.

The concerto features a solo instrument, frequently the piano or the violin, with the full symphony orchestra. It is typically in three movements. The dance movement is the one omitted, for the texture of solo with orchestra does not lend itself to the spirit of dance. A classical concerto typically features a **cadenza**, in which the orchestra stops and the soloist engages in an extended virtuoso passage, highlighting the soloist's technical abilities. The cadenza frequently has an improvisatory character and includes long passages in free rhythm.

The symphony is a work for full symphony orchestra, usually in four movements and featuring the varied tone colors of all the orchestral instruments.

The most common chamber music ensemble of the classic era is the string quartet (two violins, viola, and cello). It has already been mentioned that chamber music as a genre encompasses works for a variety of small ensembles from trios to octets, including some that combine strings and piano and some that involve wind instruments.

L istening Guide   *No.* 57

Symphony No. 39 in E♭ Major (IV)

Composed in 1788 by Wolfgang Amadeus Mozart.

Performed by the Bavarian Radio Orchestra, Rafael Kubelik, conductor.

CD4, Tracks 13–19, 5:43 (SCD) CD2, Tracks 16–22, 5:43

This movement is in sonata form. The most important principles of this form are (1) contrast and repetition and (2) development; this movement clearly exemplifies both principles. Sonata form consists of exposition (two thematic areas), development, and recapitulation.

Goals

Understand the basic characteristics of sonata form.

Be aware of the principles of stability and instability, tension and release, and contrast and repetition.

Recognize the strong, identifiable nine-note motive at the beginning, and be aware of the development of that motive.

Be aware of modulation (change of key) and return to the home key (tonic).

—*Continued*

Listening Guide — *Continued*

Finale
Allegro

Figure 12.1

Part of a conductor's score from Mozart's Symphony no. 39 (IV). Reprinted by permission of Edwin F. Kalmus & Company, Inc., Opa Locka, FL.

—**Continued**

Guide

Count in a moderately fast two. The movement starts with the opening theme. Refer to the score (fig. 12.1).

0:00	Exposition	
	a 8 bars	main theme area; diatonic melody; soft; strings; open cadence;
	7 bars	loud; full orchestra; closed cadence on the first bar of the next section;
	26 bars	starts simultaneously with end of previous phrase; first eight bars repeated, then extends to cadence; extended material serves as bridge to second theme.
0:37	b 6 bars	second theme area is in new key; soft; motive adapted from first theme; thin texture; violins answered by woodwinds;
	20 bars	modified theme leads into dialogue between flute and bassoon and strong cadence in the key of the dominant (B-flat major)
1:02	Concluding section—37 bars	
	First segment (11 bars)	loud; thick texture (full orchestra);
	Second segment (20 bars)	thin texture; dialogue between oboe and bassoon
	Third segment (6 bars)	full texture to final cadence of exposition.
1:36	Exposition is repeated.	
3:12	Development—motivic development; main motive passed around from instrument to instrument, altered in many ways; modulating; unstable; varying textures.	
3:58	Recapitulation—return to material, style, and form of exposition.	
4:58	Concluding section—47 bars in the tonic key of the movement (E-flat major)	
	First segment (14 bars)	loud; thick texture (full orchestra)
	Second segment (20 bars)	thin texture; dialogue between oboe and bassoon
	Third segment (14 bars)	full texture to final cadence of movement.

Reflections

Recognize changes, contrasts, and returns, particularly the return to the stable, tonic key after the unstable development section. Equate instability with tension and stability with release of tension.

Identify and remember the initial motive in order to recognize it in its many manifestations as the piece unfolds.

The primary vocal, choral, and dramatic genre of the classic period was opera. Composers continued to write oratorios, masses, and other sacred choral music. However, although these genres had reigned supreme in the time of Bach and Handel, this was no longer true in the musical developments of the late eighteenth and nineteenth centuries.

Vocal, Choral, Opera

The opera of the classic era strengthened the relationship between music and drama and between singers and orchestra. The trend was toward ongoing music and continuous drama arranged in scenes, rather than a series of recitatives, arias, and choruses interrupting the natural flow of the dramatic action that had been common in baroque opera. The recitative and aria were still used (see Listening Guide 58 below), but their accompaniment was now more complex and was intended to enhance the atmosphere of the text rather than be totally subservient to the singer. The recitative provided narrative; the aria provided commentary on the plot; and the solo ensembles and choruses, along with staging, costumes, and orchestral accompaniment, enhanced the plot and added musical and dramatic interest. In the classic period, more than in the baroque era, the opera orchestra was used to create a mood that would support the drama. The orchestra was given lyrical melodies rather than mere accompaniment patterns and became a more integral part of the drama.

L istening Guide   *No.* 58

"E Susanna Non Vien! . . . Dove Sono"

Recitative and aria from Act III of the opera *Le Nozze di Figaro* (*The Marriage of Figaro*). Composed in 1785 by Wolfgang Amadeus Mozart (1756–1791).

Performed by Kiri Te Kanawa, soprano, and the London Philharmonic Orchestra; Sir Georg Solti, conductor — **CD4, Tracks 20–21, 4:45**

This is Italian *opera buffa*, a type of comic opera. The libretto, by Lorenzo da Ponte, the imperial court poet in Vienna, was based on Beaumarchais's play *Le Mariage de Figaro*. The story involves love and conflicts between the aristocracy and lower classes. The complex plot is laid out in Act I and developed and resolved in subsequent acts. This is an opera with a unified story about human beings whose feelings and behavior are delineated and developed and whose major problems are resolved in the end. The substance, subtleties, and nuances of Mozart's music support the character development and give the story a timeless quality.

Figaro and Susanna, who plan to be married, are personal servants to the count and countess Almaviva. The count pursues Susanna. Figaro finds out and plots against the count. The countess, though not comfortable with subterfuge—wishing only that her love for the count were enough to keep him fulfilled—conspires against the count. Susanna, although promising to comply with the Count's wishes, joins the Countess in conspiring against him. In this recitative and aria, the countess Almaviva is onstage alone; she contemplates this turn of events while waiting to hear from Susanna.

—Continued

Goals

Describe the vocal style of a great opera singer; compare it with the style of a great folk, jazz, or pop singer.

Describe the range of expression in this aria.

Describe vocal techniques that exemplify the text and those that have little to do with the text.

Guide

0:00	Recitative	Free rhythm, dictated by the words and their meanings; dramatic and declamatory, yet with wide range of expression; thin texture in orchestral accompaniment
2:12	Aria	Duple meter in a very slow two, perhaps better felt in four; some changes of tempo; wide range of expression but essentially lyrical and melodic
	Section I	a Two phrases (8 + 10); phrase 2 modified; an open-closed cadential pattern
3:09		b Two phrases (9 + 9); vocal and instrumental dialogue; section ends on fermata rest
4:10		a Main theme returns; phrase 2-fade

Reflections

Discuss a variety of manifestations of music in drama and drama in music.

Discuss the various roles of individuals who make opera, such as the composer, librettist, producer, costumer, designer, conductor, orchestral musician, stage director, and vocal coach.

The most famous operas of the classic period are those by Mozart, including *The Marriage of Figaro, The Magic Flute,* and *Don Giovanni.*

Classical choral works include Haydn's oratorio *The Creation,* Mozart's *Requiem,* and Beethoven's *Missa Solemnis.*

Forms

The following formal structures, all related to instrumental music, were common in classical music but were seldom adhered to in a strict sense. They became flexible models used as the basis of much nineteenth- and twentieth-century music. The challenge for listeners is to learn to recognize the factors that create form, such as contrast and repetition and changes in mood, tonality, or instrumentation.

During the classic era, the **sonata form** was commonly used as the basis of the first movement of sonatas, symphonies, concertos, and string quartets. A typical first movement form would include an exposition, development, and recapitulation and sometimes an introduction and coda.

The exposition presents the primary theme in the tonic key, followed by a secondary theme in a contrasting key, sometimes in a contrasting mood. Sometimes a short transition section would move the music from one key to the next. The second section ended in the new key; that is, it did not return to the tonic key but ended with a feeling of expectancy. The exposition was sometimes repeated.

In the development section, the composer's imagination could flourish. This was music based on prior material, such as a melodic fragment of the first theme or perhaps the second theme or even both themes. The fragments became the basis of experimentation, in which the composer would use an idea and let it grow. Tonal centers might be obscure or might change frequently. The pitch contour of melodic fragments might be altered. Dynamics, rhythms, harmonies, and tempos might be modified, or a fragment might be passed from instrument to instrument, from a high- to a low-pitch area, from the brass to the woodwinds. Contrapuntal imitation might be inserted in an essentially homophonic texture, or the density (thickness) of the texture might be varied by increasing or decreasing the number of instruments playing at any time. Any or all of these devices created unstable, restless music, a dramatic sense of conflict and tension that at some point demanded a return to stability.

The recapitulation provided the return to stability, a return to the tonic key, the primary theme of the exposition. Sometimes it was a literal repetition of the exposition, except the second theme area usually was kept in the tonic key rather than modulated to a new key as in the exposition. At other times the recapitulation was modified in a variety of ways, particularly at the point of bringing the movement to a close.

A coda was the concluding section, in effect serving as an extension of the tonic ending but building up to and creating anticipation of the final cadence.

The formal structure of the sonata form can be outlined as follows:

Introduction.

Exposition: often repeated.

    A Home key—stability.

    B Contrasting key—instability and expectancy relative to section A.

Development: an expansion of the exposition, that is, music derived from previous material—instability and expectancy.

Recapitulation: return to the tonic key—stability.

    A Home key—stability.

    B Home key—stability.

Coda.

Any large instrumental work or movement of a work that is built on the statement of a theme followed by a series of variations on that theme is known as **theme and variations** form. Variations were achieved in numerous ways, such as by changing tempo, dynamics, articulation (separated or connected notes, known as staccato or legato), tonality, mode (a shift from major to minor), instrumentation, and texture. The variations might have been continuous, without clear stops; or sectional, with clear breaks between variations.

Sonata Form

Theme and Variations

*L*istening Guide   *No.* 59

String Quartet in C Major, op. 76, no. 3 (II) (excerpt)

Theme-and-variations form.

Composed by Franz Joseph Haydn (1732–1809).

Performed by the Tátrai Quartet — **CD4, Track 22, 6:40**

The "Emperor" is one of the last of Haydn's 82 string quartets. It was composed in 1797 when Haydn was 65. The second of the four movements includes a hymn that Haydn was asked to write for the birthday of Emperor Francis. It became the Austrian national anthem.

Goals

Describe theme-and-variation form.

Recognize the sounds and musical lines of each instrument.

In each variation, recognize and describe how Haydn varies the setting of the theme.

Distinguish between staccato and legato styles, and between simple and elaborate melodies.

Identify uses of tension and release.

Guide

Second movement—theme and variations (comments are provided for the theme and the first four of seven variations); a hymnlike melody; in a moderately slow four, starting with two-beat pickup on third beat.

	Main theme		
0:00	a	4 bars	primary phrase
0:15	a	4 bars	repeat
0:30	b	4 bars	contrasting phrase
0:47	c	4 bars	new melodic motive starts on high note, then descends to V—I cadence
1:03	c	4 bars	repeat
1:19	Variation 1		For two violins; melody in second violin; fast-moving; florid first violin part; shifting staccato and legato passages
2:28	Variation 2		Melody in cello; legato harmonization in second violin; harmonic "fill" in viola; more elaborate, syncopated countermelody in high first violin part
3:46	Variation 3		Melody in viola; polyphonic setting involving other three parts in equal, independent melodic lines
4:58	Variation 4		Melody in first violin; first phrase in a choralelike setting; second, third, and fourth phrases each shift to higher, more intricate interplay of parts; ends with four-bar extension, descending to a quiet cadence in which all parts hold one dissonant chord until tension is resolved on the final tonic.

—Continued

Reflections

Be aware of the varying roles or styles given to the instruments, considering such issues as foreground and background roles, simple and elaborate lines, or melody and countermelody.

Recognize polyphonic and homophonic textures.

Discuss the values of the theme-and-variations form.

The **minuet and trio** is a stately dance movement in triple meter. It is usually the third movement of a symphony or string quartet. The minuet is a carryover from the stylized dance forms popular during the baroque period. In fact, this dance was the only one that remained popular during the classic period. In the nineteenth century, this form was often replaced by a scherzo and trio, also in triple meter but played at a fast tempo with great rhythmic drive.

Minuet and Trio

The minuet is in two parts with repeats; the trio is in a contrasting mood, also in two parts with each part repeated. The minuet returns but is traditionally played without repeats. Again, contrasting key relationships and returns to the tonic are important in this form. A common minuet and trio form can be depicted as follows:

Minuet (Part I)	A	a	Repeated
		b a	Repeated
Trio (Part II)	B	c	Repeated
		d c	Repeated
Minuet (Part I repeated)	A	a b a	

The minuet. An eighteenth-century royal ballroom scene.

Rondo

The principle of contrast and return is integral to the **rondo**. It is based on two or more contrasting theme areas, in which changes are made in melody, mood, and tonality, each change followed by a return to the original section. The concluding movement of a sonata, symphony, or string quartet is frequently in rondo form, which might be depicted structurally as follows:

a b a c a   or   a b a c a b a   or   a b a c a d a

Listening Guide   No. 60

Piano Sonata no. 8 in C Minor, op. 13 ("Pathétique") (III)

I. Grave; Allegro di molto e con brio
II. Adagio cantabile
III. Rondo: Allegro

Composed in 1799 by Ludwig van Beethoven

Performed by Vladimir Horowitz, piano — **CD4, Tracks 23–30, 4:28 (SCD) CD2, Tracks 23–30, 4:28**

The "Pathétique" sonata is one of Beethoven's most respected and best-known works. It maintains many of the traditional classic ideals of clarity and balance. However, with its dramatic contrasts, its powerful chords, and its range of emotions, this sonata foreshadowed the nineteenth-century romantic spirit. It also foreshadowed the intensely personal expression of Beethoven's own later, more mature works.

Goals

Recognize the contrasting moods in the first movement of this sonata.

Discuss the musical characteristics that effect these changes.

Recognize shifts in major and minor tonalities.

Describe melodic contour as a means of identifying motives and themes.

Guide

Third movement: rondo form (a b c a b a); lively, dancelike; in the tonic key of C minor.

0:00	a	The opening statement (theme) in the key of C minor—extended phrase
0:21	b	Contrasting material in a major key; a strong chord is followed by an ascending, then descending motive, then aggressive triplet patterns, then simple, quiet, blocked chords; the aggressive triplet patterns return and conclude with a climb to a high note over a dominant chord and a scale descending to this unstable chord that is resolved with the return of the opening statement—a pattern that is to recur several times
1:16	a	In the tonic minor key

—Continued

1:35	c	Second contrasting section; in a major key; legato motive with wide skips and mild syncopation; staccato scales; arpeggio patterns that build in energy and intensity; an ending similar to the end of the second theme, with a long high note and descending scale to a sustained, unstable chord
2:30	a	In the tonic minor
2:55	b	Derived from triplet patterns in section B; modified motive
3:30	a	In the tonic minor
3:44	Coda	Derived from b motives, a return of the opening statement, and the descending scale that moves quickly to the final tonic chord

Reflections

Why do classical pieces tend to be long and popular pieces short? Discuss exceptions.

Describe the character of the coda. How is it different than the previous part of the movement? What are characteristics that cause it to bring the movement to a close in a convincing manner?

As in the baroque period, many composers were active and successful. Some of them laid the groundwork for the most illustrious composers: in the baroque era, Bach and Handel; and in the classic era, Haydn, Mozart, and Beethoven.

Composers

Among important late eighteenth-century classic composers were the following:

- Carl Philipp Emanuel Bach (1714–1788), a son of J. S. Bach. C. P. E. Bach was an important composer of concertos, chamber music, sonatas, symphonies, and particularly keyboard works.
- Johann Christian Bach (1735–1782), the youngest son of Johann Sebastian Bach. J. C. Bach was an important composer of symphonies, chamber music, keyboard works, and operas.
- Christoph Willibald Gluck (1714–1787), a composer of highly influential operas.
- Marianne von Martinez (1744–1812), a composer of music in virtually every genre common at the time except opera—more than two hundred known works.
- Maria Theresia von Paradis (1759–1824), a blind Viennese composer. Paradis composed songs, operas, and cantatas and gained an illustrious reputation as a composer and as a touring concert pianist.
- Johann Stamitz (1717–1757), a pioneer in the development of symphonic music and orchestral style.

The most significant composers who flourished during the classic period were Franz Joseph Haydn, Wolfgang Amadeus Mozart, and Ludwig van Beethoven. Haydn and Mozart were Austrians; Beethoven was born in Germany but from the age of 22 spent the rest of his life in Austria. Their music continues to be performed today, after 200 years, by virtually every amateur and professional symphony orchestra, chamber group, choral organization, and opera company throughout the world. Their music is also available on audio recordings numbering in the thousands. In fact, as of this writing, more than 2,000 compact discs or sets featuring the works of Haydn, Mozart, and Beethoven were available. Almost 1,000 of these recordings were by Mozart alone.

Franz Joseph Haydn (1732–1809)

Haydn is the best example of a composer who worked successfully within the aristocratic patronage system. For 30 years, he was court composer to the prince of Esterhazy in Austria. He wrote music for every occasion the court demanded and had a court orchestra and opera company at his disposal—an ideal situation for a composer.

Haydn was not a revolutionary, but he devised many new ways of putting music together to the delight of the people who bought his compositions and attended his concerts. His works were known throughout the German-speaking world and in France, Spain, Italy, and especially England, where he achieved his greatest fame and fortune. His imagination, inventiveness, craftsmanship, and productivity are most evident in his sonatas, symphonies, and string quartets.

Haydn built on the past, absorbed romantic impulses just beginning to emerge, and brought the classical style of the late eighteenth century to a pinnacle of sophistication and perfection. He was innovative and a champion of new forms, yet his music was logical and coherent. He drew on the folk songs of his native Austria and on the dance music of the baroque era. He also drew on the dramatic power of modulation and changes of tonality and took to new heights the concept of thematic development and motives as building blocks of composition.

Haydn enriched the literature of Western classical music. His compositions include 104 symphonies, approximately 35 concertos for various solo instruments, 82 string quartets, and 60 sonatas for solo piano. His most famous symphonies are no. 94, the "Surprise"; no. 100, the "Military"; no. 101, the "Clock"; no. 103, the "Drum Roll"; and no. 104, the "London." Of his string quartets, perhaps op. 76, no. 3, the "Emperor," is his most famous. Best known among his many concertos are those for cello, harpsichord, organ, trumpet, and violin. Finally, he composed several widely performed masses and two oratorios, the most famous being *The Creation.*

Wolfgang Amadeus Mozart (1756–1791)

Mozart was a prodigiously gifted child and a product of the Austrian aristocratic system. Since art music in the last quarter of the eighteenth century was not the sole province of the church or the aristocracy, Mozart was willing to sacrifice the security of the patronage system for personal freedom and the risks of earning a living from commissions, concerts, and the sale of his published music. He had a superior education, both from his father, Leopold, a court musician, and from his extensive travels in Italy, France, England, Germany, and the Austrian imperial court in Vienna. His childhood was serene, but his adult life was more tumultuous. He had to struggle for recognition and income and died in poverty.

Mozart was a genius with few peers in Western music. He was prolific and inventive, and he composed in virtually every popular form of the day. He brought to his music an unmatched lyricism and a profound expressiveness. Devoted listeners can gain deeper insights into his music from repeated hearings. His works convey the elegance of court music at its best. They are sophisticated and urbane, reflecting the cosmopolitan culture of Salzburg and Vienna.

In his short life, Mozart created more than six hundred compositions. The final six symphonies are especially noteworthy. The last three—no. 39, no. 40, and no. 41 (the great "Jupiter" Symphony)—were not commissioned, nor were they performed in his lifetime. Yet they now rank among the most substantial of his instrumental works.

Mozart wrote 25 piano concertos, 7 violin concertos, and concertos for bassoon, clarinet, horn, flute, flute and harp, and oboe; his "entertainment" music—the divertimentos and serenades—continues to be popular, especially the Serenade in G, commonly known as "Eine kleine Nachtmusik." His most unusual works may well be those written for glass harmonica, an instrument invented by Benjamin Franklin; the sound was similar to that created by musical glasses.

Mozart's chamber music continues to be widely performed; it includes 23 string quartets, a quintet for clarinet and strings, a quintet for piano and winds, and piano quartets and quintets (piano with strings). Professional solo pianists will likely have at least one of his 17 piano sonatas in their repertoire. His *Requiem* stands out among his many excellent choral works.

The Magic Flute, The Marriage of Figaro, and *Don Giovanni* are Mozart's most famous operas. He had an affinity for opera and was able to combine the best of the Italian and Germanic traits that dominated opera styles of this era. His gift for creating beautiful, lyrical melodies was combined with a strong sense of drama. With his collaborators, he infused opera with a sense of humanity, deep feeling, and character development. Real, recognizable human beings rather than stereotypical caricatures were central to Mozart's operas. More than lively tunes with light accompaniment, his music provided emotional and dramatic support for the characters and the plot.

Beethoven's earlier music is in classical style, but his later works—and, for many scholars, his superior works—have many characteristics associated with the romantic period that followed. For this reason, he is frequently considered both a classic and a romantic composer or, perhaps more accurately, a composer who exemplifies a transition from the classic to the romantic style.

Ludwig van Beethoven (1770–1827)

Beethoven holding his *Missa Solemnis.*

Beethoven began his career in the employment of the court at Bonn in his native Germany. At the age of 22, he moved to Vienna, where he would spend the rest of his life. Beethoven earned a comfortable living from the sale of his compositions; thus he was independent of the exclusive patronage of the aristocracy.

The creative lives of many great composers can be divided into discrete periods. In Beethoven's case, scholars identify three periods: (1) his first 32 years—his education and formative years—when he became established as a great composer; (2) his middle life, when he produced many of his most famous works; and (3) his final period, when he produced fewer but intensely serious and personal works.

Beethoven freed music from the restraints of classicism by creating works that are models of subjective feeling and personal expression. His works influenced not only his contemporaries but also numerous composers of later generations. He made significant contributions to virtually every musical form and every medium of musical expression, from the solo sonata to the symphony to grand opera.

Beethoven's music can be beautiful and tender, but much of it is described as heroic, tempestuous, and powerful. It can be energetic, unpredictable, and highly emotional. His techniques for creating his powerful, personal statements include fragmentation of themes, harmonic clashes, and sustained tension. His later works, compared with those of Mozart and Haydn and his own early works, can be lengthy. In fact, the first movement of his ninth symphony lasts longer than his entire first symphony. Beethoven was an innovator in many ways: his outstanding innovations include his use of the voice in a traditionally instrumental work, as in his ninth symphony; and his dramatic, coloristic use of the piano, as in his "Appassionata" sonata.

His numerous famous works include 9 symphonies, of which nos. 3, 5, and 9 are considered monuments of symphonic literature; 5 piano concertos, of which no. 5, the "Emperor" concerto, is best known; a widely performed and recorded violin concerto; 32 piano sonatas, of which the "Pathétique" (see Listening Guide 60 p. 270), the "Appassionata," and the "Moonlight" are best known; chamber music, including 16 string quartets, 9 piano trios, and a quintet for piano and winds; numerous concert overtures, including *Egmont* and *Prometheus*; an opera, *Fidelio*; and a great choral masterpiece, *Missa Solemnis*.

istening Guide   *No.* 61

Symphony no. 9 in D Minor (IV) (excerpt)

Composed from 1817 to 1823 by Ludwig van Beethoven (1770–1827).
Performed by the Philadelphia Orchestra; Eugene Ormandy, conductor.

CD4, Tracks 31–34, 8:47

This musical example, lasting about nine and a half minutes, includes only about a third of the final movement of this symphony. The entire symphony lasts about 1 hour and 10 minutes. In contrast, Beethoven's entire first symphony, composed in 1795, lasts twenty minutes. His music not only became longer but also became more complex, more dramatic, and more personal.

Beethoven was willing to depart drastically from the common practices of the time. The most obvious departure was his use of singers and German poetry in the final movement of this symphony. The ninth symphony unquestionably represents the romantic spirit more than the classical spirit.

—Continued

At times, this symphony is powerful, exciting, even thunderous. But sometimes it is quiet, tender, and introspective. At times, it is abstract, fragmented, without an identifiable melody. At other times, long folklike melodies appear. Changes of style and mood can be quick and abrupt.

Beethoven was deaf when he wrote this symphony. The music reflects both personal tragedy and pathos, a troubled spirit. But it ends triumphantly. Listen to the entire movement to gain a sense of Beethoven's dramatic intensity and how he expresses Schiller's "Ode to Joy."

Goals

Describe differences between legato and staccato styles.

Recognize theme-and-variations structure, describing ways a setting may be varied.

Describe ways Beethoven changes moods in this excerpt.

Recognize the timbres of the various instruments and voices.

Identify countermelodies.

Guide

0:00	Powerful passage	Brass and winds with timpani
	Instrumental "recitative"	Basses and cellos
	Powerful passage	Brass and winds with timpani
	Recitative	Basses and cellos
0:46	Quiet passage	Full orchestra; descending motive with wide skip
	Recitative	Cellos and basses
1:25	Scherzo passage	Fast; triple meter, counted one beat to the bar; staccato
	Recitative	Basses and cellos
	Quiet passage	Winds
	Recitative	Basses and cellos
2:24	Transitional passage	Legato, sustained; a hint of the main theme to come
	Recitative	Cellos and basses; strong V—I cadence
2:56	Main theme ("Ode to Joy")	Cellos and basses; duple meter, counted in a moderate two; legato; simple setting; bassoon countermelody

	a	4 bars	Question (dominant ending)
	a	4 bars	Answer (tonic ending)
	b	4 bars	
	a	4 bars	Syncopated beginning
	b	4 bars	
	a	4 bars	Syncopated beginning; tonic ending

—Continued

3:37	Variation 1	24 bars	Legato; melody in violas and cellos; countermelodies in bassoon and basses
4:17	Variation 2	24 bars	Melody in first violin; countermelodies in violin and in violas and cellos
4:57	Variation 3	24 bars	Loud, majestic setting; melody in winds, with harmony part moving in same rhythm; staccato background in strings
5:36	Extension		Ends with suddenly quiet passage followed by suddenly loud lead-in to the return
6:19	Return to opening		Powerful passage, this time followed by vocal recitative sung in German:

> "*O friends, no more these sounds continue*
> *Let us raise a song of sympathy, of gladness*
> *O Joy let us praise thee.*

7:18	Variation 4	Orchestra with vocal soloist
	Soloist	a *Praise to Joy, the God descended* *Daughter of Elysium,*
		a *Ray of mirth and rapture blended,* *Goddess, to thy shrine we come.*
		b *By thy magic is united* *What stern Custom parted wide*
		a *All mankind are brothers plighted* *Where thy gentle wings abide.*
	Chorus	b and a repeated
	Interlude	Four bars

8:06	Variation 5	Orchestra with vocal soloists and chorus
	Soloists:	a "*Ye to whom the boon is measured* *Friend to be of faithful friend,*
		a *Who a wife has won and treasured* *To our strain your voices lend,*
		b *Yea, if any hold in keeping* *Only one heart all his own,*
		a *Let him join us, or else weeping,* *Steal from out our midst, unknown.*
	Chorus	b and a repeated
	Interlude	Four bars (fade)

Reflections

What factors contribute to the sense of drama in this symphony?

Discuss the relationship of music and poetry in this excerpt.

Become aware how a symphony such as this influences composers of later generations.

What factors make this a recognized masterpiece of music?

The classic period was an outgrowth of the aristocratic life of Austria, but it also saw the decline of the aristocracy throughout Europe, the rise of the middle class, the beginnings of the Industrial Revolution, and the urbanization of Western societies. *Summary*

Musically, Bach and Handel exemplified a culmination of all that went before; their deaths marked the end of an era. With the music of many Germans, Austrians, and Italians, but particularly that of Mozart, Haydn, and Beethoven, a new style emerged, resulting in a tremendous wealth of literature: the so-called masterworks. These masterworks are still in common use today: music for piano; for orchestral instruments and the symphony orchestra, the development of the sonata, symphony, concerto, and chamber music genres; and the standardization of the sonata-allegro and other forms.

In many respects, the mid-eighteenth century—the classic period—signals the beginning of the modern age in music.

E x a m p l e *No.* **13**   *Additional Listening*

"Blue Rondo a la Turk"

Jazz in a modified rondo form.

Performed by the Dave Brubeck Quartet: Dave Brubeck, piano; Paul Desmond, alto sax; Eugene Wright, bass; Joe Morello, drums.

From the album *Time Out*: 1997; original LP: 1963; original recording session: 1959.

CD4, Track 35, 6:43

The Dave Brubeck Quartet achieved phenomenal success with *Time Out* and its emphasis on mixed meter at a time when most jazz was in 4/4, occasionally in 3/4. Dave Brubeck was a pioneer in opening up jazz to many new rhythmic possibilities, some influenced by cultures from beyond the western European tradition.

The first part of "Rondo a la Turk" is based on the concept of a classical rondo (a b a c a). It follows the pattern of multiple themes, always returning to the original or, in this case, to a second basic but related theme (a b a c b c b). Interestingly, Mozart also wrote a Turkish rondo: Rondo alla Turca—the third movement of his Piano Sonata in A Major, K. 331. Mozart's connection was his interest in Turkish Janissary music and military band music, particularly its cymbals and strong downbeats. Brubeck's interest stemmed from his experiences in Istanbul while on tour with his jazz group. His interest, however, related to rhythm—compound meters such as 6/8 and 9/8, common in Turkey but rare in jazz.

"Blue Rondo a la Turk" also reflects the classical aesthetic in its restrained, controlled emotion and its emphasis on formal structure. Listen also to Listening Guide no. 4: the third movement Rondo of Beethoven's "Pathétique" piano sonata.

Goals

Listen for patterns of repetition and contrast in a modified rondo structure.

Recognize mixed meters and alternating metric patterns in this example.

—Continued

Example *No.* 13 — *Continued*

Guide

The first part of "Blue Rondo a la Turk" is in modified rondo form. It includes 9/8 meter in different configurations. Each of the first three bars is counted: 12 34 56 789 at a very fast tempo, or 1–2–3–4—(stretched beat on 4); the fourth bar is 123 456 789—each beat the same as the previous fourth beat.

Parts of "Blue Rondo" which follow the above pattern are solo choruses, some in mixed meter (4/4 and 9/8 in alternation) and others in a traditional 4-beat meter. It begins with the 9/8 meter. Again, the modified rondo is the first section only (a b a c b c b).

0:00   a   Main theme
      b   The same melody but at a higher pitch level (in a higher key)
      a   Repetition
      c   A new theme
      b   Repetition
      c   Modified repetition—listen carefully to the piano
      b   Repetition
1:18   d
1:52   4/4 and 9/8 Sax and piano: shifting meters
2:13   Sax lead: traditional 4/4
3:53   Piano lead: traditional 4/4
5:34   Sax and piano: shifting meters

Reflections

How is this music jazz? How is it classical music?

What does the classical aesthetic mean in relation to other classical music examples in this chapter? What does it mean in relation to "Blue Rondo a la Turk?"

If to be jazz, the music has to swing, does this music swing? What makes it swing? In what contexts can it be jazz if it doesn't swing?

CHAPTER

Music of the Romantic Period (Nineteenth Century)

Goals for Listening

- **Recognize** diatonic melody.
- **Recognize** diatonic consonant harmony.
- **Identify** expressive qualities.
- **Recognize** chromatic tension and resolution.
- **Recognize** chromaticism in melody.
- **Identify** rubato.
- **Identify** inner and outer "voices".
- **Identify** arpeggios.
- **Identify** tremolos.
- **Identify** sequences.
- **Describe** thematic organization.

Summary

Additional Listening

Terms and Concepts

Absolute and program music

Ballet

Chamber music

Libretto

Art songs: Lied and Lieder

Opera

Piano music

Program symphonies

Composers

Franz Schubert

Felix Mendelssohn

Frédéric Chopin

Johannes Brahms

Richard Wagner

Giuseppe Verdi

Pyotr I'yich Tchaikovsky

Other important composers

*B*eethoven was an individualist, often defying the aristocracy and rejecting the rigidity of classical forms. Caught up in the spirit of the French Revolution and the rise of the capitalistic middle class, he sought to express his own convictions in his music with emotion and with imagination. Beethoven desired to be different.

These attributes of Beethoven also summarize the attributes of the romantic period—highly individual and personal, highly emotional. Often, one composer's beliefs and practices were in opposition to those of another composer's. The romantic period was not a time of unified musical expression. The rise of individualism and the decrease in aristocratic patronage, in effect, put composers on their own.

The business of music became an important factor in the romantic period as the patronage system shifted from the aristocracy to the public. Instead of being employed by the courts, composers and performers had to find their own audiences and publishers. They had to sell their music, literally and figuratively, to the public. This need to sell created new jobs in the music profession: concert managers (or impresarios, as they were then known), music publishers, and music critics. It became apparent that, for an artist, a dynamic and colorful personality was a significant asset.

The public craved virtuosity—dazzling displays of technical skill. The greatest virtuosos, whether performers or composers, became great stars. The orchestra conductor also became a virtuoso because of the increased size and complexity of the orchestra. Many conductors developed star personalities and became celebrities.

Music of the nineteenth century, because much of it was technically demanding, was no longer intended for amateurs. The demand for professionals created a demand for teachers. Thus in the nineteenth century the teaching of music became an established profession.

The nineteenth century was a time of polarities: tradition and experimentation, music for huge orchestras and intimate pieces for a solo instrument or voice, classical forms and new forms, nationalism and internationalism, absolute music and program music. A composer might work at one of these extremes or at any point between extremes.

Nationalism emerged in the late nineteenth century to a large extent as a reaction against the dominance of German romanticism throughout Europe; it reflected a desire for national, regional, or ethnic identity. Nationalistic music has definable national or regional characteristics. It is concert art music in which composers incorporate elements that reflect or characterize any of the following:

- Folk and popular music and traditions.

- Cultural characteristics of a national group rather than of humankind in general.

- History, tales, and legends of a nation.

- Patriotism and the glories and triumphs of a nation and its people.

Nationalist composers and compositions of this time include the following:

- Russia

    Glinka: *A Life for the Tsar*, a patriotic opera
    Borodin: "Polovetsian Dances," from *Prince Igor* (reflects the spirit of Russian music)
    Mussorgsky: *Night on Bald Mountain, Pictures at an Exhibition*
    Rimsky-Korsakov: *Scheherazade, Russian Easter Overture*

- Czechoslovakia
    Smetana: *Má Vlast* (*My Fatherland*, a cycle of six symphonic poems, including "The Moldau")
    Dvořák: Slavonic Dances, Symphony no. 9 in E Minor ("From the New World")
- Norway
    Edvard Grieg: Peer Gynt Suites no. 1 and 2, Norwegian Dances
- Finland
    Jean Sibelius: *Finlandia*

- Familiar-sounding melodies and chords. Recognize diatonic and consonant melody and harmony.
- Complex-sounding melodies and chords. Recognize dissonance, chromatic tension and resolution, and chromaticism in melody.
- Expressive qualities: Identify a ritard or an accelerando, a crescendo or a decrescendo. Identify rubato.
- Structure: Recognize thematic contrasts and repetitions as a means of identifying form, and recognize changes in tonality, modality (major or minor), tempo changes, changes of mood, a strophic setting of a text, and other characteristics that composers use to organize music.
- Identify arpeggios, tremolos, and sequences as compositional devices.
- Compare a romantic style of music, such as can be recognized in any of the musical examples in this chapter, with a classical style, such as can be recognized in the music of Mozart or Haydn.

Goals for Listening

Listening examples in chapter 13 include art songs (lieder), solo piano pieces, symphonic music, chamber music, and program music.

Musical Characteristics

Music created for its own sake without any extramusical connotations is known as **absolute music**. It is characteristic of genres such as the sonata, symphony, and concerto. In the nineteenth century, **program music** became a prevailing interest. This music was created to depict moods, images, stories, and characters. Program music reflects composers' and the audiences' interest in poetry, the unity of music and words, and the use of music to create imagery suggested by a text. Romantic composers also went to greater lengths than before to create music without text that could stimulate subjective feelings, moods, and images of places or things and to associate specific musical ideas with characters in a story.

Music in the nineteenth century was primarily homophonic, with a predominance of singable, lyrical, "romantic" melodies. Folk melodies or melodies in a folk style also became common as composers sought not only new modes of expression but also ways to reach wider audiences. Melodies were usually related to underlying harmonies and harmonic progressions, particularly in the first half of the century. The second half of the century saw an increase in chromaticism and dissonance in an attempt to create musical tension and to intensify emotion. Much music was highly emotional, with strong contrasts, unexpected chords, and long buildups to exciting climaxes. The increase in chromaticism and dissonance brought with it a decrease in tonal clarity—a weaker sense of tonal center. By the beginning of the twentieth century, tonality in much music was obscure or nonexistent.

Rhythm in nineteenth-century music, compared with music from the previous century, frequently was less regular and more complex, increasingly so in the second half of the century. Composers avoided the regular stress on each downbeat and used more polyrhythms, more syncopation, and more changes in tempo. Changes in tempo included accelerandos (getting faster), ritardandos (getting slower), and rubato (a slight speeding up and slowing down that creates a flexible pulse and a highly expressive manner). The increase in complex rhythm brought with it a decrease in the sense of meter.

The nineteenth-century orchestra was bigger, more lush, and thicker in texture than the classical orchestra. The use of instrumental tone color became an art in itself—the art of orchestration. Composers used individual instruments and combinations of instruments not only to play melodies and harmonies but also to create special unique sonorities. As the Industrial Revolution dawned in the early nineteenth century, manufacturers sought ways to enhance the resonance and range of all orchestral instruments. New instruments were added to accommodate the need for new expression and new tone colors. Some new instruments carried the names of their makers or of musicians responsible for their use. Two examples are the saxophone, named for Adolphe Sax, and the sousaphone, named for John Philip Sousa.

Forms and Genres

The multimovement sonata, whether a solo piece, symphony, concerto, or chamber work, continued to be a basic structure in the romantic period, as was the sonata form and other classical forms discussed in chapter 12. These, however, were flexible models that few composers held to rigidly. Forms were not as precise or as clear and not as symmetrical or balanced as in the music of the classic composers. Phrases tended to be longer and less regular than in classical music. Internal cadences were frequently less clear, suggesting an ongoing movement or momentum rather than an obvious ending to a phrase or a section.

Many composers, especially Beethoven, Schubert, Brahms, Mendelssohn, Tchaikovsky, and Mahler, excelled at writing symphonies, concertos, or chamber works. However, becoming important during the nineteenth century were the symphonic poem, forms derived from stage productions (the overture, prelude, suite, and incidental music), and instrumental chamber groups other than string quartets and piano trios, such as string sextets and woodwind quintets (flute, oboe, clarinet, horn, and bassoon), a genre established for virtuosic wind playing.

The **symphonic poem** is a one-movement work with contrasting moods and is derived from the romantic interest in music that describes something (program music)—in contrast to most symphonies and concertos, which do not have any nonmusical associations (absolute music).

The overture or prelude begins an opera or a ballet. The suite is an orchestral arrangement of songs or dances from an opera or a ballet. Incidental music was performed between acts of a production. Many times these instrumental works were performed as symphonic concert pieces, a context in which they were more widely performed, became better known, and lasted longer than the original stage productions.

Opera, with its sense of drama and its combining of music, poetry, drama, and visual effects, had a tremendous emotional impact in the nineteenth century and was an important medium of romantic expression. The great nineteenth-century composers of opera were Verdi, Wagner, Rossini, Puccini, and Richard Strauss. Opera flourished during the eighteenth and nineteenth centuries in France, Germany, and Italy and continues to appeal to a public that enjoys music with action, plots, and spectacle—attributes that are not typical of symphonic music or chamber music. Operas continue to include arias, recitatives, solo ensembles, choruses, and orchestral accompaniment. The orchestra plays the overture, preludes to acts, any incidental music, and the accompaniments of singers and dancers.

Grand operas, with their large number of singers, elaborate scenery and effects, and serious plots, often include visual diversion such as pageantry and ballet. Comic operas and operettas, in contrast to grand operas, generally are lighter in mood, less complex, and often satirical, and they frequently include spoken dialogue.

The **libretto** is the text of an opera—the lyrics, the poetry. It is created to allow the plot to be interrupted, perhaps enhanced, by the various songs, choral numbers, and dances. Whereas singers in choruses are identified as sopranos, altos, tenors, and basses, solo singers in operas are known as coloratura, lyric, or dramatic sopranos; mezzo-sopranos; contraltos; lyric or dramatic tenors; baritones; and basses (also basso profundo, or deep bass).

Opera is very popular in the United States, where there are professional opera companies in virtually every metropolitan area. Additionally, there are performances by many regional semiprofessional or amateur companies and by departments or schools of music in colleges and universities.

Another form of stage production that became popular in the nineteenth century was the **ballet**, which at first was part of opera and then became an independent genre. It featured both solo and ensemble dancing and represented the highest form of the art of dance. Tchaikovsky composed the most memorable music for ballet in the nineteenth century, including *Sleeping Beauty, Swan Lake,* and *The Nutcracker.*

Along with the large orchestras and orchestral forms and the elaborate stage productions, there emerged new **miniature** forms: (1) short "character pieces" for solo piano and (2) the solo song with piano accompaniment. The one-movement **character pieces**, exemplified by the solo piano works of Chopin, are expressive, at times lyrical, at times dramatic, and often technically demanding. These ballades, capriccios, impromptus, intermezzos, nocturnes, mazurkas, polonaises, rhapsodies, preludes,

A scene from a nineteenth-century ballet, Tchaikovsky's *Swan Lake.*

waltzes, and études have their own distinctive mood and character. They rank among the best of solo piano literature from the nineteenth century, remain in the repertoire of all concert pianists, and are studied by virtually all advanced piano students.

The songs, known as **art songs** or **lieder** (singular **lied**), are best exemplified in the works of Schubert, who wrote over 600 of them. Most are short and are set to the works of German poets, notably Goethe. The German poets' interest in creating lyric poetry stimulated composers' interest in creating art songs. The emergence of the piano in the nineteenth century as the primary keyboard instrument in concert halls and homes also contributed to the development of the art song. Its expressive power was well suited to enhance the varying moods and images of the art song.

The German lieder are known for their beautiful, expressive melodies. Many are strophic (that is, the music is the same for each verse of the poetry), but in some songs the music changes to reflect changes of character or mood. Today, art songs from the nineteenth century are presented regularly in recitals by both professional and amateur singers.

Composers

At least twenty nineteenth-century composers are well known to large numbers of Americans, and their music is performed regularly in concerts and on stage in the United States each year. All are men. It is unfortunate but not surprising that the two most prominent women artists and composers of the nineteenth century are usually presented in history books not as musicians in their own right but in relationship to male composers who were important in their lives. These women were the concert pianist and composer Clara Schumann, who was married to Robert Schumann; and the composer and pianist Fanny Hensel, the sister of Felix Mendelssohn.

Clara Schumann (1819–1896) was born into a musical family, was given the best musical education, and married the composer Robert Schumann, who encouraged her pursuits as a concert pianist, composer, and teacher. Clara Schumann wrote mainly songs, choral works, chamber works, and piano pieces, many of which were intended to show off her dazzling skill as a pianist. She also wrote a piano concerto. Through her long career as a teacher and performer, she influenced future generations of pianists.

*L*istening Guide   *No.* 62

Trio for Piano, Violin, and Cello in D Minor, op. 11 (I) (excerpt)

Chamber music.
Composed in 1846 or 1847 by Fanny Mendelssohn Hensel (1805–1847).
Performed by the Macalester Trio — **CD4, Tracks 36–38, 5:28**
Fanny was the older sister of Felix Mendelssohn. They were devoted to each other and respected each other's music. Fanny was a gifted pianist as well as a composer. Fanny's father, Abraham, encouraged Felix to become a professional while advising Fanny that music, for her, "will always remain an ornament [and should not] become the foundation of your existence and daily life." She married a Prussian painter, Wilhelm Hensel, and became a housewife. Nevertheless, she composed more than 400 works, some of which were published under Felix's name.

—Continued

Fanny Hensel composed oratorios, cantatas, other choral works, songs, vocal and instrumental chamber music, piano pieces, and orchestral music. This trio, opus 11, was published in 1850. The piano part is extremely virtuosic; the violin and cello parts are more lyrical.

Goals

Differentiate the sound of the violin and cello.

Recognize arpeggio and tremolo passages and differentiate them from those more scalar (stepwise) passages.

Identify themes, dotted rhythms, sequences, chromaticism, and modulations.

Differentiate the harmonically stable from the less stable sections.

Guide

Sonata form in D minor. *Allegro molto vivace.*

0:00   First theme: The motive of this quiet theme, stated first by the violin and cello in octaves, is characterized by a dotted rhythm with a wide, ascending skip, answered by an equally wide descending skip; the motive occurs over ascending and descending arpeggios, then fast shimmering scale passages on the piano

0:52   The lengthy transition to the second theme begins with a brilliant descending scale passage on the piano, followed by a descending sequence and a harmonically unstable section settling quietly in F major

1:35   Second theme: In F major; this lyrical melody, stated first in the cello, then the piano and violin, is related to the first theme in its wide chromatic skips: the accompaniment, however, rather than the fast arpeggios and scales heard previously, is an extended tremolo

2:34   Descending piano arpeggios, answered by a simple ascending scale motive in the violin, signal the second half of this theme, which is heard in F minor in a descending stepwise pattern; this idea soon becomes fragmented and unstable

3:46   Development: Ascending piano arpeggios signal the beginning of the development section as fragments of the first theme are soon heard

5:14   After the second theme is heard, the excerpt fades

Reflections

What special skills, if any, are required to listen to chamber music?

In what ways is this music classical? Romantic?

This music has not been performed very often. Why? Does it deserve more hearings?

Fanny Mendelssohn Hensel (1805–1847) was a prolific composer and a skilled pianist who was encouraged to develop her talent but not to become a professional musician or to have her compositions published. Most of her works were songs and piano pieces, although she did write a few choral, orchestral, and chamber works (see Listening Guide 62, p. 284).

All who claim even a minimal knowledge of western European classical music have some acquaintance with the most prominent romantic composers. Seven of these composers are discussed below; these discussions are followed by a brief listing of other important composers.

Franz Schubert (1797–1828)

Schubert was endowed with a prodigious natural gift for music. He composed 143 songs before he turned 19 and 179 more works the following year, including major choral and symphonic pieces. His entire adult life, however, was a struggle against illness and poverty. Without position or patronage, he had a precarious existence, depending on the generosity of friends, a few commissions, the sale of a few pieces to publishers, and some private teaching.

Schubert is best known for his more than six hundred lieder. These art songs embody a wide range of feelings, from elegant simplicity to bold, dramatic expression and from simple folklike songs to elaborate ballads of great musical sophistication. The outstanding qualities of his compositions are lyrical melodies, colorful harmonies, and sensitivity to the poetic expression of the texts. "The Erlking," "Who Is Sylvia?" (see Listening Guide), and "Serenade" are among his best known solo songs, although some of his most important songs are found in his two song cycles (sets of songs with a common unifying factor), "Die schöne Müllerin" and "Winterreise."

His nine symphonies reflect the classical ideals of form and structure yet are infused with the songlike qualities of Viennese romanticism. Of these works, no. 8, the "Unfinished" (a symphony in two movements), and no. 9, "The Great," are the most important. His short piano pieces, including the impromptus, the 22 solo piano sonatas, and "Moments Musicaux," are widely performed today. His best chamber works include the quartet "Death and the Maiden," the "Trout" piano quintet, the Quintet in C for strings, and 2 piano trios. Among his well-known choral works is *Mass in G*.

Listening Guide   *No.* 63

"An Silvia" ("Who Is Sylvia?")

Art song.

Composed by Franz Schubert (1797–1828).

Performed by Fritz Wunderlich, tenor; Hubert Giesen, piano — **CD4, Track 39, 2:45**

Schubert had a remarkable gift for creating melodies that were expressive, emotional, dramatic, sad, or mysterious. Such melodies epitomize the essence of romanticism. His songs, for solo voice and piano accompaniment, ranged from short, simple pieces to extended, more dramatic, emotionally complex works.

The text to "An Sylvia" was taken from Shakespeare's *Two Gentlemen of Verona*. The music is elegant and simple.

—Continued

Goals

Recognize diatonic melody.

Recognize diatonic, consonant harmony.

Be aware of expressive qualities in music.

Use the terms lied and lieder correctly.

Guide

A simple accompaniment combining a bass ostinato in the left hand and repeated chords in the right hand supports one of Schubert's most beloved songs. It is strophic (the same music is used for each verse of poetry). Three musical phrases make up each stanza. Solo piano introduces and concludes the song and separates each stanza.

The text is from Shakespeare and was translated into German by one of Schubert's friends. It honors Sylvia, extolling her beauty, her grace, and her kindness, but it does not tell us who Sylvia is! The text follows:

Who is Sylvia? What is she
That all our swains commend her?
Holy, fair, and wise is she,
The heaven such grace did lend her
That she might admired be.

Is she kind as she is fair?
For beauty lives with kindness:
Love doth to her eyes repair
To help him of his blindness:
And, being help'd, inhabits there.

Then to Sylvia, let us sing,
That Sylvia is excelling;
She excels each mortal thing
Upon the dull earth dwelling;
To her let us garlands bring.

Reflections

Why are such simple pieces called art songs rather than folk songs?

Describe the accompaniment.

Differentiate between a song that is strophic and one that is not. Discuss the advantages and disadvantages of each.

Felix Mendelssohn
(1809–1847)

Mendelssohn came from a wealthy, educated German family of high social and cultural status. His home was a gathering place for musicians and intellectuals. He was surrounded by the finest opportunities for an aspiring musician, including the resources of a private orchestra. He was widely traveled and became famous throughout Europe and England.

His music had wide appeal. It was traditional and closely aligned to the classical ideals of form and structure. His classical spirit was reflected in his orderly, elegant, graceful expression; his romantic spirit showed through primarily in the emotional expressiveness and sentimentality of his melodies. He is best known for his "Scotch" and "Italian" symphonies, the oratorio *Elijah*, the Violin Concerto in E Minor, the Hebrides Overture, and incidental music to *Midsummer Night's Dream*.

Frédéric Chopin
(1810–1849)

Chopin was born and educated in Poland, but spent his entire professional life in Paris. He was a virtuoso pianist but did not seek to develop an extensive concert career. He preferred private performances in the aristocratic salons and intimate gatherings of wealthy Parisians. In Paris, Chopin was profoundly influenced by his lover, George Sand (her pen name). She was a cigar-smoking feminist with whom he lived for nine years. Many of his greatest and best-known works were created during this period.

Chopin is known almost exclusively for his short, one-movement piano compositions: études, preludes (see Listening Guide 64, p. 289), mazurkas, waltzes, scherzos, impromptus, polonaises, nocturnes, and ballades. He also wrote three solo piano sonatas and two piano concertos. His piano "miniatures" included stylized dances (not intended for dancing), pieces that reflected the spirit of the Polish people, and virtuoso pieces with beautiful melodic invention. He expanded the concept of pianism chromaticism by creating more elaborate, decorative melodies, particularly in subsequent repetitions of a theme. He incorporated bold, colorful harmonies with daring dissonances, unresolved tension, and unusual modulations. He freed himself from the pulse by increased application of rubato, and he developed new uses of the pedal that allowed a smooth, sustained quality. He also enhanced the harmonic texture through innovations in left-hand technique.

Frédéric Chopin playing in the salon of Prince Radziwill. Painting by Siemisadszki.

istening Guide   *No.* **64**

Preludes, op. 28, no. 6 in B Minor

Composed in 1839 by Frédéric Chopin (1810–1849).

Performed by Murray Perahia, piano — **CD4, Track 40, 1:52 (SCD) CD2, Track 31, 1:54**

Chopin's 24 preludes, each in a different major or minor key, have no structural or stylistic similarity, whereas his other sets of pieces, such as his polonaises, nocturnes, and ballades, have common musical characteristics.

The preludes are varied in style and mood. They may be short, miniature pieces or extended works having contrasting moods, and they may range in emotion from quiet serenity to chromatic restlessness. They are examples of absolute rather than program music.

Goals

Differentiate between absolute and program music. Compare this prelude with Schubert's art songs.

Recognize chromatic tension and resolution. Identify chromaticism in melody.

Recognize rubato, arpeggios, inner and outer voices on the piano, and left-hand and right-hand pitch areas on the piano.

Guide

Differentiate between the left-hand melody (rubato and a rising-and-falling contour within each phrase) and the right-hand accompaniment (many repeated chords).

Listen for the phrase structure and points of repetition, contrast, and return.

Reflections

What makes the Prelude absolute music? Give it a programmatic title. Can it now be classified as program music? Is the determining factor only the title?

What musical characteristics in this piece allow us to classify it as romantic?

In what ways is the Prelude different from a piano sonata?

Discuss the relationship between right-hand and left-hand functions in this example.

Brahms was born in Germany but moved to Vienna at the age of 30 and lived there for the rest of his life. He worked mostly as a freelance composer and pianist. He became world-famous and was part of a mid-century controversy between the traditionalists, of which he was the acknowledged master, and the musical revolutionaries, led by Richard Wagner. Such controversies were fed by the propensity of composers like Schumann and Wagner to function also as music critics and essayists.

While touring, Brahms met and became friends with Robert and Clara Schumann, friendships that shaped the course of his artistic and personal life. He fell in love with Clara and was torn between his love for her and his loyalty to Robert. Evidently, he was

Johannes Brahms
(1833–1897)

Johannes Brahms.

also torn between love and freedom, for after Robert died, Brahms never married Clara (or anyone else). Still, his friendship with Clara continued until her death in 1896.

Brahms's music is passionate. It is often introspective, mellow, and full of rich, dark sonorities. His melodies are lyrical, even when they have complex rhythms or intricate polyphonic textures. His phrases can be irregular, at times conflicting with the prevailing meter. He was a romantic in his emotional expressiveness but a classicist in his formal organization—he was devoted to the principles of the sonata form. His orchestral music was full and massive. He was interested in absolute music, writing little program music except for his songs and choral works.

Brahms is best known for his four symphonies; a violin concerto; two piano concertos; Hungarian Dances; the *Liebeslieder* waltzes; important trios, quartets, quintets, and sextets; two serenades; the *German Requiem*; sonatas for piano, cello, violin, and clarinet; and numerous short piano pieces, songs, and choral works.

**Richard Wagner
(1813–1883)**

Wagner was a German composer of opera who was caught up in the revolutionary movements of his time. He was raised in a theatrical family but was virtually self-taught as a musician and composer. He studied the scores of previous masters, notably

Beethoven. Active in the revolution of 1848, he was forced to flee his country and took up exile in Switzerland. While there, he set forth his theories about art, describing an ideal art form in which music, drama, poetry, and stagecraft would all have equal emphasis. He called this form *music drama* rather than *opera*. In the German town of Bayreuth, a theater designed by Wagner was built to produce his operas, and to this day it serves as a center for lovers of Wagnerian opera. As a composer and author, Wagner expressed an artistic philosophy that influenced both contemporary and future musicians as well as other artists and writers.

Wagner's music dramas were symphonic in nature, with strong emphasis on orchestral color, notably the powerful brass instruments. The music was continuous, and the dramatic flow was not interrupted by arias, recitatives, and ensembles in the traditional sense. Wagner used chromaticism, dissonance, vague cadences, and unresolved tension. Much of his music had virtually no sense of tonality and no sense of symmetry or balanced phrase structure. He made extensive use of the leitmotiv, a recurring musical motive associated with a character or a mood. It contributed unity to his music in the absence of more traditional forms and structures.

Wagner's theories are exemplified in his cycle of four operas known as *The Ring of the Nibelung*, which took 20 years to complete, and in *Tristan and Isolde*, a work of great beauty, sustained tension, and dramatic expression. Wagner was his own librettist, further contributing to his ability to fuse the arts into a unified whole. He was aided greatly by a wealthy patron, King Ludwig of Bavaria, who helped him complete *The Ring* and create a lavish production of the cycle in Munich in 1876.

Giuseppe Verdi (1813–1901)

Verdi was the greatest figure of Italian opera, a national hero. He had a wealthy patron and a secure job, and he became world renowned. He was famous in America and was invited to help open Carnegie Hall in 1891.

Verdi composed for a population whose main source of musical enjoyment was opera. He maintained the traditions of the aria and recitative and included choruses and ensembles as in earlier operas. Conventional harmonies and predictable rhythms and meters characterize most of his music, but he enriched his operas with superb melodies and a strong theatrical sense.

Verdi's early operas had little continuity of dramatic action and in some cases were nationalistic and political. His next operas, *Rigoletto, La Traviata,* and *Il Trovatore*, are among his best-known and most durable works. They are in the repertoire of virtually every opera company today. These operas portray violent emotions and dramatic actions, such as dishonor, seduction, and murder. His last operas, including *Aïda*, provide more drama and spectacle, richer harmonies, and a more important orchestra than his earlier operas. In these later works, he lessened the differences between the aria and the recitative. The librettos are invariably unhappy with tragic endings. Real-life passions and emotions are conveyed through both heroes and villains. The dramatic action is typically swift moving, energetic, and full of conflict and tension.

Among Verdi's few nondramatic works are two large, successful choral compositions: the *Te Deum* and the *Requiem*.

Pyotr I'yich Tchaikovsky (1840–1893)

The most famous Russian composer, Tchaikovsky, was appointed a professor of composition at the Moscow Conservatory at age 25. He had a wealthy patroness, Mme. Von Meck, whose support enabled him to leave his teaching position to devote his life to composition.

Tchaikovsky's music is both nationalistic and international, capturing the spirit of Russian folk song but also influenced by Italian opera, French ballet, and German symphonies and songs. His music is tuneful, accessible, sometimes exciting, and sometimes sentimental, and it has remained tremendously popular to this day. It has an appealing directness and a wide range of emotional expression. This is music full of beautiful melodies, striking contrasts, powerful climaxes, and passionate emotions.

Tchaikovsky's best-known works include his violin and piano concertos; his symphonies, particularly nos. 4, 5, and 6 (the "Pathétique"); the "Overture 1812"; and "Romeo and Juliet," a symphonic overture-fantasia (see Listening Guide 65, below). His ballets, *Swan Lake, Sleeping Beauty*, and *The Nutcracker*—and orchestral excerpts taken from these ballets—are also very well known.

L istening Guide *No.* 65

Romeo and Juliet (excerpt)

Overture-fantasia (concert overture).

Composed in 1869 by Pyotr I'yich Tchaikovsky (1840–1893).

Revised and published in 1881.

Performed by the Chicago Symphony Orchestra; Claudio Abbado, conductor.
CD4, Tracks 41–43, 8:55 (SCD) CD2, Tracks 32–34, 10:12

The concert overture is a favorite musical genre of many nineteenth-century composers. It is a one-movement concert piece that is not associated with a stage production but is based on a nonmusical idea such as a literary work. In this sense it is considered program music. One can appreciate *Romeo and Juliet* on its own merits, however, whether or not one knows its relationship to Shakespeare's play.

Goals

Describe the style and character of the two primary themes.

Recognize the thick, lush texture of the romantic orchestra.

Describe musical climaxes and how they are achieved.

Guide

Composed for large symphony orchestra; in sonata form.

Introduction

0:00   a   Opens with slow, somber melody in chordal texture played on the clarinets and bassoons; features an ascending stepwise motive in a simple, direct rhythm

0:34   b   Mysterious, dramatic passage begins in the low strings; rises to thick texture with full orchestra; ends with a series of sustained high pitches in the woodwinds over ascending harp arpeggios

2:00   a   Descending pizzicato strings introduce a restatement of the opening theme in a new guise; theme is stated in the woodwinds to the accompaniment of pizzicato, running notes in the strings

—Continued

Listening Guide— *Continued*   *No.* **65**

2:49   b   Mysterious second theme suddenly reappears in the lower strings; moves to higher strings

4:07   Transition. Introduction is extended to its greatest point of intensity; loud chords derived from the opening theme; suddenly quiet; intense, repeated chords lead to the exposition

Exposition

5:25   a   Conflict theme: sharp, crisp, syncopated motive; loud, fast; full orchestra; extends with full orchestra, then drops out suddenly at transition to the second theme; features an ascending three-note motive in thin texture; restless harmonies; resolution repeatedly delayed and finally resolved at the beginning of the love theme

7:43   b   Love theme: first part. Lyrical, romantic—one of the best known melodies in classical music; opens with English horn and viola; light texture, small orchestra; simple chordal accompaniment in horns (see additional listening example no. 14)

8:05   Love theme: second part. Provides a gentle, rocking motion; violins; straight rhythm in groups of four beats, but each group starts on the fourth beat of each bar

Reflections

Discuss in what ways this is program music and in what ways it is absolute music.

How is this music—the rhythm, phrasing, cadences, textures, and so on—different from that of Mozart or Haydn? What makes this music romantic in character?

Listen to the work in its entirety to appreciate the range of Tchaikovsky's musical expression, such as the ways he develops and extends the themes and builds musical climaxes and massive sonorities.

Other Composers

Other important composers of the romantic period included Hector Berlioz, Aleksandr Borodin, Anton Bruckner, Antonin Dvořák, Edvard Grieg, Fanny Mendelssohn Hensel, Franz Liszt, Gustav Mahler, Modest Mussorgsky, Giacomo Puccini, Serge Rachmaninoff, Nicolay Rimsky-Korsakov, Gioachino Rossini, Camille Saint-Saëns, Clara Schumann, Robert Schumann, Jean Sibelius, Bedřich Smetana, and Richard Strauss.

Summary

The nineteenth century produced an amazing number of great composers and great works that are known, loved, and listened to by people worldwide. The purpose of this chapter has been to draw attention to the characteristics of nineteenth-century romanticism and to the composers and their compositions that best exemplify these characteristics.

For many people, nineteenth-century music is their introduction to the world of classical music. It is this music, along with the music of Mozart and Haydn in the classic period, that we usually listen to first, because these sounds are familiar and the music is to a great extent accessible at first hearing. Also, these works wear well. They can unfold subtleties and reveal new insights on repeated hearings, and their ability to communicate feelings and to evoke responses among large numbers of people has spanned generations, even centuries. These are the factors that distinguish a great work of art in any medium or style from the trite, the obvious, and the predictable—that is, from lesser works.

 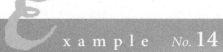

Additional Listening

Example No. 14

"Our Love"

A romantic ballad derived from classical music of the romantic period.

Performed by Dinah Washington—a jazz, blues, R&B, and pop singer.

The melody is the love theme from Tchaikovsky's *Romeo and Juliet* (see Listening Guide no. 65).

Music arranged by Don Costa.

Recorded in 1962.

From the album *In Love* (1991) **— CD5, Track 1, 2:45**

Songs from the classics are common. Bach's music has been set in a jazz style by the Swingle Singers (see chap. 11, Additional Listening Example no. 12) and by the Jacques Loussier Trio, a jazz combo. Classical melodies have become hymns, such as "Joyful, Joyful We Adore Thee," from Beethoven's Ninth Symphony (see chap. 12, Listening Guide no. 61), and "Glorious Things of Thee Are Spoken" (Austrian national hymn), from Haydn's String Quartet, op. 76, no. 3 (see chap. 12, Listening Guide no. 59). Classical melodies have become American pop standards, though of a previous age; here are a few of many examples, with major artists who recorded them: "Moon Love," from the second movement of Tchaikovsky's Symphony no. 5 (Glenn Miller); "Full Moon and Empty Arms," from the third movement of Rachmaninoff's Piano Concerto no. 2 (Frank Sinatra and Sarah Vaughan); "My Reverie," from "Rêverie" by Claude Debussy (Ella Fitzgerald and Glenn Miller, among many others), and "I'm Always Chasing Rainbows," from Chopin's "Fantasie-Impromptu" for solo piano (Judy Garland, Tony Bennett, Perry Como, and many others).

Dinah Washington first attracted attention nationally in the mid-1940s while playing with the Lionel Hampton orchestra. She left Hampton to pursue a solo career, mostly as a nightclub singer. Her many recordings include blues, standards, novelties, pop covers, and jazz sessions with big bands and combos.

—Continued

E x a m p l e   *No.* 14 — *Continued*

Goals

Describe the style of the orchestral introduction.

Describe the piano part in the first phrase of the song.

How is the accompanying texture different in the second phrase?

Describe the vocal style. How is it distinctive?

Guide

A romantic ballad with large orchestra—a lush orchestration. Vocal backed by jazz combo (thin texture) in first phrase and full orchestra (thick texture) thereafter— string section predominant throughout. Count in a moderate four. In a a b a a form.

0:00		Instrumental introduction
0:22	a	Jazz combo: thin texture—notice the piano line; bass: 2-beat rather than 4-beat meter
0:50	a	Full texture: full string sound
1:18	b	Contrasting melody: full string sound
1:39	a	Full texture: similar in style to the second phrase of the song
2:07	a	Full texture: tempo slows; an elaborate, lush ending

Reflections

Describe your reaction to romantic ballads with large orchestras and lush sounds. Other than the large ensemble, what makes the sound lush?

This is popular music derived from classical music. What about classical pieces derived from popular music? Discuss possible formats and styles. Name existing pieces.

CHAPTER 14

Music of the Twentieth Century

Goals for Listening

- **Develop an understanding** of texture and timbre.
- **Recognize** asymmetrical rhythm and phrasing.
- **Identify** polytonality.
- **Identify** angular melody.
- **Recognize** tone clusters.

Summary

Additional Listening

*T*he music of the twentieth century is presented in two chapters. Chapter 14 introduces several important trends in music and the composers associated with these trends. Chapter 15 emphasizes classical music in America and presents musical examples by American composers that further illustrate the trends discussed in chapter 14.

Music, like the other arts, reflects the society in which it was created. Thus, music in the twentieth century was characterized by complexity, experimentation, a multiplicity of styles and directions, new forms, new symbols for expressing musical language (new notational systems), and multicultural influences. The uncertainty of our global society, moreover, is reflected in uncertainty as to what styles, forms, musical language, and composers will withstand the test of time and survive to influence twenty-first-century composers, performers, and listeners.

The nineteenth century was a time of great diversity of musical styles. Composers took a more personal approach and many of them were interested in creating program music, depicting images, moods, and other nonmusical associations. We see all these characteristics, and more, in the music of the twentieth century.

Some twentieth-century composers returned to the classical ideals of order and objectivity, and there was a renewed interest in polyphonic texture. Modern music, as might be expected, has been affected by advances in technology. It also reflects good and bad aspects of the society in which it was created, as music has always done.

Many contemporary composers cannot be easily classified. In their search for originality, they will sometimes experiment and discover new possibilities but at other times return to certain practices of the past. When a composer returns to an old style, the music usually combines elements of the old with the new musical languages of the day. Other composers—the **avant-garde**—branch out into new directions, perhaps minimizing influences from the past and developing new musical language, compositional techniques, or aesthetic ideas. As radical and extreme as much contemporary music may seem, it most likely does not represent any greater extreme than some of Monteverdi's music relative to Palestrina's; or Beethoven's music relative to Haydn's; or Wagner's music relative to Brahms's. Stravinsky's ballet music of 1910–1913 was considered radical and barbaric at the time but is now ranked among the classics of the twentieth century.

Classical music from all historical periods is readily available on broadcasts, in recordings, at concerts, and over the Internet. Through recordings, scores, books, and musicological research, present-day audiences for classical music know the music of the past, and for the first time in history they prefer the music of the past to the music of contemporary, living composers. In fact, many twentieth-century composers created music not for the general public but for highly trained professional musicians and scholars and other composers. This has been an ironic aspect of contemporary Western classical music: It speaks in a contemporary language to a public that prefers eighteenth- and nineteenth-century language.

What will the musical environment of the twenty-first century be like, and how will audiences respond to the new music of the new century?

In this chapter you will notice   *Goals for Listening*
- More emphasis on texture and timbre, more than on melody and harmony—new instruments and new uses of old instruments.
- Less emphasis on regular rhythm and balanced phrases.
- More than one key sounding simultaneously (polytonality), obscure tonality, or no sense of tonal center.
- Melodies often jagged, with wide skips (angular).

- **Tone clusters**: three or more adjacent tones (no tones in between) sounding simultaneously.

Listening experiences include impressionistic program music by Debussy; neoclassical music by the Russian-French-American composer Stravinsky; atonal music by the Austrian American composer Schoenberg; an excerpt of early electronic avant-garde music by Varèse; and nationalistic music by the Brazilian composer Villa-Lobos.

General Characteristics

About the only generalization one can make about modern classical music is that it is diverse and often complex. Contemporary composers have written for every conceivable medium from a single solo instrument to a huge symphony orchestra. They have written for conventional orchestra instruments, expected performers to play conventional instruments in unconventional ways, and written for unconventional instruments, adding them to the orchestra or creating new ensembles.

Contemporary composers have written for a tremendous diversity of instrumental combinations, some involving only a few instruments and some incorporating the solo voice. When composers write for a large orchestra, the texture is frequently thinner and more transparent than was common in orchestral writing toward the end of the nineteenth century.

By the end of the romantic period, the typical symphony orchestra had become more than twice the size of the orchestra of Mozart's time. Composers wrote for larger numbers of string instruments and also added brass, woodwind, and percussion instruments. Instrumental compositions had become much longer and more involved, but new short forms for both piano and voice had also emerged.

Chromaticism had increased and harmony had become complex, at times blurring tonality so much there was no tonal center. Melodies were longer, phrases were less clear, and form was more difficult to discern.

To a great extent, twentieth-century composers emphasized timbre and rhythm rather than melody and harmony, creating a need for a different way of listening to music. Silence has become a conscious compositional device in modern music, not simply a time for a performer to rest. Silences frequently have a powerful aesthetic impact because of their length and their place in the music.

The organization and form of music are also diverse and often complex; music ranges from totally controlled to free and improvisatory. In controlled music, the composer gives minute instructions about how the music should be played. In music that is more free, sometimes performers are instructed to improvise some passages, though usually within certain guidelines and restrictions. Much of this music is organized in time segments, measured in seconds rather than bars and phrases.

The horizontal pitch organization is typically angular and disjunct, moving in wide intervals or skips rather than in the smooth, conjunct manner of traditional-sounding melodies with a stepwise contour. Melodic lines span wide, even extreme ranges. Frequently, these melodies cannot be described as singable. In modern music, it is less common than in earlier music to find balanced phrases, symmetrical patterns, forward energy culminating in clear cadences, and regular meter. Traditional tonic-dominant chord progressions are rare. Dissonance is the rule, and unresolved dissonances and sustained tension are common.

Modern music may be tonal, but typically the sense of a major or minor key is obscure. Some music lacks any sense of key; some may be in two or more keys at the same time. Frequently, pitches are based on scales other than major or minor. They may incorporate scales found in other cultures or scales invented by the composer.

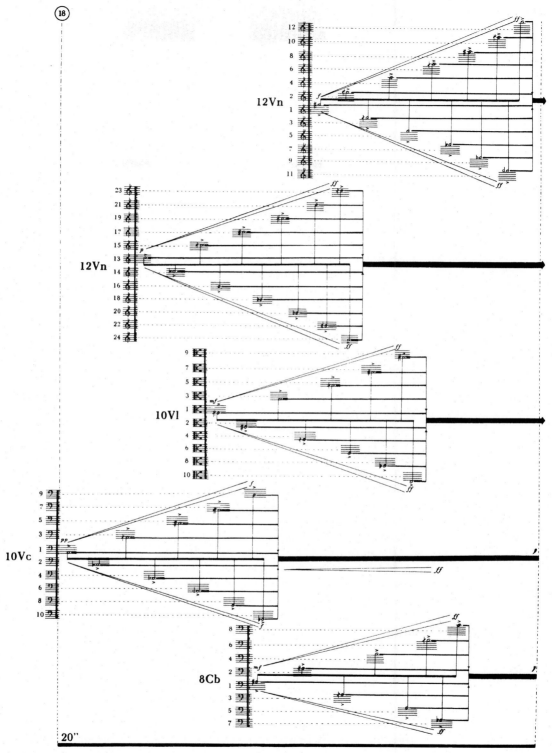

Figure 14.1

A page from a contemporary classical piece using a new musical language—a new notation. *Threnody for the Victims of Hiroshima*, by Kryzystof Penderecki.

The five-tone pentatonic scale and a whole-tone scale which excludes half steps are common in some modern pieces. Many modern composers, however, are experimenting with a return to tonality.

Essentially, the musical language of today is extremely different from the language common in the nineteenth century. For much contemporary music, new notations had to be devised (see figure 14.1) to accommodate new sounds and new concepts. It is a language with which many people feel uncomfortable, perhaps because it is a language they haven't completely come to understand.

Experimental Music

In every generation, a small group of composers will try new styles, techniques, forms, timbres, or concepts in order to develop a new approach to composition, new aesthetic notions, or a new language for expressing music. These composers are said to be in the avant-garde. Their pieces, being experimental, will have varying impacts. For some experimentalists, the musical outcome of an experiment is far less significant than the process of the experiment itself. In other words, such compositions were viewed as more important as musical ideas than as music.

It is through the work of experimentalists that the history of music moves on. However, musical styles through history are usually represented not by specific experimental pieces but by pieces that follow. These later pieces show the influence of the experimentalists but more likely blend new concepts with tried and acceptable practices. It is not unusual for pieces by an experimentalist to gain wide acceptance as concepts and techniques are refined in his or her own subsequent compositions.

The creative process, as such, suggests a certain amount of experimentation, but composers have ranged from creating in bold, innovative ways to creating in a language that is known and proven acceptable. Typically, composers settle into one end or the other of the continuum, depending on where they feel most comfortable and have the best prospects for success.

Music history evolves, sometimes very gradually, sometimes quite suddenly. Compositional style is always influenced by experimental music but also builds on acceptable practices of the past. No new musical developments totally reject the past. (Refer to experimentalism in American music, chap. 15, page 327.)

Stylistic Developments

Most developments in the history of Western art music have come logically from past practices, as composers sought to create music in new, inventive ways while building on existing forms. The continuum ranged from conservatives such as Mendelssohn and Brahms to radical innovators such as Berlioz and Wagner.

New developments occurred because composers reacted against what they considered excesses of the past or against a particular style then in common practice. New developments also occurred because of external circumstances: economic factors, shifts in patronage, or political upheavals.

As we move through the early years of the twenty-first century and look back on the twentieth century, we can identify the most important composers and see a number of styles and techniques that influenced other composers and that rightfully are considered major new developments in the history of Western music. The reader of this text can assume that all the composers discussed or listed created works outside the category under which they are presented, but all are best known for their influence in that category. It should also be noted that important composers are numerous and many could not be included in this text.

Impressionism is derived from the philosophy and practice of a group of French painters, notably Monet and Renoir, toward the end of the nineteenth century. Impressionism in music was a reaction against the massive intellectual Germanic music of Brahms, Wagner, and Mahler. This new impressionistic music is best typified in the works of Claude Debussy (1862–1918) and is marked by the delicate sonorities of flute, harp, and strings rather than massive sounds of brass and by subtle shadings rather than dramatic contrasts of tone color. Impressionistic music is sensuous, beautiful, and seldom harsh.

Debussy was an adventurous French composer who rejected many of the established musical styles, forms, and techniques. Although he is considered an impressionist composer, he did not set out to compose impressionistic music; others gave his music that label.

Debussy sought to evoke moods and to convey impressions of images and feelings rather than to produce literal descriptions. In fact, he also was influenced by the symbolist poets, notably Mallarmé, and by Asian music, especially the gamelan music of Indonesia (see chap. 9, page 204).

Debussy, perhaps more than any other composer, represents the transition from nineteenth-century romanticism to the diverse and more complex practices of the twentieth century. He wrote in virtually every medium, but his piano and orchestral music stand out. Among his best-known works are *Prelude to the Afternoon of a Faun* (1892–1894) for orchestra; *Nocturnes* (1893–1899), a set of three descriptive pieces for orchestra; *La Mer* (1903–1905), a large programmatic three-movement orchestral work (listen to Listening Guide 66 below); *Syrinx* (1912) for unaccompanied flute; *Images for Piano*, Books 1 and 2 (1905, 1907); and *Preludes for Piano*, Books 1 and 2 (1910–1913). He also composed one string quartet, one opera, and his most popular piece, "Clair de Lune." Also well known during this time was the composer Maurice Ravel.

Impressionism: Claude Debussy

Listening Guide — No. 66

La Mer (II)

I. De l'aube a midi sur la mer (From Dawn to Noon at Sea)

II. Jeux de vagues (Play of the Waves)

III. Dialogue du vent et de la mer (Dialogue between the Wind and the Sea)

An impressionistic orchestral work for large symphony orchestra composed in 1903–1905 by Claude Debussy (1862–1918).

Performed by the New Philharmonic Orchestra; Pierre Boulez, conductor.

CD5, Tracks 2–8, 7:17 (SCD) CD 2, Tracks 35–41, 7:17

The orchestra, in addition to the normal string section and winds in pairs, includes piccolo, English horn, a third bassoon and contrabassoon, two additional horns, a third trombone, and a tuba. The percussion section includes three timbales, gong, cymbals, triangle, two harps, and a glockenspiel.

This "symphony" paints a tonal landscape, evoking Debussy's impression of the wind and sea. The music conveys the surges and swells of the waves, with moods ranging from serene when the sea is calm to furious during the storms.

—Continued

Listening Guide — *Continued*   *No.* 66

This musical example is the second movement, Play of the Waves. It is light and playful. Listen to musical details as specified in the guide but also to the overall sounds, letting the soundscape create images in your mind.

Goals

Be aware of texture, timbre, and mood more than clearly stated melody and harmony.

Recognize chromatic and dissonant harmony.

Recognize asymmetrical meter and phrasing.

Describe impressionism.

Recognize music whose tonality is obscure and whose sounds are derived from scales other than major or minor.

Guide

Downbeats are often obscure, resulting at times in ambiguous meter.

0:00	Introduction	Quiet; sustained winds and harp arpeggios followed by descending flute; repeated staccato notes in the trumpets that signal the start of the first theme
0:16	Theme A	Stated in English horn (motive is an ascending, four-note, whole-tone scale, which is then repeated and extended); answered by oboe in high range, with ascending harp arpeggio; music builds in intensity then recedes, descending to low trills in cellos, signaling beginning of second theme
0:53	Theme B	Stated in upper strings (shimmering, flat contour); followed by harp arpeggios and horns in dialogue; repeated staccato notes in high woodwinds signal the start of the third theme
1:34	Theme C	Long, legato theme stated in English horn; joined soon by solo horn; short, loud brass figures accompanied by flurry of descending, ostinato figures passed between high woodwinds and high strings; solo clarinet, then solo violin, then solo horn followed by increasingly animated passage; suddenly quiet as oboe line is accompanied by countermelody in flute and horn; legato strings and horns with flute arpeggios; staccato horns and trumpets signal return of theme C; theme C restated in cellos; staccato figures continue; music builds and subsides
3:26	Theme A	Stated in oboe and clarinet; builds to peak—solo trumpet—then subsides; dialogue in the upper woodwinds, beginning with oboes and English horn, then clarinet and flute; descending string scales answered by ascending scales in the woodwinds with horn melody; occasional brief trumpet solos; builds to climax; subsides to quiet sustained trills in upper strings

—Continued

Listening Guide — *Continued*   *No.* 66

4:44	Theme B	Stated in flute then oboe; legato passage in violas and cellos; horns and clarinets soon added; theme restated in oboes and bassoons; many lush ascending and descending passages in strings over ascending pizzicato scales in cellos, contrasting with fragments in upper woodwinds, horns, and trumpet solos; builds to huge climax; sound subsides and texture thins
6:02	Coda	Ascending and descending harp arpeggios; answered by sustained horns with fragments of the first theme; ends with slow harp figures and one final statement of theme A in oboe; short ascending lines by the harp, then flute in the low range, a glockenspiel arpeggio, and finally a single tone on the harp

Reflections

The music is chromatic, with little sense of tonality or traditional chord progression.

Melodies seem to emerge and recede, flowing in and out of the sound fabric, ranging from a light, airy texture to the sonority of the full orchestra, which is never brassy or percussive.

Many twentieth-century composers have valued form and structure, in many cases returning to the common practices and aesthetic values of the past. These composers are known as **neoclassicists**. Other composers as well have created one or more pieces in a neoclassical style.

Neoclassical music may be derived from past practices, but its language is not. A neoclassical piece by Stravinsky, perhaps the best-known neoclassical composer, does not

Neoclassicism: Igor Stravinsky

A scene from Stravinsky's *The Rite of Spring (Le Sacre du Printemps)*, a twentieth-century ballet.

sound like Mozart, but it may reflect the classic ideals of control, order, emotional restraint, adherence to formal structure, minimal instrumentation, and transparent texture.

Igor Stravinsky (1882–1971) was a Russian composer who lived and worked in Russia, Switzerland, France, and, for the last 32 years of his life, the United States. He became an American citizen in 1945. He became a legendary figure, and for many generations to come he undoubtedly will continue to be regarded as one of the great composers of the twentieth century.

Stravinsky's fame began around 1910 in Paris, where he composed three large-scale ballets for Diaghilev and the Russian Ballet: *The Firebird, Petrushka*, and *The Rite of Spring*. The collaboration produced revolutionary ballet and ballet music. As frequently happens, however, his ballet music has been kept alive mainly through orchestral versions of these three major works. Each became a classic of the twentieth-century symphonic repertoire.

Because the economy had been adversely affected by World War I, Stravinsky then turned to smaller works, such as *The Soldier's Tale* (1918), a theater-piece with an "orchestra" of seven solo instruments that incorporated elements of jazz, ragtime, marches, a waltz, a tango, and a fiddling dance.

Stravinsky's neoclassical music began in the early 1920s and included *Symphonies of Wind Instruments* (1920) and *Concerto for Piano and Wind Orchestra* (1924). Other neoclassical works include the opera-oratorio *Oedipus Rex* (1927); *Symphony of Psalms* (1930), a three-movement sacred work for chorus and orchestra that omits violins, violas, and clarinets (listen to Listening Guide 67B, p. 306); and *Symphony in Three Movements*

A pen and ink sketch of Stravinsky by Jean Cocteau: *Le Sacre du Printemps*. Reprinted with the permission of Corbis-Bettman, New York, NY.

(1945), one of Stravinsky's most original works. An opera, *The Rake's Progress* (1951), written when he was nearly 70, was the culmination of Stravinsky's neoclassic period.

He then began his modern period, during which he produced more experimental works. He continued his compositional activity into the 1960s, but most critics agree that his greatest and most memorable works came from his earlier neoclassical period.

Stravinsky's contributions lie in several areas:

- Rhythmic imagination and complexity. He explored irregular meters and shifting accents to create imbalance, minimizing the effect of the pulse and regular metric feeling.
- Innovative approaches to orchestration. He used extreme ranges and unusual combinations of instruments.
- His ability to produce tonal music in new ways.
- His success in creating new music from old material, particularly baroque and classic forms and techniques, and from other existing styles, such as jazz and ragtime rhythms and Russian folk melodies.

Another important composer of this period was Paul Hindemith.

Listening Guide   No. 67

"Le Sacre du Printemps" and "Symphony of Psalms"
CD5, Tracks 9–12, 11:42 (SCD) CD2, Tracks 42–44, 3:22

Two pieces by Igor Stravinsky (1882–1971)

A. *Le Sacre du printemps* (Rite of Spring)—opening scene

Ballet composed between 1911 and 1913; first performed by *Ballets Russes* in Paris in 1913.

Orchestral version recorded by the Cleveland Orchestra; Pierre Boulez, conductor (1991).

Le Sacre du printemps is Stravinsky's third ballet. Although its first performance caused a riotous response, the work has become a classic of twentieth-century music. The harsh dissonance, sharp rhythms, irregular meters, and unusual use of conventional instruments used in this ballet and in his other early works influenced countless composers throughout the twentieth century.

Le Sacre du printemps is in two parts. This example includes the beginning of part 1 (the entire concert version lasts more than 33 minutes).

Goals

Recognize dissonant harmonies, unusual melodies, and asymmetrical rhythm and phrasing.

Recognize ostinato patterns.

Be aware of varying degrees of tension and how they were achieved.

—Continued

Listening Guide — *Continued*   *No.* 67

Describe neoclassicism in relation to *Symphony of Psalms.*

Describe various timbres and instruments.

Guide

A. (*Le Sacre du printemps*)

0:00	Introduction	Thin texture; quiet; woodwinds: high bassoon solo
0:41		English horn solo
1:11		Clarinet solo; then oboe solo; then English horn solo with bass clarinets; sound diminishes
1:52		Motives passed from instrument to instrument
2:21		Oboe, then joined by clarinet and English horn; trumpet enters. Texture thickens and energy builds; ends suddenly
3:00		Solo bassoon returns
3:32	Omens of Spring: Dances of the Youths and Maidens	Harsh dissonant chords with off-beat accents sound in the strings followed by an English horn ostinato; more dissonant chords; descending trumpet line; texture thins but energy intensifies; off-beat dissonant chords return with a different accompanying motive, primarily in trombones and bassoons
4:51		Patterns move from instrument to instrument creating fragmented texture; previous motives are heard, especially the English horn ostinato; a lyrical melody is heard in the horn—then, after descending trumpet lines, on the flute; texture thickens; loudness increases, then softens and builds again gradually to its greatest intensity
6:45	Ritual of Abduction	Begins with strings—answered by low thuds in timpani and bass drum; followed immediately by fast notes on solo trumpet; frenetic energy—motives passed around quickly from instrument to instrument; many punctuated chords, percussion thuds; ends with a loud string tremolo and a quiet flute tremolo.

B. (*Symphony of Psalms*—Part I)

Multimovement neoclassical work for chorus and orchestra composed in 1930. Performed by the CBC Symphony; Igor Stravinsky, conductor, and the Festival Singers of Toronto; Elmer Iseler, director.

Symphony of Psalms was composed "to the glory of God" and dedicated to the Boston Symphony Orchestra on its fiftieth anniversary. The instrumentation is for

—*Continued*

symphony orchestra but excludes violins, violas, and clarinets. The text is from Psalms in the ancient Latin version of the Bible: the Vulgate.

The musical style is neoclassical in that it is restrained and controlled; is in clear form; and uses consistent, cohesive patterns and traditional unifying techniques, such as repetition, ostinato, and fugue. Additionally, the piece somehow evokes a sense of the past, perhaps through melodic suggestions of ancient traditional chant. Yet the work is unmistakably derived from the musical language of Stravinsky's time. It is one of the great works of the twentieth century.

Guide

Part I: Moderate tempo in mixed meter with slow rhythmic activity in the choir.

0:00	Introduction	Broken chords punctuated by occasional single blocked chords; ascending ostinato in piano followed by strings to introduce the first theme, a two-note melody
0:34	Verse I	Chorus enters with main theme in alto voice over constant patterns of two different ostinatos, followed by soprano, tenor, and bass voices
1:03	Interlude	Features a fast descending oboe line
1:09	Verse 2	Choral parts incorporate increasingly wide melodic intervals; music increases in intensity
1:29		Music continues mainly in block chords over the double ostinato; builds to a great climax
2:24		Sustained pitches in the chorus, along with pungent arpeggios in the trumpets
2:32		Suddenly soft as the final section begins; approaches the final cadence through slow, powerful, dissonant chords whose tension is resolved at the final major chord, a chord that gives an expectation of continuing

Reflections

In listening to either of these works, one will not hear many dominant-tonic chord progressions. Functional harmony had not been a large part of twentieth-century musical language. This is unconventional tonal music, but any sense of key center is achieved by ways other than through traditional chord movement and cadences.

To a large extent, this music, particularly *Le Sacre*, avoids regular pulse and metric feeling. One at times may have a sense of suspension in time, of stasis, of a lack of forward energy. At other times, the music moves forward, building to powerful climaxes.

This music deviates from the common practices of the eighteenth and nineteenth centuries and helped pave the way for a twentieth, if not a twenty-first, century western European language for classical music.

Atonal Music and
Serialism: Arnold
Schoenberg

In traditional tonal music, compositions are usually organized around patterns of whole steps and half steps that establish key centers: the major or minor scales. **Atonality** results when establishment of a tonal center is deliberately avoided. This provides an alternative approach to the major-minor tonal system.

Serialism, known as **serial composition** or **12-tone technique**, evolved as a systematic means of organizing atonal music, a formula that served as the basis for creating a piece of music. It emerged in the 1920s and revolutionized music.

The essence of serialism is a set of pitches typically consisting of the 12 tones of the chromatic scale, that is, each half step within the octave. This set of pitches, a tone row, is the basis of the composition; by its nature, it avoids key centers. The tone row is subsequently used in various forms in its entirety, never repeating a tone until the entire row is completed. In addition to its original order of pitches, the row may be used backwards, upside down, or upside down and backward. The art is in the imaginative manipulation of the row: rhythmically, melodically, harmonically, in varying textures and timbres, and in contrasting dynamics. The first and most important composer associated with this means of organizing sounds in music was Arnold Schoenberg, although few composers, including Schoenberg, adhered to it strictly except, perhaps, in a few pieces.

Arnold Schoenberg (1874–1951), an Austrian, became a leader of contemporary musical thought in the 1920s. He assumed an important post as professor of composition in Berlin in 1925. After the rise of Hitler, he moved to the United States in 1933. His longest post was as professor of composition at the University of California at Los Angeles where he remained until his retirement at age 70. He became an American citizen in 1940.

Schoenberg's first compositions were in the highly chromatic but tonal postromantic style reminiscent of Brahms, Mahler, and especially Wagner. His most important early work is *Verklärte Nacht* (1899). In his next stage as a composer, Schoenberg rejected the major-minor tonal system entirely and created atonal pieces. Schoenberg's outstanding pieces from this period are *Five Pieces for Orchestra*, op. 16 (1909), and what is perhaps his most popular work, *Pierrot Lunaire* (1912), for female reciter and an ensemble of five players playing eight different instruments (listen to Listening Guide 68, p. 309). The reciter "sings" in an unusual style that combines speech and singing. From 1914 to 1920, Schoenberg produced few works. Instead, he contemplated ways of organizing the 12 tones of the chromatic scale in some cohesive system, ultimately serialism.

Schoenberg's most famous serial compositions date from the late 1920s. His first composition based solely on a single row is *Suite,* op. 25, for piano. *Variations for Orchestra* (1928) is considered one of his best serial compositions. An entire opera, *Moses and Aaron* (1930–1932), is based on a single tone row. He continued to write serial music throughout his career, at times experimenting with combinations of tone row technique and tonality in the same piece.

In Schoenberg's atonal and serial music, the melodies tend to be predominantly disjunct rather than stepwise; the texture is sometimes polyphonic. Rather than the huge resources of postromantic music, Schoenberg preferred small orchestras and chamber ensembles of both standard and unconventional instrumental combinations. His phrases are of irregular length, and he deliberately avoided melodic repetition and chord progressions. The music sounds complex and fragmentary. Unity is achieved in different ways in different pieces, often through some transformation of short motives.

In Vienna, Schoenberg gathered students around him, the most talented being Anton Webern and Alban Berg, both of whom became significant composers. In fact, composers since Schoenberg have experimented and produced important compositions in which other musical factors have been serialized, basing their compositions not only on tone rows but on specific sequences (rows) of nonrepeated, contrasting dynamic levels, note values, or timbres. When several factors have been serialized, the music is said to be **totally controlled**. Little creativity is left to the composer once the serial decisions are made; that is, the growth of the composition is determined in great detail by the previous decisions establishing the various rows.

Atonality and serialism are controversial. Some people think that this music is too cerebral, too complex, and without emotion. Others feel that serial composition is the logical path on which to base future musical developments. However, few composers in the late twentieth century based entire compositions on a single row of 12 tones; instead, most worked more flexibly as they applied the principles of cohesive organization suggested by Schoenberg's revolutionary system.

Other important composers of this period were Alban Berg and Anton Webern.

Listening Guide   *No.* **68**

Pierrot Lunaire

1. "Mondestruncken"
2. "Columbine"

Atonal song cycle composed in 1912 by Arnold Schoenberg (1874–1951).

For voice and ensemble of five performers.

Performed by Yvonne Minton, *sprechstimme*; Pinchas Zukerman, violin and viola; Lynn
    Harrel, cello; Michael Debost, flute; Anthony Pay, clarinet; Daniel Barenboim,
    piano; and Pierre Boulez, conductor.

Poetry by Albert Giraud — **CD5, Tracks 13–14, 3:20**

This song cycle consists of 21 numbers grouped by sevens into three parts. The musical example includes the first two songs of part I.

The music is atonal and includes *sprechstimme*, then a new way of fusing music and words. It is a technique of pitch declamation that is half-spoken, half-sung, and sung on approximate pitches.

Goals

Be aware of unusual treatment of words and music.

Recognize thin texture, angular melody, and polyphonic interplay of voice and instruments.

Identify various instrumental timbres.

Guide

Follow the phrases of the text. Be aware of various musical characteristics and the changes of mood. The German and English texts follow:

—Continued

Listening Guide — *Continued*   *No.* **68**

Part I

1. "Mondestruncken" (for voice, flute, violin, cello, and piano)

2. "Columbine" (for voice, flute, clarinet in A, violin, and piano)

German

Den Wein, den man mit Augen trinkt,
Giesst Nachts der Mond in Wogen nieder,
Und eine Springflut uberschwemmt
Den stillen Horizont.

Gelüste schauerlich und süss.
Durchschwimmen ohne Zahl die Fluten!
Den Wein, den man mit Augen trinkt,
Giesst Nachts der Mond in Wogen nieder.

Der Dichter, den die Andacht treibt,
Berauscht sich an dem heilgen Tranke,
Gen Himmel wendet et verzückt
Das Haupt und taumelnd saugt und schlürit er
Den Wein, den man mit Augen trinkt.

Des Mondlichts bleiche Blüten,
Die weissen Wunderrosen,
Blühn in den Julinächten—
O bräch ich eine nur!

Mein banges Leid zu lindern,
Such ich am dunklen Strome
Des Mondlichts bleiche Bluten,
Die weissen Wunderrosen.

Gestillt war all mein Sehnen,
Dürft ich so märchenheimlich,
So selig leis—entblättern
Auf deine braunen Haare
Des Mondlichts bleiche Blüten.

English

"Moondrunk"
Pours nighttimes from the moon in waves,
And its springtime tide floods over
The horizon's quiet bowl.

Aching lusts, shocking and sweet,
Float beyond measure in the gushing philter!
The wine that only eyes can drink
Pours nighttimes from the moon in waves,

The poet, under piety's cover,
Gets fuddled on the holy brew;
Towards Heaven, rapt, tilts back his head
And giddily reeling laps and swills
The wine that only eyes can drink.

The wine that only eyes can drink
The moonlight's pallid blossoms,
The white and wondrous roses,
Bloom in midsummer midnights
O! could I pluck but one!

To still my luckless grieving
I seek in Lethe's murky stream
The moonlight's pallid blossoms,
The white and wondrous roses.

All my yearning would be sated
could I, in fairytale secret,
In gentle bliss . . . rip petal from petal
And scatter in your auburn hair
The moonlight's pallid blossoms.

Reflections

Discuss ways that Schoenberg's melodies differ from the nineteenth-century concept of melody.

Discuss cadences and phrase structure.

Notice the role of the instruments before and after the poetry.

Notice that angular melodies have many wide intervals. Stepwise motion is minimized.

Nationalism, introduced in chapter 13, became a major stylistic feature among a number of late-nineteenth-century composers, particularly from Russia and eastern Europe (page 280). Nationalism in American music is discussed in chapter 15, page 330.

Many twentieth-century composers in Europe and America incorporated nationalism in their music. Among the most noted of these is Béla Bartók.

Béla Bartók (1881–1945), the greatest of Hungarian composers, taught piano at the Budapest Academy of Music for 27 years (1907–1934) and gave recitals throughout Europe. In the early years of his career, he did not gain much acceptance as a composer in his native land. As an intense anti-Nazi, he felt compelled to leave Hungary and emigrated to the United States in 1940. He settled in New York City, where he died in 1945.

In the early part of his career, Bartók became interested in the nationalist movement that had spread throughout Europe. He sought to preserve the folk music of Hungary and let the world know that Hungary possessed a traditional folk repertoire which included more than Gypsy music. He, with Zoltán Kodály, went into small villages and rural communities during the first decades of the twentieth century and recorded the people's songs on cylinder machines. Bartók and Kodály succeeded because they lived with the peasants, gaining their confidence and trust. As a result, they were able to develop a treasury of folk songs numbering in the thousands, including songs collected and recorded as they moved into other parts of eastern Europe and Northern Africa. This folk music was to have a profound effect on Bartók's compositional style.

Bartók's highly individual style combines the spirit of eastern European folk music, forms of the classic era, and the musical language of contemporary Europe, a language he expanded in exciting and innovative ways. His music transcends many styles, techniques, and systems. It is tonal, often modal, sometimes polytonal. It frequently slides into highly chromatic atonality because Bartók did not adhere rigidly to the major-minor tonal system. His harmony is dissonant and often harsh, and his rhythms are vital and often pounding, nonsymmetrical, and syncopated. He often treats the piano as a percussion instrument, using pounding chords and tone clusters as elements of rhythm. His scoring for instruments brings imaginative tone colors, particularly from the many percussion instruments that he frequently uses.

Bartók's greatest compositions include those for piano and for orchestra. *Mikrokosmos* (1926–1937) is a set of 153 piano pieces in six books at varying levels of difficulty. They not only have pedagogical value but summarize his compositional styles and the styles of European composition flourishing at the time. Music for Strings, Percussion, and Celesta (1936) is another of his greatest works. His six string quartets (1908–1939) rank among the finest works in the chamber music repertoire.

His best-known compositions are from the years he spent in the United States, although these were not happy years. He was poor, felt isolated and unaccepted, could not get his music performed, received few commissions, and developed leukemia. While he was hospitalized, he received a commission from Sergey Koussevitsky, for which he composed Concerto for Orchestra (1943). This was to become his most popular work. It led to a series of other commissions. Unfortunately, he was to live only one more year. His last completed work was his Third Piano Concerto (1945). Ironically, Bartók became famous after his death, and his music came into demand in the United States.

Additional important composers of this period included Ralph Vaughan Williams (England), Zoltán Kodály (Hungary), Alberto Ginastera (Argentina), Heitor Villa-Lobos (Brazil) (see Listening Guide 70, p. 317), and American nationalists discussed in chapter 15.

Nationalism and Folk Music: Béla Bartók

Electronic Music:
Edgard Varèse

Although primitive electronic instruments existed in the first half of the twentieth century, electronic music as a medium did not appear until the 1950s. The impetus came from the development of magnetic tape recording. Technicians in Paris experimented with ***musique concrète***, a name given to the technique of manipulating tape-recorded sounds from existing natural sources. Recorded sounds generated from musical instruments or voices could be altered by changing the speed of the tape, playing it backward, and cutting and splicing it. The altered sounds, perhaps combined with natural sounds, could then serve as sources for a composition.

The next development in electronic music was sound-generating equipment and synthesizers in which the electronic sound generation was combined with sound modification. Composers could now control every detail: rhythm, dynamics, pitch organization, timbre, reverberation (echo), and even how a tone is begun and released (attack and decay). What the composer created was immediately on tape, ready for any listener; no performer was necessary. Synthesizers are common today. They are greatly reduced in

One of the best known of early electronic instruments, the *Ondes Martenot*, with its inventor, Frenchman Maurice Martenot. Dating from the 1920s, the instrument produces a single note at a time and has been used by Varèse, Messiaen, Boulez., and Honegger among other composers.

size and operational complexity and are used in the performance of classical, jazz, rock, and commercial music.

Most electronic music today is created to be used with live performance. The performance may include one or more standard instruments with prerecorded tape or a standard instrument using tape for sound modification, such as digital tape delay. Early experiments involved not only live performers with electronically generated sounds but also real or modified tape-recorded sounds from nature, such as the sound of fire, water, birds, or whales.

A relatively recent development, which may dominate the field for generations to come, is computer-generated music. Here the composer plots desired sounds in numerical sequence, feeds them into a digital-to-analog converter, and records on tape. Software programs now make this process easy for professionals and amateurs through MIDI (Musical Instrument Digital Interface), which connects a computer with a synthesizer to store sounds (samples) and to produce sounds for recording or immediate playback in live performance. One of the prominent early composers of electronic music was Edgard Varèse (1883–1965).

Edgard Varèse was born and educated in Paris, but in 1915 he came to the United States, where he spent his entire career. Like Henry Cowell, Aaron Copland, and others, Varèse actively promoted new music.

Varèse accepted any sound—whether perceived as pitches or noise—as potential material for musical composition. In the 1920s, he used a wide variety of percussion instruments and even sirens. In the 1950s, he incorporated electronically taped sound sources. His music is frequently described as static, sound masses, or collages of sound having little to do with chord progressions or melodic movement.

His most influential music was composed in the 1920s and 1950s. The earlier music, reflecting his lifelong interest in science and technology, included *Hyperprism, Octandre, Intégrales, Arcana, Ionization, Density 21.5,* and *Ecuatorial* (see Listening Guide 69). His later music, incorporating manipulated taped sounds, is best represented by *Déserts* and *Poème électronique.* Listen to *Ecuatorial,* a unique piece composed in 1934 that uses primitive electronic instruments: originally a theremin and, in a later version, an ondes Martenot.

Other important composers of this period included Milton Babbitt, Mario Davidovsky, and Morton Subotnik.

*L*istening Guide   *No.* 69

"Ecuatorial" (excerpt)

Composed in 1934 by Edgard Varèse (1883–1965).

Performed by the Contemporary Chamber Ensemble; Arthur Weisburg, conductor.

For bass voice, 4 trumpets, 4 trombones, piano, organ, 2 *ondes Martenots,* and 5 percussion.

CD5, Track 15, 3:16

Varèse, one of the most important innovators in musical composition in the first half of the twentieth century, wanted to link music with science and technology. The text for *Equatorial* (not in musical example) is a setting of a Spanish translation of a Mayan prayer. The ondes Martenot (heard in the example) is an electronic instrument invented in the

—Continued

late 1920s by the French musician, Maurice Martenot. It has an extremely wide range (over seven octaves), plays one note at a time, and can produce sliding pitches (like a siren; not like a piano).

Goals

Describe this musical organization, which is based on sound masses rather than melody, harmony, rhythm, form, or other traditional Western ways of making music.
Describe elements of unity and cohesion, contrast and repetition, thematic development, tension and resolution—ways the musical elements interact.
Identify by sound the various instruments and instrumental combinations, specifying which sonorities are dominant.
Describe the aesthetic and cultural values of this music.

Guide

The excerpt is the first part of the composition. Instruments are specified on page 313. The high register of the *Ondes Martenot* and the low notes of the contrabass trombone extend the playing range of this ensemble. The composer contrasted timbres and loudness levels (Varèse called these "zones of intensities"). The zones below refer to evident points of contrast (timbres, dynamic levels, textures, and so on).

0:00	Zone 1	Piano and trumpets predominant; quiet mood; highly disjunct and fragmented
0:33	Zone 2	All brass; percussion soon enters; flat contour; many repeated notes; quiet mood which intensifies as it leads into the next zone
0:54	Zone 3	Brass and percussion, then organ, then *ondes Martenot*; quickly contrasting sonorities
1:40	Zone 4	Percussion throughout; starts with loud, low trombones; then *ondes Martenot*; mood quiets only to be interrupted by loud blasts in the trombones; then piano and organ; loud brass and percussion
2:15	Zone 5	Quiet brass soon explode with percussion; both *ondes Martenots*, then piano, enter softly; excerpt ends with strong brass and organ

Reflections

Does this music seem to be derived from Western civilization, another culture, another world?

Is this piece without rhythm? Without form?

If you can't sing the tune, you can't tap the rhythm, and you can't hear the chord progressions, what are the musical attributes and aesthetic and cultural values that make this music important as a creative work?

Chance music, sometimes called *indeterminate music,* represents a compositional style at the opposite end of the spectrum from totally controlled serial music. The composer does not control all the details of a composition. Chance music allows the performer to participate in the creative process.

This process can include the random selection of sounds, selection by chance, or improvised passages within the structure of a composition. However, it is not uncontrolled music. Although details are left to the performer, the overall structure will be indicated in a score. A work in which techniques of chance are applied will never be performed the same way twice. The most noted exponent of chance music is John Cage (1912–1992).

Cage's influence is not only through his music but also, and perhaps more, through his writings. Like his predecessors, Cage explored new sounds and new ways of organizing sound. He is best known for areas of influence broadly symbolized by the following terms: prepared piano, chance music, and silence.

Whereas some composers extended concepts of serialism to gain total control of every nuance of sound, Cage reduced control, allowing the outcome of a performance to be unpredictable. Rather than put things together, Cage was willing to let things happen. He is well known for a piece for multiple radios set at different places on the dial, including static. He accepted the sounds, whatever they were, as the piece of music.

Cage's early work emphasized percussive sounds, including the piano. His best-known technique was to alter the sound of the piano by placing screws and other things inside,

Chance Music: John Cage

John Cage with a prepared piano.

touching the strings in ways that affected the sound. His most famous work in this manner is Concerto for Prepared Piano and Chamber Orchestra (1951).

Cage became aware that there is no such thing as silence, that we always will hear sounds—of our own body, air circulating, and people moving, breathing, or coughing. These sounds become sources of sound for music. Today, more than at any time in music history, silence has become a conscious part of composition. Cage has helped us understand it better.

Minimalism

Minimalism is a style of composition that seeks the greatest effect from the least amount of material. It emerged in the late 1960s with music by Philip Glass (b. 1937), in part as a reaction against the complexities of serialism and other twentieth-century styles that lacked melodic shape, tonal clarity, and perhaps audience appeal.

The technique of minimalism is to take a musical pattern or idea and repeat it incessantly, creating slow subtle changes in rhythm, chord movement, or other musical elements. The rhythmic activity may be fast, but the speed of change in the activity will be slow. The technique represents a way of controlling music other than through serialization, and it also represents a return to tonal music in that the repetition generates clear centers of tonal feeling.

Minimalist music allows the listener to concentrate on few details, thus enhancing perception. Its adherents have a kinship with jazz, rock, and the music and ideas of India and Africa. Time will tell if minimalism will have a significant impact on the long-term development of Western classical music.

Other important composers of this period were Steve Reich, Terry Riley, John Adams, and LaMonte Young.

Traditional Sounds

Not all twentieth-century music is abstract, complex, or challenging to listen to. In the early part of the twentieth century, such neoclassicists as Stravinsky returned to practices of the past, yet their music was put in a context and a fresh musical language that made it sound like it belonged in the twentieth century. Other composers preferred a return to nineteenth-century romantic aesthetics, forms, and techniques. They wrote program music, symphonies, or concertos, and they created personalized, expressive music with singable melodies. Their music is tonal with relatively simple rhythms, conventional playing or singing ranges, and traditional instrumental combinations. Their harmonies are colorful, even bold, but generally within the accepted techniques of the major-minor tonal system.

Composers may have adopted a traditional style because of their own comfort with accepted practices or perhaps from a desire to counter the complexities of other modern music by simplifying musical language. They were also probably motivated by a desire not to alienate audiences but rather to provide music that listeners would find accessible and enjoyable, and, of course, would pay to hear in concerts or on recordings.

Folk songs and regional ethnic music have inspired many composers. Bartók, as mentioned previously, became intimately involved in folk music. Whereas some composers, such as Bartók, incorporated the spirit of folk music rather than specific songs, others used specific folk material—melodies, rhythms, and dances—as the basis of a composition. Because of the literal reference to folk material, such music frequently was tuneful, rhythmically comfortable or even exciting, and created in a traditional rather than an experimental context.

Many of the great composers found a balance between innovation and a style that would find wide acceptance. Interestingly, such acceptance at times comes decades later, even after a composer's death. Those whose music is never forward looking seldom contribute much to the development of music. It is the great innovators—Monteverdi, Beethoven, Wagner, and Stravinsky—who give vitality to music.

Other important composers of this period included Heitor Villa-Lobos (Brazil) (see below), Samuel Barber (United States), Alberto Ginastera (Argentina), Serge Prokofiev and Dmitri Shostakovich (Russia), and Ralph Vaughan Williams (England).

Listening Guide   *No.* **70**

"Bachianas Brasileiras," no. 5—II. Dansa (*Martelo*)

Composed for soprano voice and eight cellos in 1938 and 1945 by Heitor Villa-Lobos (1887–1959).

Performed by Arlene Auger, soprano, and the Yale Cellos; Aldo Perisot, conductor.
CD5, Tracks 16–17, 5:08

This lively Dansa is evocative of a Brazilian folk dance, the *martelo*. It is in duple meter and has the formal pattern a b a. The text is by the Brazilian poet Manoel Bandeira.

Goals

Describe nontraditional and traditional musical language.

Describe the nationalistic elements in this music.

Recognize sequential patterns (ascending or descending sequences).

Compare this musical language with that used in other classical pieces you have studied.

Guide

For phrasing and structure, follow the numerical groupings. Each number represents one bar felt in duple meter (in two) at a moderately slow tempo. Each bracket ([ ) denotes the beginning motive of a sequence. Each line of numbers represents a phrase. The rhythm is energetic and active.

Section 1

0:00	1 2 3 4	Instrumental
0:05	1 2 3 [4 5 6 7 8 9	Vocal; ascending sequence of three patterns starting in bar 4 and ending in bar 7
0:16	[1 2 3 4 5 6 7 8 9 10 11 12 13	Two-bar descending sequence (three patterns ending on bar 6); slower tempo with long holds in bars 12 and 13
0:41	1 2 3 4	a tempo
0:47	[1 2 3 4 5 6 7 8 9 10	Descending sequence (two patterns ending on bar 4); ritard in last two bars
1:00	1 2 3 4 5 6 7 8	a tempo (divided 4 + 4)

—Continued

| 1:10 | 1 2 3 4 5 6 7 8 9 10 11 | Instrumental vamp begins in bar 8 |
| 1:24 | 1 2 3 4 5 6 7 8 9 10 | Instrumental; slight ritard at end, setting up next section |

Section 2

1:37	More complex; asymmetrical rhythm and phrasing; changing styles and moods; several new motives and themes
2:21	Intense instrumental rhythmic pattern introduces a contrasting second part
2:33	Lyrical motive—vocal
3:26	Cello motive provides the transition to the return

Section 1

| 3:32 | Return, with a different ending |

Reflections

Recognize the vamp and sequential patterns in the middle part of the second section.

In what ways does this music reflect twentieth-century musical language and culture? To the extent that it does not, is it therefore to be considered old-fashioned, traditional, and perhaps unworthy music? Is new and experimental music worthy music, and is traditional, noninnovative music unworthy music? Does traditional mean not innovative? In what ways might this piece be innovative?

To what extent is the element of enjoyment a factor in judging worth?

Summary

The twentieth century was the first time in music history in which the public was more interested in dead composers than in those still living and writing music—the contemporary composers. One major reason for this circumstance is that this century has seen advances in scholarly research on old music and in the accessibility and availability of all kinds of music in their published form as well as on recordings.

Another reason for the popularity of music of the past is that the twentieth century was an age of experimentation in the sciences and the arts. The strategy called for composers to "do their own thing"—express as they feel, try new techniques, and create new notations—while valuing artistic integrity above the need to appeal to the masses or sell more music. For the most part, the audience is less important to the twentieth-century composer. Likewise, the modern composer's music is less important to the contemporary audience.

Yet another reason is the kind of society the twentieth century generated: two world wars, the atomic age, a continual threat of more devastation, and rapidly advancing technology affecting every facet of our lives. Communications and the media provided immediate information about tragedy and turmoil wherever in the world they occurred, and a highly mobile society made us feel insecure. In music as well as the other arts, the production of works reflected this unsettled world. Society is not all pleasant, a state reflected in its arts. Has society changed in these early years of the twenty-first century?

x a m p l e   *No.* 15

La Création du Monde, op. 81 (excerpt)

The first piece of classical music to incorporate jazz elements—in the early 1920s.
Composed by Darius Milhaud (1892–1974).

Performed by Branford Marsalis, alto saxophone, and the Orpheus Chamber
Orchestra.

From the album *Creation* (2001) — **CD5, Track 18, 7:15**

Branford Marsalis is a jazz musician, having performed with great jazz artists during
the 1980s, such as Art Blakey, Clark Terry, his brother Wynton Marsalis, and
Herbie Hancock. By 1986, he headed his own quartet. In 1985, he joined Sting's
pop/rock group, and in 1992, he became musical director of Jay Leno's Tonight
Show. As of this writing, his versatility is demonstrated on five classical CDs—
including *Creation.*

La Création du Monde ("The Creation of the World") was premiered in 1923,
before the jazz-influenced pieces of George Gershwin: *Rhapsody in Blue* (1924) and
Porgy and Bess (1935). *La Création* was originally a ballet but is now more
frequently heard as a concert piece. This is an excerpt; the total work lasts over
17 minutes.

Goals

Listen carefully to parts other than the solo instrument and describe how they
support the melody.

Describe Marsalis's playing style in this piece.

Discuss the effect of the last chord of the excerpt in relation to the preceding
material.

Guide

0:00	Part 1	Alto sax solo; gentle rocking pattern supports the melody; soft syncopated pattern in the trumpets provides contrast; notice strong percussion beats
0:50		Similar to above—repetition of style and mood
1:36		Long ascending scale increasing in loudness followed by descending scale in different style, decreasing in loudness and speed
2:14		Slow—quiet mood—moving parts supporting the melody; ends with ascending scale pattern in upper strings
2:39		Suddenly loud—change of mood, part of it like a fanfare; brass, percussion
2:54		Quiet mood—descending, tempo slows
3:14		Extended quiet section—sax solo—rocking accompaniment; double bass countermelody; descending scales; tempo slows to full cadence

—Continued

E x a m p l e   *No.* 15 — *Continued*

4:21	Part 2	More jazzy style: increased energy; percussion; double bass solo; syncopated polyphonic texture, solo entrances: trombone, alto sax, trumpet, clarinet, trumpet; suddenly quiet ending
6:00		Transition—somber mood
6:27		As at the beginning: quiet mood; flute solo, rather than alto sax— double bass countermelody; steady drumbeat; alto sax enters, then oboe; soft cadence: music in a minor key, but excerpt ends quietly.

Reflections

In what ways is this piece classical and in what ways is it jazz? Or is it both or neither one? Would you answer differently if considering only part 1 or only part 2?

To the extent that you feel *La Création* is effective as a jazz-influenced piece, would it have been equally as effective if the primary solo material had been written for an instrument other than alto saxophone, such as violin, clarinet, or trombone? What other instruments would have worked as well as the alto saxophone?

CHAPTER 15

American Classical Music

Goals for Listening

- **Increase** vocabulary.
- **Refine** listening skills.
- **Describe** nontraditional pitch relationships (melody, harmony).
- **Recognize** nontraditional rhythms.
- **Recognize** nontraditional timbres.

Summary

Additional Listening

Terms and Concepts

Cultivated music and a dichotomy

Vernacular music

The ticket-buying public

Eclectic taste

Virtuoso—star personalities

German and French influences

Contributions of immigrants

Women and minorities as composers

Americans' view of classical music

Music instruction

Experimental (avant-garde) music

Nationalism

Composers
  Ives
  Copland

ne goal of this text is to present a broad spectrum of music that is important to our time and to our nation. Therefore, this chapter will continue the presentation of contemporary music, emphasizing American classical music. The chapter will explore issues related to the development of American classical music, particularly in the twentieth century. It will present a sampling of important works by American composers who sought to create interesting, important music—some experimental, some traditional, and some unquestionably American.

Goals for Listening

In this chapter you will learn to

> Increase ability to use vocabulary.
>
> Refine listening skills.
>
> Describe musical elements used in nontraditional ways.
>
> Recognize unique piano sounds.
>
> Recognize electronic sounds.

Perspectives on American Classical Music

This section draws attention to a number of issues related to the history and development of classical music in the United States:

- Varying relationships between cultivated high art music (classical) and vernacular, folk art, or commercial music (popular).
- Varying relationships of American music to foreign influences, particularly to the creation of music that is based on European styles as opposed to that which reflects uniquely American qualities (nationalistic qualities).
- The impact of immigration on American classical music (already indicated in chap. 14, with regard to the contributions of Stravinsky, Schoenberg, and Bartók).
- The dichotomy between sophisticated, complex music for professional virtuoso performers and simpler, more accessible music that can be understood and appreciated by the ticket-buying public.
- The development of music conservatories and their relationship to American classical music.

The Classical and Popular Dichotomy

In American music history, the relationship between cultivated, high art music (classical) and vernacular, folk art or commercial music (popular) has shifted. In the eighteenth and early nineteenth centuries, very little distinction was made between classical and popular music. The most loved and best-known songs were from the classics or similar in style to classical art songs or songs from operas, especially English ballad operas. These operas included songs, waltzes, marches, and an overture. They were very popular in the United States, and the music was tuneful and appealing.

It was in the second half of the nineteenth century that the separation took place, as popular songs took on a more rhythmic, syncopated feel—most evident in the minstrel songs. New songs emerged from the cross-cultural interaction among Anglos, Blacks, Creoles, and all sorts of immigrants. This new music widened the gap between the classical and the popular with regard to musical styles and people's acceptance of these styles. The dichotomy became established: classical music became an elite art, and popular music, given stimulus by an increasingly sophisticated and powerful music industry, was for mass audiences.

A factor in this dichotomy was that the United States was always a middle-class, rather than an aristocratic, society. Music involved amateurs and professional performers whose financial support came from paying audiences. This circumstance affected the repertoire, which had to appeal to the largest possible audiences. More advanced, complex modern pieces became something for the elite, and this separated composers from mass audiences. In turn, more demand was created for accessible eighteenth- and nineteenth-century music. Many modern composers, however, resisted innovation and complexity in music so that their music would be more widely accepted or sought a style that would be both sophisticated and appealing.

Another factor was the rise of the music industry, particularly sales of sheet music and tours by virtuoso artists and performing groups. Marketing and promotion affected and continue to affect peoples' taste, what they will buy, and what kinds of concerts they will attend.

The dichotomy became even more pronounced by the mid-twentieth century, as some classical composers consciously created innovative, complex music. Universities had become their patrons, employing them to teach and compose as they saw fit, without depending on the patronage of the public.

Today, however, there is ample evidence of a more eclectic taste among the general population and of a lessening of the dichotomy. Several factors have contributed to crossover and fusion styles in pop, rock, country music, jazz, and classical music:

- The recording industry, film, live concerts, and the broadcast media, particularly public radio and public television, have made music in many styles widely known and available.
- Electronic music began in the classical context, then branched out to rock, jazz, and popular music.
- Increased influences from world music have affected classical music and, in recent years, jazz and rock.
- Music courses and curricula have expanded beyond their traditional focus on classical masterworks.
- The natural cycle of changing tastes was affected by the manipulation of the media through marketing and advertising.
- Since 1965, the federal government, through the National Endowment for the Arts, has expanded audiences for music in many styles, particularly classical music, and stimulated interest in folk, jazz, and ethnic music.

For these and perhaps other reasons, an increasing number of musicians and listeners are involved in more than one style within the jazz, classical, and popular repertoires. The result has been a broadening of taste or at least a greater awareness of other music and a lessening of the view that classical music is an elite art. It may be useful to consider the extent of this broadening of interests and taste and its effect on how Americans view classical music.

The initial immigration to the United States came primarily from the British Isles, and so the first main musical influence was English music. Immigrants brought their folk songs, their psalmody, and their love of music making. These immigrants settled in cities on the East Coast (Boston, Charleston, Philadelphia, and New York) and developed centers of musical activity for both professionals and "genteel amateurs." Among the early American gentleman musicians were Thomas Jefferson, Benjamin Franklin, and Francis Hopkinson.

The
Preoccupation
with Europe

Public concerts and opera were prevalent by the mid-eighteenth century. The most popular art music included songs, waltzes, and marches—not what we call "highbrow" music. The first important classical genre popular in the United States was the English ballad opera. Other popular genres included overtures, variations on familiar tunes, and program music. In the nineteenth century, the piano became the most important household instrument. It was valued not only as an instrument but also as a cultural symbol.

As more immigrants came from mainland Europe during the early part of the nineteenth century, the music of the German and Austrian composers—Haydn, Mozart, and Beethoven—became known and appreciated. Much of their music was made available by American publishers. These immigrants contributed significantly to the shaping of America's taste in art music.

Romanticism and the Virtuoso

By the mid-nineteenth century, romanticism was at its peak in Germany. Americans valued the romantic ideals of individualism, personal freedom, and the virtuoso performer (see chap. 13, page 280). European artists began to present concerts in America; many became popular as star performers and entertainers. Musically naive American audiences became enamored of the artists' personalities and technical proficiency more than the quality of their music.

Among the performers who achieved great success in America in the mid-nineteenth century were the Norwegian violinist Ole Bull and the "Swedish nightingale," Jenny Lind. Americans were in awe of Europeans' virtuosity, and Americans who aspired to become professional musicians went to Europe, especially Germany, for their education. They returned knowing European music; thus those who were composers created music in the European style.

Americans inferred from this that the music created in America was inferior to European music, that America's educational system had not yet developed sufficiently to prepare professional musicians, and that German music represented the ultimate in art music.

This love of German romanticism and European music created a dilemma for American music: personal freedom and individualism came into conflict with the taste of the ticket-buying public. The public, then as now, tended to want the tried and true, the familiar, and the simple, rather than what is innovative and individual.

Symphony orchestras began to tour the United States, and their conductors, like the instrumental and vocal virtuosos, often became stars. In imitation of the Europeans, large Eastern cities soon established their own symphony orchestras: New York in 1842, Boston in 1881, and Chicago in 1891. Most American orchestras hired European conductors. Again, this may have reflected an inferiority complex or a belief that the American educational system had not yet developed sufficiently to prepare professional conductors. It must be pointed out, however, that the infatuation with European artistry continued into the mid-twentieth century. (Name contemporary virtuosos with star personalities.)

The French Connection

With regard to art, relations between the United States and France had improved by the early part of the twentieth century. By the 1920s, American composers were flocking to France, not Germany, for reasons that included the following:

- The environment in France, especially Paris, encouraged artistic interaction among poets, composers, dancers, and intellectuals.
- France also provided a sense of the exotic, and many American and French composers were influenced by the cosmopolitan music found in Paris: Russian folk music, Asian and North African music, Latin American sounds and rhythms, and jazz.

(a)

Twentieth-century virtuosos (a) Leonard Bernstein; (b) Luciano Pavarotti with Zubin Mehta.

(b)

- Many American composers were receptive to the new French impressionistic music as an alternative to the excesses of German romanticism and the conservatism of many Germanic composers such as Brahms and Schumann.

Composers studied at the Paris Conservatory, the Schola Cantorum, and later at the American Conservatory in Fountainebleau. The American Conservatory was originally a music school for American soldiers serving during World War I. It was established in 1918 to give musically talented soldiers a world-class education. The school closed in 1919, at the end of the war. However, through the efforts of Walter Damrosch, then conductor of the New York Philharmonic, it reopened in 1921 as the American Conservatory.

The conservatory's most notable teacher was Nadia Boulanger, probably the twentieth century's preeminent teacher of American composers. An unusually large number of American composers went to France to study with her. Many, such as Aaron Copland, Elliott Carter, Roy Harris, Roger Sessions, and Walter Piston, now are considered among America's most illustrious composers.

By the 1920s, European composers had been exposed to jazz and American popular music during their trips to the United States; also, jazz was already being performed in Europe. Well-known pieces by composers such as Debussy, Ravel, Stravinsky, and Milhaud included these American vernacular sounds, and it became respectable to incorporate American idioms into classical music.

American classical music matured considerably after the 1920s. Americans had gone to Europe; Europeans were now coming to the United States. American composers since the 1940s have sought to become part of an international musical style rather than to continue seeking a uniquely American music. This effort was given impetus by the arrival of a number of important European immigrant composers.

Immigrants

Millions of immigrants have come to the United States since the late nineteenth century. Many were fleeing persecution and hardship and were seeking a new life in the "land of opportunity" (see chap. 8, page 156). Some immigrants were peasants, laborers, and farmers rather than members of the educated upper classes. But in the 1930s the political climate in Russia, Germany, and eastern Europe—a climate inimical to Jews—caused artists, craftspeople, scientists, and other educated people to emigrate. They came to the United States seeking the freedom to practice their skills and to continue developing their knowledge and careers.

Through the years, composers who faced political or religious persecution or who were deprived of artistic freedom have come to the United States, which by the mid-twentieth century was a center of musical excellence offering abundant opportunities. Among these immigrants were several of the world's most renowned composers: Igor Stravinsky, Arnold Schoenberg, Paul Hindemith, and Béla Bartók. Their influence was felt through their music and, in several cases, through their writing and teaching in American universities.

Music Instruction

Americans in the nineteenth century understood the importance of music instruction, both formal and informal. As discussed previously, singing schools (see chap. 5, page 66) were established to raise the standard of hymn singing in America. Secular counterparts of the singing school were the choral and instrumental organizations established in the Eastern cities to promote and perform the new European music. The first and most famous of these organizations was the Handel and Haydn Society of Boston, founded in 1815.

Private instruction was common. In 1838 in Boston, Lowell Mason established the first formal music program in the public schools. Today, music education in our schools reflects the pedagogical influence of two twentieth-century composers: Carl Orff, from Germany; and Zoltán Kodály, from Hungary.

At the college level, music conservatories were founded to develop professional virtuoso performers of European classical music. The most famous of these conservatories exist to this day: Peabody Institute of Baltimore, founded in 1860; and conservatories in Oberlin, Boston, and Cincinnati, founded in 1865. The first music curriculum in an American university began at Harvard in 1875. It was taught by John Knowles Paine, America's first professor of music.

American Composers

The material that follows includes brief information about the most influential and best-known American composers of the twentieth century. Others, such as John Cage and Edgard Varèse, are discussed or at least mentioned in chapter 14.

Experimentalism: Charles Ives

To a large extent, one must listen differently to twentieth-century experimental music. The emphasis is more on texture, color, and rhythm than on melody, harmony, or thematic development. By definition, when the music of the experimentalists is new, it is not in the mainstream repertoire known and appreciated by the general public, although some of it gradually becomes part of the mainstream. Experimental music is performed and recorded and is thus available for others to study, particularly composers who help shape the course of musical development.

Charles Ives (1874–1954) was perhaps the first great innovator in twentieth-century American classical music. He was followed by Edgard Varèse and Henry Cowell who continued the line of composers who shaped the mid-twentieth-century avant-garde movement, particularly in America. In the 1950s, experimentation was given an impetus by the music and writings of Cowell's student John Cage and by Varèse's work in the newly developing electronic medium.

Charles Ives, symbolic of America's rugged individualists, felt that he could be more free and independent as a composer if he did not have to depend on music for his livelihood. He became very successful in the family insurance business. Ives was well educated in music; in fact, he received a degree in music from Yale. Working in Connecticut and New York, far from the major European music centers, he developed a style that was outside the generally accepted European tradition. His music represents virtually every major compositional innovation in the twentieth century, but Ives "discovered" the new techniques decades ahead of everyone else.

Ives experimented musically but was guided by larger issues. To him, music was more than sounds. It was the spirit that emanated from its creator. It was a musical manifestation of life itself. Ives's music was infused with quotations of melodies or fragments of melodies from familiar American vernacular music, mostly hymns, patriotic songs, and marches—recreating sounds from life. He did not think of this use of quotations as producing nationalistic music; rather, he was using available materials to create something larger. He recognized that all of life is vital and substantial and that art and life do not need to be separate. In this way, his music synthesized American classical and vernacular traditions.

Ives stopped composing in 1921, and he has been well known only since the 1940s. Full recognition of his work came even later, after his death in 1954.

Although much of Ives's music is extremely complex and some of it hard to perform and listen to, his works now are widely recorded and performed, particularly some choral pieces and songs from the nearly two hundred that he wrote. His instrumental music is widely recognized. Particularly noteworthy are his four symphonies, the third of which was awarded the Pulitzer Prize in 1947; *Three Places in New England*, a set of tone poems (see Listening Guide below); and *The Unanswered Question*, for trumpet, four flutes, and an offstage string orchestra. Of his two piano sonatas, Sonata no. 2 ("Concord") is best known.

Other important composers of this period were Henry Cowell, Edgard Varèse, and Milton Babbitt.

Listening Guide   *No.* 71

Three Places in New England (II)

I. The "St. Gaudens" in Boston Common (Col. Robert Gould Shaw and His Colored Regiment)

II. Putnam's Camp, Redding, Connecticut

III. The Housatonic at Stockbridge

Nationalistic work composed by Charles Ives (1874–1954).

Performed by the Philadelphia Orchestra, Eugene Ormandy, conductor.

CD5, Tracks 19–21, 5:34

Three Places in New England is a set of three pieces for large orchestra. It was begun in 1903, completed in 1914, and revised in 1929 for chamber orchestra.

The work was first performed publicly in 1931 in Boston's Town Hall by the Boston Chamber Orchestra under the direction of Nicholas Slonimsky. In that year, other performances took place in New York, Havana, and Paris. The original performance was initiated by Henry Cowell, and partial financial support was provided by Ives.

This piece was Ives's first commercially published work. Although it was published in 1935, it was not performed again until 1948, when it was revived by the Boston Symphony Orchestra, Serge Koussevitsky, conductor, at the urging of Slonimsky. In 1974, it was revised by James B. Sinclair for large orchestra; Sinclair combined the best of the 1914 and 1929 versions.

In 1931, Ives wrote a letter of encouragement to Slonimsky's musicians in Paris, who were beset by problems in rehearsal:

> The concert will go alright. Just kick into the music as you did in Town Hall—never mind the exact notes, they're always a nuisance. Just let the spirit underneath the stuff sail up to the Eiffel Tower and on to Heaven.

The instrumentation for the 1974 version of "Three Places" is the common large orchestra of winds in pairs plus piccolo, English horn, contrabassoon, two additional horns, one additional trombone, and one tuba as well as piano, celesta, organ, harp, and a gong.

Goals

Identify unresolved dissonances, mixed meter, and asymmetric phrasing.

Recognize Ives's selection and use of melodic motives.

Identify the many sounds of individual instruments.

Be aware of the range of expression in this piece.

—Continued

Guide

II. Putnam's Camp, Redding, Connecticut
In the winter of 1778–1779, General Israel Putnam's soldiers were camped near Redding, Connecticut. At this location there is now a small park preserved as a Revolutionary War memorial.

Ives's inspiration for this movement was derived from the following story:

A child went to this park on a picnic. Wandering away, he hopes to catch a glimpse of some of the old soldiers. As he rests on the hillside of laurel and hickories, the tunes of the band and the songs of the children grow fainter and fainter. Over the trees on the crest of the hill, he sees a tall woman standing who reminds him of a picture of the Goddess of Liberty. With a sorrowful face, she pleads with the soldiers not to forget their cause and the great sacrifices they have made for it. But they march out of camp with fife and drum. Putnam is coming over the hills in the center—the soldiers turn back and cheer. The little boy awakens, hears the children's songs, and runs down past the monument to listen to the band and join in the games and dances.

A number of fragments of popular children's and patriotic songs are heard in this movement. They provide continuity and cohesion and some familiar sounds in this dissonant, complex, though highly programmatic music.

The music can be traced to Ives's two pieces for theater orchestra composed around 1903: the "Country Band" march and the overture and march "1776."

The movement is mostly loud and marchlike, in mixed meter, and at times with several different melodies (and different tonalities) all happening at once. It is a cacophony, just like the real-life sounds of a picnic and a band concert in a town park—a variety of unrelated sounds all happening at once.

0:00	Introduction	Marchlike in quickstep time.
0:10	Section 1	First theme stated in the violins, the first phrase ending with a few syncopated piano chords. The next phrase is an interplay of two melodies in the woodwinds and strings
0:51		Then, Ives introduces his first cacophony. Different songs are played by the trumpet; the trombone and tuba; the oboe, first clarinet, and violas; the flute and second clarinet; and the violins.
1:11		Suddenly, a lovely, quiet children's song appears in the first violin, followed by an interplay among the various instruments.
1:42		This section ends with a low, static passage in the clarinets and violins that decreases in pitch, dynamics, and texture. A quiet, dissonant passage prepares us for the next section.
2:26	Section 2	Soft and sustained. Quiet strings interact with melodic fragments in the upper woodwinds. Both soon are supported by short, syncopated piano chords.

—Continued

3:15   Section 3   The music builds with fervor to huge climaxes, once suddenly returning to the quiet children's song heard in the first section. The movement returns to the town band and picnic sounds before building to its most intense, most furious climax.
The movement ends on a highly dissonant, unstable, crashing chord.

Reflections

Discuss aesthetic benefits of cacophony (noise) in music.

Discuss communication in music, Ives's musical language, and his selection of musical materials in relation to his aesthetic intentions.

Discuss the extent, nature, and purpose of dissonance in Ives's music.

Discuss the range of expression in this piece—the dramatically contrasting moods.

Nationalism: Aaron Copland

Nationalism in music emerged in the late nineteenth century among a group of composers from eastern Europe and Russia—Rimsky-Korsakov, Mussorgsky, and Dvořák, among many others (see chap. 13, page 280). Charles Ives was one of the most prominent of American nationalistic composers; another was Aaron Copland (1900–1990).

Composers of nationalistic music will at times quote directly from folk literature or will compose in a manner that reflects folk rhythms or the moods of this music. For example, an "Indianist" approach to nationalistic composition would use native Indian melodies and rhythms. Another approach would incorporate native instruments—for example, claves, guiro, or bongos—and rhythms in an orchestral piece based on Cuban dances.

Before the 1920s, American composers may have quoted folk tunes, spirituals, and other vernacular music, but European-style music dominated. Since the 1920s, certain composers, notably Aaron Copland, sought a style that would be immediately recognizable as uniquely American. Their style would become a matter of national pride and would also reach a broad audience. One begins with the premise that something American is in some way suggestive of events, places, or characteristics, musical or other, that are important and known to a large segment of Americans. It is something that does not apply to other nations or regions, because it is national rather than universal.

American nationalistic music might convey a sense of the wide open spaces; might reflect vernacular elements, such as the syncopated rhythms of jazz and popular music; or might connote religious, folk, or patriotic songs. Perhaps the ideal of a distinctively American musical style was derived from the notion that America was a melting pot where various cultures blended into one "American" society. However, America already was too diverse for such a blending. Perhaps many immigrants—individuals and groups—were thoroughly assimilated into mainstream society, but other groups retained distinctive characteristics such as their taste in food, their songs and dances, their dialect, and their values.

The music of mainstream America and that of its ethnic groups were a mosaic of styles, diverse and enriching. The mosaic also included the many American composers who developed their own style without a consciously American flavor. These composers focused more on abstract, experimental music, perhaps electronic and, more recently, computer music. Others focused on atonality and serialism and still others on a return to earlier styles and structures—neoclassical or neoromantic. Many of these composers produced works with more than one focus. Yet, all this was American music, created in America by Americans. Diversity is the core of the American musical language.

Aaron Copland (1900–1990), without a doubt, is the best-known and most successful American composer of classical music. His nationalistic music has been especially successful. He was the first of the idealistic Americans in Paris in the 1920s who wanted to elevate American music and help shape the American musical personality. He is one of a number of American-born Jews—including George Gershwin, Irving Berlin, and Leonard Bernstein—who contributed to the development and vitality of American music.

Copland was interested in merging elements of classical and vernacular music. He wanted to do more than quote hymns, spirituals, or American Indian chants, as others before him had done. His genius was in using vernacular, often regional, elements to formulate more universal thoughts that could represent the whole country.

Copland was interested in innovation, but not at the expense of the past. He felt that although music had to move ahead, it should be built on past practices. He was influenced, as were other Americans in Paris in the 1920s, by Stravinsky, whose first musical achievements had taken place in Paris 15 years earlier. Stravinsky's influence was neoclassicism—he combined a new musical language with old forms, structures, and values.

In the 1920s and 1930s, along with Henry Cowell, Roger Sessions, Edgard Varèse and others, Copland organized concerts that featured new, often experimental, works by American and sometimes contemporary European composers. Copland also wrote about this music to help people understand it. There was an audience for these concerts for awhile, but in the mid-1930s the audiences began to dwindle. The gap between composer and listener began to widen, as composers became ultramodern, abstract, and separated from the tastes of the public. As audiences for new music declined, Copland became concerned about composing in a vacuum. In the late 1930s, he began to explore ways of reaching a wider public, of composing with artistic integrity but in a more accessible language.

Listening Guide   *No.* 72

Billy the Kid (**excerpt**)

Composed in 1938 by Aaron Copland (1900–1990).
Performed by the New York Philharmonic; Leonard Bernstein, conductor.
CD5, Tracks 22–23, 3:58 (SCD) CD2, Tracks 45–46, 4:00
This example, an excerpt from an orchestral version of music to Copland's ballet of the same name, is derived from the western European concert music tradition. It is American music in one sense because the composer is American. It is American in another sense because the story and many of the tunes Copland uses in this ballet are derived from the songs and traditions of the American people and from American folk traditions.

—Continued

Goals

Recognize and describe texture, timbre, and dynamics.

Describe various layers of sound, such as bass lines, inner voices, and other supportive lines.

Recognize patterns in the music as it develops, particularly patterns in the treatments of meter, repeated musical ideas, and contrast.

Be aware of rhythmic vitality, and identify ways in which it is achieved.

Distinguish between the sound of a solo instrument and of a group of instruments.

Guide

0:00   The first theme, a four-note motive, sounds soon in the solo horn, then the flute. The oboe answers.

0:21   As this section begins to extend and expand, building on the original motive, the quiet mood is accompanied by a two-note descending interval featuring offbeat thumps in the timpani and other low instruments.

0:59   It then increases in intensity and loudness, culminating in cymbal crashes, timpani, and brass instruments.

1:14   The energy suddenly diminishes, builds again in a similar manner with the two-note motive appearing melodically in higher-range instruments, and then ends abruptly as the next section begins.

2:04   The contrasting section features a folklike melody introduced by the piccolo. The wind instruments then enter a dialogue with the brasses, passing parts of the melody back and forth. Pungent dissonances add interest and excitement.

2:56   The section extends in a more regular dancelike style, followed by irregular rhythms and much syncopation.

3:07   The strings present the melody; the trombones answer. The strings play it again but this time are followed by the trumpets. Soon only fragments of the melody are heard in various instruments. The section subsides to a quiet ending.

Reflections

Be aware of the density of instrumentation. Describe the sound—a few instruments produce thin texture while many instruments usually produce a full, thick texture.

Listen for contrasting sections and changes of tempo (speed), range (high or low pitch areas), and musical thoughts (phrases).

The folklike melodies, usually presented only in fragments, are often passed from instrument to instrument. Identify the instruments from their sounds.

Describe the meter and rhythm. Can you tap your foot to the music? Is there a regular beat? Is it danceable music, or does much of it have only the "feel" of music to be danced to?

Discuss the texture of a string quartet (Listen to Guide 3, p. 33 and Guide 59, p. 268), and compare it with that of a symphony orchestra as heard in this example. Is one texture always thin and the other full?

From this approach came Copland's tone poems, ballet music, music for films and radio, and patriotic works reflecting the American spirit and drawing on vernacular forms. This music includes cowboy songs, popular Mexican songs, church music, jazz, and blues. It was the music of rural America with urban rhythms and harmonies. It allowed Copland to develop a distinct and enduring style.

Copland's best-known ballets are *Billy the Kid* (listen to Listening Guide 72, p. 331), *Rodeo*, and *Appalachian Spring*. His patriotic music includes *Fanfare for the Common Man* and *Lincoln Portrait*. His best-known movie music was for *Red Pony* and *Our Town*. Copland also experimented with serial technique, particularly in the 1950s, and his piano music ranks among his best abstract modern works.

Additional American Composers

This section begins with the work of several women and black composers who were pioneers in the history of American music. The following women and men were among the first successful American composers. (For additional insight into the historical circumstances facing women composers in Western culture, refer to the Introduction to Part IV, p. 211).

Amy Cheney Beach (1867–1944) pursued a successful career as a performer and composer, a significant accomplishment in her time. Her "Gaelic" Symphony was the first symphony by an American woman. She was also the first woman to have her music premiered by the Handel and Haydn Society of Boston and the New York Philharmonic Orchestra. Much of her music is recorded and still available.

Beach's compositions for solo piano, in particular, may sound conservative to our contemporary ears. They incorporate impressionistic sounds and are programmatic, titles such as "By the Still Waters" and "From Grandmother's Garden." Her instrumental music, including a piano concerto, a string quartet, and a piano quintet, is more innovative and complex.

Ruth Crawford (1901–1953) was an active and important composer when, in the early 1930s, she married Charles Seeger, a distinguished ethnomusicologist and folk song collector. She then stopped composing because of family responsibilities and to concentrate, along with her husband, on American folk music.

Crawford was in the vanguard of musical developments such as the serialization of elements other than pitch. In 1930, she was awarded a Guggenheim Fellowship, the first woman to win one. It enabled her to study in Berlin and Paris. She composed songs, suites for various instruments, nine Preludes for Piano, a well-known string quartet, and a woodwind quintet.

Listening Guide   *No.* **73**

Preludes for Piano, no. 8 ("Leggiero")

From a set of nine preludes composed in 1928 by Ruth Crawford (1901–1953).
Performed by Virginia Eskin, piano — **CD5, Track 24, 2:24**
Ruth Crawford was important in the American avant-garde scene during the 1920s. Among her most important works are a string quartet (1931) and these piano preludes, some of which use compositional techniques that were rare at the time but later became commonplace.

—Continued

Listening Guide — *Continued*   *No.* 73

Goals

Describe the rhythmic characteristics and the approach to melody and harmony.
Recognize motives and patterns of repetition that give the piece cohesion (unity).

Guide

The piece, in a b a form, is bold and innovative. It has imaginative rhythms and
harmonies. First comes a lively, dancelike part with irregular, crisp rhythms; then a
contrasting, quiet, middle section followed by the return.

0:00	a
0:35	b
1:41	a

Reflections

Compare this work with other piano pieces, such as Gershwin's prelude (Listening
Guide 75, p. 336), Chopin's prelude (chap. 13, Listening Guide 64, p. 289), and
Beethoven's sonata (chap. 12, Listening Guide 60, p. 270). Discuss how each work
was appropriate for the age in which it was created.

William Grant Still (1895–1978) had a career that took him from his home state of
Mississippi to New York and Boston. He worked or studied with W. C. Handy in Memphis, Eubie Blake and Noble Sissle on Broadway, George Chadwick at the New England
Conservatory, and Edgard Varèse in New York. While Still was a staff arranger and
composer for radio stations in New York City, he came into contact with such famous
entertainers as Artie Shaw, Sophie Tucker, and Paul Whiteman.

Still's Guggenheim Fellowship, awarded in 1934, enabled him to devote more of his
time to classical composition. Settling in Los Angeles, he had pursued an active career in
composition. He produced operas, many orchestral works, and vocal, keyboard, and
chamber pieces. His style, conservative and consonant, combined elements of French
impressionism and Afro-American music. His most representative and perhaps best-
known work is the *Afro-American Symphony*, composed in 1930 (see below).

Ulysses Kay (1917–1995) was one of the most honored of American composers. He
received a Fulbright, a Guggenheim, and the Prix de Rome. He had a successful career as
a moderately conservative tonal composer. Much of his music is in small forms, but he
also composed operas and music for television and films. Much of his work could be
considered neoclassical because of its form and orchestral balance. Interestingly, William
Grant Still encouraged Kay to become a composer.

Other important American pioneers include Henry Cowell, Louis Gottschalk, and
George Gershwin.

Henry Cowell (1897–1965) was influential as a composer, a teacher, an author, and a
promoter of new music. Some of his values and practices, which he developed in the
1920s, became commonplace by the 1950s.

Afro-American Symphony (III)

Composed by William Grant Still (1895–1978).

Performed by the London Symphony Orchestra; Paul Freeman, conductor.

A four-movement work composed in 1930 (revised, 1969) — **CD5, Track 25, 3:23**

This symphony, the first composed by a black American, is rooted in the blues and in the syncopated popular music of the time.

Goals

Recognize blue notes and the call-and-response technique in symphonic music.

Recognize diatonic and tonal American music.

Identify the principal motive and recognize its modifications and variations as the piece progresses.

Guide

The syncopated motive on which the entire movement is based is stated in the introduction and at the beginning of the predominant theme. The movement is basically a series of variations of that motive. It is passed throughout the orchestra, often in a question-answer, call-and-response format.

Reflections

This movement, diatonic and tonal, has songlike themes. It is lighthearted and bouncy. The dancelike, regular rhythm is enhanced by the strumming of the banjo. Notice the abundance of blue notes.

Cowell was committed to exploring ways of merging Western music with the folk and traditional music of other cultures. He searched for new sources of sound and new ways of organizing sound, and he created new notation to communicate his new techniques.

One of his most famous compositional devices, dating from as early as 1912, is the tone cluster, several adjacent pitches played simultaneously. On the piano, a cluster is often achieved by depressing the keys with the fist or the entire forearm. Cowell found new sources of sound in numerous percussion instruments and in using the piano as a percussion instrument—by means of tone clusters and also by plucking, strumming, scraping, and hitting the strings inside the piano.

The best known of Cowell's more than five thousand compositions includes a number of symphonies, a series of pieces entitled Hymn and Fuguing Tunes, and music for solo piano.

Louis Gottschalk (1829–1869), the first well-known composer of American classical music, was a virtuoso pianist, a well-known composer of piano music, and a star in Europe and throughout the United States, Canada, and South America. He grew up in New Orleans but lived and studied in Paris for almost eleven years. Thus, much of his music is based on Negro and Creole songs but set in a European, virtuosic context that demonstrated his pianistic skills to the utmost. However, his Americanist music does not seem to have worn well and has had little lasting influence on later composers. His best-known works are two solo piano pieces, "The Banjo" and "Bamboula." After Gottschalk, it is Charles Ives, Aaron Copland, and George Gershwin who rank at the top among those composers who incorporated American vernacular elements or otherwise attempted to capture the American spirit.

George Gershwin (1898–1937) is known as a successful Tin Pan Alley composer of songs, musicals, and film music (Additional Listening Example 16, p. 345). He is also known as a successful composer of jazz-oriented classical music. Indeed, he was one of the most popular and most effective of all American composers. His classical music is widely known, universally loved, and extensively performed. It includes

Rhapsody in Blue for piano and orchestra (1924); Concerto in F for piano and orchestra (1925); *An American in Paris* for orchestra (1928); three Preludes for Piano (1926); and *Porgy and Bess*, a folk opera (1935) (see "Summertime," from *Porgy and Bess*, Listening Guide 21, p. 104).

Listening Guide   *No.* 75

Preludes for Piano, no. 1

From a set of three preludes composed in 1926 by George Gershwin (1896–1937).
Performed by Michael Tilson-Thomas — **CD5, Track 26, 1:26**
These preludes were composed for Gershwin's own recital at the Hotel Roosevelt in New York City. They are usually performed as one 3-movement composition in a fast-slow-fast order. The movements are in contrasting keys.

Goals

Recognize jazz and Latin elements in a classical context.
Recognize the vamp.

Guide

The first movement opens with a blue note motive. The left-hand vamp precedes the entrance of the opening theme, and the accompaniment takes on a distinctively Spanish flavor.

Reflections

The movement is in a classical form and context but incorporates the syncopated, bluesy sounds of the popular music and jazz of the 1920s.
Compare this prelude with the preludes by Chopin, Chap. 13 Listening Guide 64, p. 289; and Crawford, chap. 15, Listening Guide 73, p. 333.

The next guide is to illustrate unusual organization of musical elements and nontraditional uses of a traditional instrument. Emma Lou Diemer's Toccato for Piano calls for these unusual pianistic techniques: (1) strings damped by a hand inside the piano, (2) strings strummed by a hand inside the piano, and (3) hitting undamped strings.

istening Guide No. **76**

Toccata for Piano

Composed in 1979 by Emma Lou Diemer (b 1927).

Performed by Rosemary Platt, piano — **CD5, Track 27, 5:52**

Diemer, a prolific American composer who has received many awards and grants, has composed in the electronic medium and for virtually all standard and many nonstandard vocal and instrumental ensembles.

Goals

Be aware of the expanded coloristic uses of the piano.

Recognize a variety of contemporary compositional techniques.

Guide

0:00 Repeated notes; close intervals; syncopation; middle range

0:23 Fast ascending and descending ostinato; fades into damped sound, then returns to normal piano sound

0:49 Low-register rumble, then several short wide-ranging ascending and descending passages

1:16 Back to first motive—undamped-damped (percussive)—undamped trills

2:02 Descending motives, then short, widely separated patterns on undamped strings, leaving the tones to resound after they have been played at the keyboard

3:20 Energetic, syncopated pattern

3:52 Wide-ranging arpeggios

4:10 Thumping rhythm in low register

4:21 Original motive

4:44 Scrapes of sound and low rumbles played inside the piano; fades away to end the piece

—*Continued*

Reflections

Unusual compositional techniques in this piece include:

- Percussive use of the piano
- Wide range of pitches, using the entire keyboard
- Lack of traditional melody and harmony
- Fast, staccato repeated notes
- Melodic contour ranging from a flat shape with a narrow range of pitches to a wide-ranging, angular use of pitches
- Energy ranging from a flurry of activity to considerable silence

What was your overall response to this music?

What aspects of this music did you respond favorably to? Unfavorably?

The next three pieces were composed by winners of the Pulitzer Prize in music: George Crumb in 1968; Ellen Taaffe Zwilich in 1983, and Shulamit Ran in 1991.

Echoes of Time and the River (I) (excerpt)

I. Frozen Time

II. Remembrance of Time

III. Collapse of Time

IV. Last Echoes of Time

Four processionals for orchestra composed in 1967 by George Crumb (b. 1927).

Performed by the Louisville Orchestra; Jorge Mester, conductor

CD5, Track 28, 3:21 (SCD) CD2, Track 47, 3:23

Echoes of Time and the River was premiered by the Chicago Symphony Orchestra and won the Pulitzer Prize for Music in 1968. Crumb is a Pennsylvanian and has received grants from the Rockefeller and Koussevitsky foundations and a Guggenheim award. He has been on the faculty at the University of Pennsylvania.

In live performance, *Echoes* has a double impact—both aural and visual. The audience sees the performers, at times, move about onstage, marching in varying steps to the music they are performing. The percussionists play numerous instruments, and other instrumentalists also play certain percussion instruments; for instance, a violinist plays the antique cymbal.

—Continued

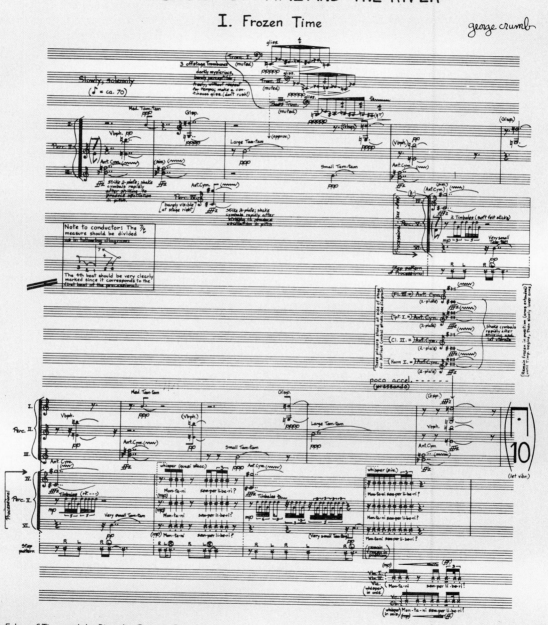

Echos of Time and the River, by George Crumb.

—*Continued*

The orchestration calls for three flutes and three clarinets but no oboes; all the brass instruments except tubas; a full string section; two pianos, a harp, and a mandolin; and many regular and exotic percussion instruments, including cymbals of different types and sizes; two sizes of gongs; glockenspiel, vibraphone, and xylophone; bamboo wind chimes and Chinese temple gongs and bells; conga drums, bongo drums, and timbales; and cowbells, sleigh bells, and tubular bells.

The composer has indicated every detail in the score: what notes are to be played and how but also where performers are to be placed on the stage—there is a different placement for each of the four movements.

Goals

Be aware of the organization of music by time segments as opposed to bars and phrase structure.

Describe the musical language in terms of melody, harmony, and rhythm.

Identify glissandos.

Identify altered tones produced inside the piano.

Guide

The following outline specifies prominent musical events, showing the time lapsed from the beginning:

:00   Loud bell sound—antique cymbal

:17   Low register glissandos by three trombones

:27   Timbales

:42   Voices: staccato whispers, only approximate pitches; timbales continue; bells

1:12   Timpani: up-and-down glissandos; voices reenter

2:14   Loud chord: all previous instruments sound at once, starting with the antique cymbal, followed by eight pitches altered by touching strings inside the two pianos

2:28   Loud chord begins a long series of rising and falling glissandos in strings that move from the high-pitch area of the violins down to the low-pitch area of the basses

Reflections

Discuss musical language and describe how this excerpt is in nontraditional language.

Discuss the instrumentation. Is this orchestral music, chamber music, or something else?

Discuss silence in music. What role does it have in this music?

L istening Guide   *No.* 78

Symphony no. 1 (III)

A three-movement work composed by Ellen Taaffe Zwilich (b. 1939).

Performed by the Indianapolis Symphony, John Nelson, conductor.

CD5, Track 29, 3:58

Zwilich won the Pulitzer Prize for Music in 1983 for this work—she was the first woman to win this coveted prize. She has composed solo works, chamber music for various ensembles (her *String Quartet* of 1974 received much acclaim), and music for orchestra. Her style combines modern musical language with links to the past. She likes to develop large-scale works based on a germinal idea, and she values the richness and variety of modern orchestras.

Goals

Recognize main motives and elements of contrast and repetition.

Identify entrances of main theme areas.

Be aware of the sounds of modern, tonal music.

Guide

0:00	First theme area	Fast, vibrant, forceful; begins with timpani, followed by the main ascending motive and by many staccato repeated-note patterns as well as wide-ranging passages; ends with a bell
1:14	Contrast	Slow and quiet; descending, stepwise pattern
1:38	Return	Timpani, then the original ascending motive
1:52	Second contrast	Begins with a bell; legato, soft, and slow
2:34	Return	Fast and sprightly, making use of the earlier repeated-tone patterns; intensity builds; the range of the violins is at times extreme; the piece ends conventionally, providing a clear sense of tonic

Reflections

This movement has characteristics of a rondo (a b a c a), but not with traditional sounds or formal clarity.

Compare the musical characteristics of this piece, particularly the orchestral sonorities, with those of Stravinsky, Brahms, and Bach.

L istening Guide

"Private Game"

Composed by Shulamit Ran (1979) for clarinet and cello.

Performed by members of Da Capo Chamber Players: Laura Flax, clarinet; André Emelianoff, cello — **CD5, Track 30, 4:02**

Shulamit Ran was born in Israel and moved to the United States to study music when she was 14. Her distinguished career includes piano performances and performances of her works with major orchestras worldwide. She was the first woman appointed composer-in-residence with a top-five symphony orchestra—the Chicago Symphony Orchestra, a position she held for seven years. She is professor of composition at the University of Chicago, where she has taught since 1973. Among her numerous awards, fellowships, and commissions are those from the Martha Baird Rockefeller Fund and the Guggenheim Foundation. Ran received the Pulitzer Prize for Music in 1991 for *Symphony*.

"Private Game" is a short piece that uses "strict repetition, without giving the appearance of arbitrary formalism" (from her own liner notes). She describes repetition as the "essence of comprehensibility." Repetition is "essential for [giving] a piece coherence, but it may not be "consciously perceived as repetitions on first hearing." That is her "private game."

Goals

Listen for static melodic ideas (many repeated notes) as well as sweeping angular lines (wide-ranging arpeggios).

Listen for sections of repetition and contrast.

Describe the interaction of the clarinet and cello.

Distinguish between bowed and plucked cello lines.

Guide

0:00	Theme A	Motive stated in the clarinet; bold, angular, wide-sweeping arpeggios
0:34	Theme B	Quiet and delicate, yet also somewhat angular
0:47	Theme A	Wide-ranging clarinet motive
1:08	Theme C	Lively, ascending motive followed by a brief descending line
1:54	Theme B	Motive restated; section extended
2:50	Theme C	Lively, ascending motive followed by descending line

Reflections

Are angular motives and themes appealing? Why or why not?

Ran described her composition as her private game—strict repetition but not necessarily perceivable at first hearing. With my guide, I have shared my solution— one person's analysis. What is your analysis—your own "private game"?

(a) Ethel Leginska, 1928. A leading pianist from England, an important conductor of symphony orchestras during the 1920s, and an ardent proponent of feminist issues in music; (b) JoAnn Falletta is part of a new generation of orchestra conductors.

(a)

(b)

Summary

Chapter 15 focuses on classical art music in the United States. The classical tradition has been dominated by western European culture but in the twentieth century has become a worldwide phenomenon, with the United States taking a place at the forefront of modern developments.

An "American musical language," to some, means nationalist music that reflects aspects of American life. This chapter suggests that modern American music is more than that; the music has been created by people who value explicitly American idioms but also by Americans who continue to cultivate European styles, who experiment while searching for a new musical language, or who write in a personal style that fits no particular label and is perhaps neither American nor European. American music is the sum of all the music making up the American musical language.

Finally, twentieth-century America has raised the social consciousness of its citizens in matters of race relations and minority and women's concerns, a fact that has permeated every aspect of our society, including music. This chapter has drawn attention to American music by women and minority composers by focusing on a few representative composers and their works.

The Kronos Quartet, a contemporary performance ensemble, with Foday Musa Suso, playing the *Kora,* an African lute-type stringed instrument.

x a m p l e *No.* **16**

"Porgy and Bess"

A blend of American music: classical-opera-jazz-popular-music theater

A. "Summertime"
B. "It Ain't Necessarily So"
C. "I Loves You, Porgy"

Composed by George Gershwin.
Lyrics by Ira Gershwin.
Arrangement by Marty Paich.

Performed by Sarah Vaughan, vocal; a jazz trio of piano, bass, and drums; and the Los Angeles Philharmonic; Michael Tilson-Thomas, conductor.
You will find this piece on the student **CD set. (SCD) CD2, Tracks 48–50, 6:06**

Goals

Describe the singing style of Sarah Vaughan and her interpretation of "Summertime."
Compare the styles and moods of each song.
Enjoy this final listening example in *The World of Music*.

Guide

Count in a slow four; flexible pulse

Introduction	Strings
A. ("Summertime")	Vocal
B. ("It Ain't Necessarily So")	Vocal
C. ("I Loves You, Porgy")	Vocal

Reflections

Which genre or genres does this music most easily fit: Jazz? Opera? Popular? Music theater? Classical? Give reasons for your choice or choices.

16 Music in American Society

Summary

*T*his chapter seeks to promote an understanding of those cultural factors common in the United States that can enrich the study of music. It will focus on the following points:

- Ways music functions in the United States, that is, how music is used by Americans.
- Roles Americans play as creators and performers, as listeners, and as supporters of the musical life in their community, their region, or the nation.

The information is organized in three broad areas:

1. *The music industry.* Consists of merchandising (making and selling things for profit) and performance (producing and selling live or recorded music for profit or as a service).
2. *Music and the media.* Includes broadcasting, film, and advertising.
3. *Music in our communities.* Encompasses professional, semiprofessional, and amateur musical activities and the promotion and development of music and the other arts.

Music is big business, one of the largest and most complex businesses in the United States. The music industry, as has been stated, consists of selling products and live and recorded music. It can be broken down into five overlapping categories that can help us understand what the industry is and how it functions. These categories are manufacturing, publishing, merchandising, performance, and management.

The Music Industry

The making of goods includes research, design, and development. The following listings of manufactured goods that are essential to the music industry will suffice to illustrate its scope, its variety, and its impact on our lives.

Manufacturing

Musical Instruments

- Band and orchestra instruments for thousands of school, community, and professional bands and orchestras.
- Electronic instruments—mostly keyboards, guitars, drums, and synthesizers with their links to computers through MIDI technology—for a vast number of professionals, semiprofessionals, and amateurs.
- Pianos and pipe organs for homes, schools, churches, and concert halls.
- Traditional folk instruments such as dulcimers, autoharps, and acoustic banjos and guitars for mostly amateur or semiprofessional music making that varies from region to region.
- Educational instruments such as recorders, various drums and tone bars or other mallet instruments, guitars, and keyboard instruments that are used especially in elementary school music classes.

Audio Equipment

- Stereo systems (home entertainment centers) that include record and/or playback capability for cassette tapes (DAT—Digital Audio Tape), compact discs, videotapes, and DVDs (digital versatile discs).
- Receiver capability for stereo FM, AM, and TV broadcast.
- Audio reinforcement and enhancement from amplifiers, graphic equalizers, and speaker systems.
- CD-ROM technology for playback and recording.

    CD-ROM—Read Only Memory (for prerecorded CDs)

    CD-R—Recordable (can be recorded only once)

    CD-RW—Rewritable (can be recorded multiple times)

Uniforms and Robes

- Uniforms and robes—for thousands of school, college, and community choirs, orchestras, and bands.
- Accessories—for all musicians who need supportive goods, such as replacement strings for guitars and violins, music stands, lubricants, patch cords, disc and tape cleaners, and other goods that for the most part represent high-profit items for music stores.

Publishing

The heart of the music publishing industry is the popular song in its recorded (not printed) form. Everything is related to making a hit and realizing the full commercial potential of a song.

From the days of the minstrel shows in the second half of the nineteenth century, America became enamored of a vernacular music that we call *popular music*. By 1900, with the establishment of large publishing houses and the development of sophisticated merchandising methods, the music industry was big business. It was a business based on the "hits," a concept still central to the industry today. By the 1920s, hits were made with the aid of Tin Pan Alley song pluggers and songs from musical theater and vaudeville shows. The primary means of disseminating a song and determining its level of popularity was the sale of sheet music. In the swing era of the 1930s, songs were plugged by the lead singers of the big bands. In the 1940s and 1950s, many former big band singers became independent solo performers and promoted their own songs. Since the 1950s, the disc jockey and airplay have become the indicators of a hit. Since the 1980s, video airplay remains a significant part of making a song commercially successful.

With the establishment of the copyright law in 1909, composers, lyricists, and publishers became the copyright owners of popular songs and were able to make a profit from the royalties earned when these songs were performed live and in recordings. Copyright holders were granted exclusive rights to authorize the use of their music for a limited time and to collect fees for such use. Anyone performing copyrighted material had to obtain *performance rights* by paying for a license or by paying a royalty. Anyone recording copyrighted material had to obtain *mechanical rights* and pay the established fees. Anyone using copyrighted material in a film had to obtain *synchronization rights* and pay the appropriate fees.

Licensing agencies, such as the American Society of Composers, Authors and Publishers (ASCAP) and Broadcast Music, Incorporated (BMI) have been established to collect these fees and distribute them to the copyright holders. With the revised copyright law that went into effect in 1978, colleges and universities now pay these agencies the cost of "blanket" performance licenses to cover royalties, rather than individual works, for a year's collective use of copyrighted material controlled by the agencies. The material is then performed by school marching and concert bands, stage bands, choirs, and other ensembles.

Publishers build catalogs of music with the greatest commercial potential. They follow this process:

- Seek out composers and songwriters.
- Negotiate and obtain rights for their music.
- Manage and promote their music to realize maximum profit.
- Negotiate contracts for producing, manufacturing, distributing, and selling recordings.
- Release a song, usually after it has become a hit, in sheet music or songbooks (folios).

Some publishers specialize in printed music for churches, schools, and colleges—the Christian, educational, and concert music markets. Another market for printed music is the large group of amateur music makers who buy pianos, organs, electronic keyboards, and guitars for home use and who also need to buy sheet music, folios, and instructional "how to" books. One area of music publishing that is very large but typically is not included as part of the music industry is the music book industry, including textbooks and magazines about music. Usually, these materials are published by houses that specialize in writing, producing, and distributing books and other materials in more than one discipline.

Music merchandising is the pricing, distribution, promotion, retailing, and servicing of music and music-related products. For the most part, it is ultimately the exchange between the music store retailer and the consumer. Consumers include music teachers buying band or choral music, instruments, or instruction books; professional musicians who are always on the lookout for a better instrument or new music; parents supporting their children's interest in music; teenagers checking out the latest in electric guitars; adult amateurs who keep active musically as an avocation; and people adding to their record or tape library.

Merchandising

Such merchandising exchanges may be with a local or a mail-order music store, but they will also be found at concerts where consumers can buy merchandising "tie-ins" (posters, tote bags, T-shirts, recordings) that identify an artist or music organization. Such merchandising is common for performers of all types of music—popular, rock, folk, religious, country, and classical. Sales of tie-in merchandise add to the profits of the musician or organization, and as long as the products are used and seen, they advertise the musician or organization. Virtually all organizations producing classical music, including opera companies, consider tie-ins an essential component of their business operation.

Recorded music is sold mostly in stores specializing in the sale of CDs and tapes, but it is also sold in department stores and bookstores, in discount houses, through record clubs, and from direct offers on television. Inventories of large record stores are usually maintained by the retailer, who purchases directly from record distributors associated exclusively with a major label (record company) or distributors handling (representing) many labels. The inventory of nonspecialized stores (department stores, discount houses, and perhaps bookstores) or any store that maintains racks of records and tapes is supplied and controlled by the "rack jobber." The rack jobber pays the retailer a space rental fee, a commission on sales, or both. In large record and tape departments, the rack jobber may actually function as a retailer, controlling the sales and cash flow through his or her own checkout counter and financial management. Most record stores or departments, in responding to changing technology and changing markets, now stock videos, books, and magazines.

Specialized audio stores serve mostly semiprofessionals and sophisticated amateurs: the audiophiles. These stores provide expertise and service, and you pay for it. Department stores and discount houses that sell audio equipment usually stock the middle to low end of the quality spectrum and provide little expertise and service. You pay less and you get less.

Almost all these stores—again, responding to changing technology and changing markets—now stock video equipment, home entertainment centers, and car stereo systems. Professional consumers of audio equipment deal directly with manufacturers or through sound design consultants in maintaining sophisticated recording studios or other sound reinforcement businesses.

Printed music, band and orchestra instruments, guitars, pianos, organs, and electronic instruments of various types are sold in music stores that range from highly specialized shops to full-line, comprehensive stores maintaining a large and varied inventory. Most stores specialize to some degree. Some serve local or regional school music programs by selling band and choral music and selling, renting, and servicing (repairing) band and orchestral instruments. Some serve a local or regional amateur or semiprofessional entertainment market with an inventory of drums, guitars, and electronic instruments and equipment. Others limit themselves to the sale of pianos and organs or to a mail order market for choral music in schools and churches.

In size and scope, music stores range from small "mom and pop," family-owned shops to large mail-order houses with a national market. Most of the national stores now offer Internet sales. The largest market for music stores is the amateur market, including more than 100,000 school music ensembles with millions of members altogether and a vast amount of music making that takes place in communities, churches, and homes.

Performance

Performance, of course, permeates every aspect of the music industry and indeed of society. Thus it overlaps, relates to, and is served by every topic under consideration in this chapter. Music is performed live in concert halls, gymnasiums, parks, fairgrounds, and hotel lounges. It is recorded on discs or tapes, distributed, and sold to consumers; broadcast on radio or television; downloaded; used in films and commercials; and played in elevators, offices, and department stores.

The saying "it all begins with a song" is literally true in most parts of the entertainment industry. The business of music begins with a creative work, whether composed in notated form, created spontaneously through improvisation, or composed orally as a means of expression by someone who has no thought of writing it down. Music—whether created recently, decades ago, or even centuries ago—is presented to a paying audience who hears live music or buys recordings.

The concept of "making a hit" means commercially exploiting a song—from creating it to getting it recorded, distributed, played on the air, and sold. This process usually

A recording in progress.

The Merce Cunningham Dance Company with "pit orchestra," 1990s style.

precedes a song becoming a hit and a performer becoming well known. A song becomes a hit when enough people listen to it on the radio, hear it on television, and then buy a recording of it, either as a single or in an album. The process also must take place before a performer becomes a sufficient "name" to attract a paying audience to live concerts, perhaps as part of a tour. A career can be boosted by appearances on important talk shows and at televised award ceremonies, especially if a performer receives an award. Live concerts can provide income for a performer and can also increase sales of recordings. Live performances can be single concerts that are part of a regional, national, or international tour or multiple engagements at a single location such as a hotel lounge. Fame, sales of recordings, and successful tours are also major goals for many professional classical, folk, and jazz artists.

The biggest "buyers" of musicians include community arts organizations and colleges and universities who organize "artist series" sold preferably as packages of concerts (commonly known as *subscription series* or *season tickets*) with considerable savings over the cost of individual concerts. At present, organizations such as Affiliate Artists and Community Concerts assist communities in providing high-quality music at the lowest possible costs. Affiliate Artists—and many state arts councils—assist communities in sponsoring residencies in which musicians live in a community for an extended period of time, usually from one to six weeks. The artists give recitals and also involve themselves in the musical life of the community in as many ways as possible. Community Concerts assists in developing artist series for many small communities.

One way many communities and colleges reduce costs is by block booking—artists who can play several concerts in a region with minimal travel between locations will perform for reduced fees. This concept saves the artists time and energy because it allows a more efficient travel schedule, and it earns them more money, even with reduced fees, because it allows more concerts in less time.

Most communities offer their own local music performances in every conceivable style, depending upon the size and population mix of the area. Large cities with a diverse ethnic makeup can offer a tremendous diversity of live musical performances to appeal to every taste. Many communities sponsor special events such as folk festivals, bluegrass festivals, fiddle contests, or Renaissance fairs. Most large cities maintain symphony orchestras, community bands, and even opera companies, of which some are fully professional, some strictly volunteer.

Most community orchestras hire semiprofessional musicians who play for pay but at a level that requires them to earn their major income elsewhere, usually from teaching. Many of the performers have chosen professional careers outside music and play music for their own enrichment, enjoyment, and perhaps supplemental income. Numerous semiprofessional or amateur musicians play jazz, rock, or country music in local nightclubs, lounges, and private social clubs and for school or community dances, or they may be hired to perform church music regularly or on special occasions.

For many communities, a vital and active musical life is a source of civic pride—a symbol of a progressive attitude that stresses human, cultural, and artistic values, and a strategy for economic development that includes promoting tourism and attracting new businesses and industries.

Management

Virtually no professional musician can succeed without the assistance of people other than a paying audience. The performer needs help in finding jobs, negotiating contracts, hiring attorneys, handling the intricacies of the copyright law, creating an image, designing and writing publicity materials, organizing publicity campaigns, stimulating media coverage, obtaining recording or publishing contracts, organizing concerts and tours, and managing finances.

An aspiring professional with limited funds begins with an agent whose responsibility is to find jobs for the performer and to exploit the performer's talent. The agent may be a friend of the performer or a representative of a talent agency who handles many clients. The second step would be to hire a personal manager who will be responsible for handling the artist's money as well as every aspect of the artist's career. As the performer achieves financial success, the specialized functions described above may be assigned to more specialized people or to people who are put on the performer's payroll. The performer may establish a corporation, perhaps a publishing company, to handle the business and keep expensive fees and commissions in-house.

In the classical field, careers typically are handled by representatives of artist management firms who serve the dual roles of personal manager and booking agent for concert artists.

Music and the Media

This section will briefly explore fundamental relationships between music and various forms of communication (media), with emphasis on how music benefits the media and how the media benefit music. The media most closely aligned with musical life in our society are the mass media, those that reach the largest number of people—radio, television, and newsprint. Of these, perhaps radio has had the greatest impact on music, particularly in making a hit tune in the entertainment or popular music industry. In the

1980s, however, music videos began to change the relationship of radio to music in our society. Other relationships between music and the media are music in advertising and music in newspapers and magazines—the music journalist and the music critic.

Fundamental factors in the relationship between music and radio programming are these:

Radio

- Music remains at the core of programming.
- Music is part of virtually all advertising.
- Airplay promotes the sale of recorded music.
- Airplay provides income from royalties for jingle writers, songwriters, publishers, and other holders of copyrighted music used by stations in advertising or programming.
- Musicians are hired for the production of some commercials and recorded program material.

Soon after it began, radio was found to be a medium for reaching large numbers of people, and the best format for reaching that goal was popular music. Another common format for live programming, common through the 1940s, included comedy, drama, variety, swing music, and opera. In the 1950s, responding to television, radio settled on a format of music, news, and weather reports. The music was recorded, and the programs were hosted by DJs (disc jockeys). Typically, programming was in one-hour blocks, with news at the top of the hour followed by music and an abundance of commercials and chitchat by the DJ. Promotions, contests, gimmicks, interviews, or remotes (live broadcasts from outside the studio, perhaps at a store or shopping center) were common. Most radio shows were local, and the personality of the DJ was a valued commodity, particularly when rapport with the audience was established.

Because of the importance of the music to programming and the importance of airplay to the success of songs and their performers, music publishers were highly

A radio disc jockey.

competitive and assertive in encouraging DJs to air their clients' latest songs. The competition was fierce, for there was only so much broadcast time available for new releases. Frequent replays of songs were common, and dozens if not hundreds of new releases appeared on the market each week. Airplay was essential for a song to become a hit and for a performer to become famous and financially successful. In recent years, however, airplay has become less essential for established performers and for those concentrating on promotion by means of music videos and concerts in major, perhaps international, venues.

In the 1980s, two related factors have modified if not completely changed the format of radio broadcasting, particularly programming: automation and increased syndication. Computer technology has allowed radio stations to be partially or totally automated. Stations can program equipment to air-taped music, commercials, and station identifications or logos on reels or carts (broadcast cartridges) automatically, without the need for a disc jockey or an engineer.

Production companies (syndicators) develop prepackaged programs or "canned" material compatible with a station's programming policy and format. Many of the top-40-type shows are now syndicated as are many news and sports programs. This minimizes spontaneity and local color, since the traditional DJ has become less of a factor in local radio and in the promotion and sales of recordings.

Paid advertising is the primary source of income for commercial radio, but most regions of the United States are also served by public or noncommercial radio. Such stations, funded by grants and contributions, can program less popular material such as jazz, classical, and folk music; extended news programs; and special features that appeal to a more sophisticated audience. Many public radio stations are affiliated with colleges and universities.

Music in Advertising

Virtually all commercials on radio and television use music. That music has to be created and performed, and so it provides jobs for musicians and jingle writers (composers). Many commercials use electronic instruments only, and the creator frequently is also the performer.

It has been found, intuitively and through psychological research, that music affects listeners' conscious and subconscious emotions. Music in advertising can be in the foreground, can accompany dancing and other activities, and can serve as background for spoken material. It can create an image or a mood, establish an association, and enhance the positive and minimize the negative attributes of a product or service. Advertising attracts attention, creates unity, and makes a product, slogan, or tune memorable. The music can be catchy, simple, and repetitive, and it can serve as a catalyst for an entire ad campaign. Music for an ad may be derived from a popular song, or it may be converted into a popular song. Either way, the intent is for one form to capitalize on the exposure and popularity of the other.

Examine the qualities of familiar commercials or virtually any current commercials on radio or television. What are their attractive qualities? What makes them potentially effective? How do you respond to them? Describe music in advertising on the Internet and compare it with music in advertising on radio and television.

It is worth pointing out that the broadcast media air commercials for which they are not paid a fee. Public service announcements (PSAs) are available to nonprofit groups such as educational institutions, arts organizations, and charitable agencies. Sponsoring organizations may have to pay the production costs of PSAs, but most are produced locally and inexpensively. Many times they involve no music, only a spoken message.

A music video is a commercial for recordings, a tool for promoting a song and its performer, and another method of getting a performer before the public. Part of the attraction of music videos, in addition to the music itself, is the innovative production techniques and the imaginative visual creativity. Many videos incorporate dance, movement, dramatic action, montages, graphics, and other special effects. Such effects might be produced by means of editing techniques but also might be computer generated.

Music videos at first were distributed free to nightclubs, discos, and other places that would expose them to potential buyers of recordings. With their success and with rising production and performance costs, they are now sold not only to commercial establishments but also to the public. They originally promoted rock music and became prominent on cable television, notably MTV and VH-1, and were aired usually to coincide with the release of a commercial recording.

Computer technology continues to advance at an astounding rate: expanded memory, high-speed processors, large storage capacity, and small laptops; CD-ROM, CD-RW, and playlists; and graphics and games.

At the current rate of change in technology, it is safe to predict that by the time you read this book, much of what I am discussing will be out of date. To illustrate the fast rate of change in computer technology, the numbers in parentheses in the following sentence describe the equivalent item listed in the previous edition of *The World of Music* (1999). Today, a pentium 300 processor (150) is considered minimal, as are 64 megabytes of memory (16), a 56,600 modem (14,400), or a 20-gigabyte hard drive (1.6). Larger numbers are common. Software will continue to improve; hardware will be more advanced and perhaps very different, and the vocabulary will most assuredly change.

Music students can learn to read, hear, and analyze music better by means of computer-assisted instruction. Composers, theorists, teachers, and students can use highly sophisticated computer programs that, with an appropriate printer, provide published-quality notation for anything from a homework assignment to a symphony.

The Internet has become a major medium for communication, exchange of information, banking, shopping, and advertising. It continues to offer wonderful benefits and has become a significant presence in our lives. It has high-speed access; streaming radio and video, including thousands of stations worldwide; downloading of music and photographs, with cataloging and storage capabilities—including recording your own CDs; sophisticated search mechanisms; e-mail, Instant Messenger, chat rooms, and listservs; individual bidding, and selling—and so on. Web pages are now for consumers as well as for businesses and institutions.

Composers create computer music by manipulating sampled sound or creating new, electronically generated sounds. CD-ROM programs have largely given way to similar resources easily available on the Internet. This includes bibliographic information, encyclopedias, and other reference works that help researchers at all levels. Biographical information, reviews of music, and recorded repertoire in every genre are easily available. In fact, much of the current information used in preparing the fifth edition of *The World of Music* came from research on the Internet.

Our global culture is now experiencing a digital music revolution. It has created a new vocabulary, such as streaming and ripping; new uses of old vocabulary, such as buffering and encoding; new issues, such as downloading and piracy (copyright infringement); new acronyms, such as CD-RW (compact disc-rewritable) and CDDB (Compact Disc Database); and new products, such as Rio and Sonique (players of MP3 music files).

Music Videos

Music, Computers, and the Internet

It is significant that the practice of downloading music files and the creation of Internet record labels are having considerable impact on the way recorded music is marketed and distributed.

Newsprint

The relationship between music and the newsprint media (newspapers and magazines) involves two styles of writing:

1. *Music journalism* presents information about coming musical events and feature articles about artists and artistic developments—local, regional, or national.
2. *Music criticism* presents reviews of newly released recordings and commentary, interpretation, and criticism of musical events that have just occurred.

Music journalism typically refers to the reporting of information without personal commentary or interpretation. By contrast, music criticism, presented in a signed column or article (the author's name is identified), informs but also entertains and editorializes with the interest of the public (perhaps more than the artist) in mind.

Reviews of jazz, popular music, rock, and classical music are found regularly in music magazines and in newspapers, particularly in metropolitan areas. These reviews can provide a way for consumers to be more knowledgeable in purchasing recordings and in deciding which live performances to attend. Positive reviews are, of course, welcome to any artist, and negative reviews can be damaging, particularly for repeated presentations such as a musical show. Bad reviews have been known to cause the premature closing of Broadway shows.

Music in the Community

Making music, listening to music, and learning about music are favorite pastimes for large numbers of Americans. Most of these musical activities take place outside the formal music education programs in schools and colleges. Instead they take place in the community.

A symphonic band concert.

Outside formal education, musical activities take place in such diverse locations as streets, malls, playgrounds, civic auditoriums, community music schools, senior centers, prisons, mental health clinics, and private homes. The extent and nature of musical activities in these contexts reflect the vast amount of amateur music making in our society. These examples also suggest that Americans value and enjoy a wide diversity of styles of music, from children's songs to chamber music, from square dance music to ballet, from mariachi to blues. Additionally, considering the extent to which Americans attend live concerts and buy radios, stereos, cassettes, albums, and compact discs, listening to music as well as making music is a valued activity in our society. Again, it is easy to document the variety of musical styles people listen to by examining the programming of various radio stations in a community; record sales; the various categories used for sales "charts," such as [hot soul singles, hot country LPs, top-50 adult contemporary, jazz LPs, spiritual LPs, and classical (with the Internet, worldwide charts are available)]; and the types of concerts publicized in newspapers and arts and entertainment magazines. This is not to say that people as individuals are eclectic in their listening preferences. They probably are not—most choose to listen to a limited number of styles. However, collectively, a wide variety of music is performed and listened to in our society.

The discussion of the music industry concludes by suggesting that a vital musical life is valuable to a community. This is equally true whether it involves amateur music making or listening to music. A community's musical life, both professional and amateur, can

A Diverse
Musical Life

Charles River Concert.

help build civic pride, promote tourism and economic development, and convey human, cultural, and artistic values. A community's musical life does not happen automatically. If it is to be successful, it needs to be developed, promoted, and nourished.

Promotion and Development

In the entertainment industry, many people have nonmusical functions—agents, managers, bookers, promoters, and so on. In a community's artistic life as well, many paid professionals and many more unpaid volunteers have nonmusical supporting functions.

Government Support   Government agencies at all political levels support music and the other arts. At the national level, the National Endowment for the Arts (NEA) provides grants to performing and visual arts organizations that must be matched by the requesting agency, thus stimulating fund-raising in the private sector. NEA also provides funds to regional agencies and state arts councils that in turn support programs in their constituencies. These programs include facilitating block booking of touring groups, selecting and supporting residencies, and offering grants to worthy programs that in turn generate even more local fund-raising, since these grants must be matched by the requester. Many grants support programs of local community arts councils. Unfortunately, in the mid-1990s, funding for the NEA was drastically reduced, and a number of politicians called for its abolishment.

Nevertheless, this form of government subsidy has had a marvelous ripple effect as it filters down to the local level. When individuals support a program with money, typically they become involved personally and attend public events. Thus, NEA, since its establishment in 1965, has generated directly or indirectly dramatic increases in private and corporate support of the arts—both financial backing and audience attendance. Additionally, the support of NEA lends an air of credibility to a program and causes private and corporate contributors to feel that a gift will be a good investment. Many arts organizations, however, are well known in a community, have a track record of high-quality productions, and attract repeated contributions each year.

Street musicians.

Corporate Support   Many large corporations, such as Ford, Kresge, and Atlantic-Richfield, have established foundations to handle their corporate giving. Others contribute funds directly from their operating accounts.

Typically, business and industry support arts programs to help give their employees a better place to live. Such support sends a message that the arts contribute to an improved quality of life and are important in the workplace.

Civic Support   Local community support from the private sector comes from the volunteer work of boards of directors of professional arts organizations, committees of chambers of commerce and local government, local arts councils, and volunteer support groups (such as Friends of Music, the Symphony Auxiliary, and the Opera Guild).

Board members are appointed for their capacity to contribute money, their ability to raise money and encourage contributions from their peers, or their professional expertise, such as that of lawyers or accountants. Arts councils usually involve both professionals and nonprofessionals who work together to develop important community projects. Any volunteer groups are usually associated with a professional organization or an educational institution. The volunteers may help the parent organization in a host of ways. They may sell tickets, work with local and state government and arts councils in supporting and enacting legislation affecting the arts, promote a concert or festival, plan fund-raising activities and related social activities, usher at concerts, or schedule concerts or special programs in schools or for community organizations.

Large and active volunteer organizations also cause a ripple effect: increased contributions and larger and perhaps better-informed audiences at live concerts. Many, perhaps most, arts organizations would not exist without the dedication and hard work of the community volunteers.

Summary

Music is an aural art, either classical or vernacular, that can be studied for its own value. The way people use music, the value it has for their lives, and the function it has in society all create a cultural context that enables music to be observed and studied outside the realm of art. One example is the study of music as an industry.

This chapter has examined music as a multibillion-dollar industry that employs hundreds of thousands of people—musicians and nonmusicians. It has looked at music and its relationship to the mass media, the entertainment and advertising industries, and computer technology. It has discussed the diverse roles of music in our communities: how music functions, who is involved, and how it does or does not thrive, depending on community values about music and the extent to which consumers, patrons, and advocates become involved in their community's musical life.

Appendix A
Classification of Instruments according to Methods of Tone Production

Different cultures produce not only different musical styles but different instruments. The following material describes musical instruments from throughout the world using a common "world music" method of classification. This classification is helpful since language based on western European culture—such as *brass, woodwinds, strings*, and *percussion*—does not always suffice in describing or even including many instruments used throughout the world.

Acoustics is the science of sound. It can be applied to the construction of all sorts of performance halls, studios, and audio equipment. Acoustical principles can apply also to the construction of musical instruments, and it is on this basis that instruments worldwide are classified.

The basic sound-producing mechanism of an instrument is the vibration of the material of which it is made. Vibrations are set in motion by energy exerted by a performer through an elastic medium. This process of generating musical sound may include a bow or finger that starts a string in motion (violin or guitar), lips that vibrate ("buzz") into a cupped mouthpiece (trumpet) or cause a wooden reed to vibrate (clarinet), or sticks that are hit on a stretched skin (snare drum) or a wooden or metal bar (marimba or xylophone). The resulting sound-producing vibrations cause the material that the instrument is made of to vibrate sympathetically (at the same speed), such as a box (violin or drum) or a tube (flute or trumpet). This sets air into motion inside and outside the instrument that, if received by an aural system (the outer and inner ear), can be perceived as sound.

The basic sound-producing mechanism of string instruments is the vibration of the string by plucking or bowing. These vibrations are transmitted by a bridge to the belly and back of the instrument causing the wood to oscillate sympathetically with the frequencies present in the vibrating string.

The strands of the bow are usually hair from the tail of a horse that grips the string during bow strokes. Sound is produced when the bow grabs or a finger pulls (plucks) a string. The string, when it reaches its maximum point of elasticity, moves in the opposite direction as far as it can, then returns as far as it can, thus setting up vibrations that continue only if given additional stimulus from bowing or plucking the string.

Chordophones (Stringed Instruments)

The piano consists of individually tuned strings encased in a wooden body. The keyboard has 88 keys, 36 black and 52 white, which when depressed causes hammers to strike the strings. The upper notes of the keyboard consist of three strings per hammer, while the lower ones have single or two strings. When pressed, the left pedal (soft pedal) moves the entire keyboard slightly to the side so a hammer that would normally strike three strings only hits two strings. The middle pedal (sustain pedal) on many grand pianos (absent from most uprights and some grand pianos) sustains only those keys that are being held at the time the pedal is pushed. It simply acts as a damper pedal for the notes in the low range.

Representative Chordophones

A. Violin family
   1. Violin (fiddle)
   2. Viola
   3. Violoncello (cello)
   4. Double bass (string bass, bass fiddle)
B. Viols
C. Sāraṅgī
D. Harp
E. Zither
   1. Dulcimer (plucked, hammered)
   2. Autoharp
   3. Koto
   4. Cimbalom
F. Lute
   1. Sitar
   2. *Shamisen*
   3. Mandolin
   4. *Biwa*
G. Guitar
   1. Banjo
   2. *Guitarrón*
   3. *Charango*
   4. Tamburā
   5. Ukelele
   6. Dobro
H. Keyboards
   1. Piano
   2. Harpsichord

Aerophones (Wind Instruments)

The trumpet and trombone of the brass family use basically cylindrical tubes. As in the woodwinds, conical tubes are also used in brasses, although the acoustical difference between conical and cylindrical tubes is not as dramatic for brass instruments as it is for reed instruments. For woodwind instruments, there are three primary elements that determine the characteristic tone quality:

1. The source of the sound—for example, the vibration of the reed in clarinets and saxophones.
2. The size and shape of the bore (wood or metal tube—the body of the instrument).
3. The size and position of finger holes or keys.

A. Flute
    1. Piccolo
    2. Flute (alto flute)
    3. Panpipes
    4. *Shakuhachi*
    5. Recorder (soprano, alto, tenor, bass)
B. Reeds
    1. Single reed
        a. Clarinet (soprano, alto, bass, contrabass)
        b. Saxophone (soprano, alto, tenor, baritone)
    2. Double reed
        a. Oboe
        b. English horn
        c. Bassoon
    3. Free reed
        a. Harmonica (mouth harp)
        b. Accordion
C. Pipe organ
D. Brass
    1. Trumpet
        a. Cornet
        b. Flügelhorn
    2. Horn (or French horn)
    3. Trombone (bass trombone)
    4. Euphonium (baritone)
    5. Tuba (sousaphone)

Representative Aerophones

Of all the instrument families, the percussion family has the greatest variety of sound, both in dynamics and sound quality. Basic to percussion is sound that is produced by striking the instrument, whether it is a marimba, timpani, cymbal, or drum. Important in considering percussion instruments are the unique timbres of the many instruments and the unique attack and decay of the sound.

Idiophones

A. Clappers
    1. Claves
    2. Castanets
    3. Cymbals (also a hitter)
B. Shakers
    1. Maracas
    2. Rattles
C. Hitters
    1. Xylophone
    2. Marimba
    3. Vibraphone (vibes)
    4. Steel drums
D. Pluckers
    1. Mbira (*sansa, kalimba*)

Idiophones and Membranophones (Percussion)

Representative Idiophones and Membranophones (Percussion Instruments)

Membranophones

A. Double head
    1. Snare drum
B. Single head
    1. Bongos
    2. Timpani (kettle drums)
    3. Tablā

Electrophones (Electronic Instruments)

With the technological explosion during the last half century, many new instruments and ways to make music have been developed. In the 1950s, the tape recorder became influential in the creation of classical music. Electronic music originally resulted from the taping of sounds from nature and the environment and of sounds of both traditional and nontraditional musical instruments. Music was created by manipulating these taped sounds (for example, changing the direction and speed of the tape and by tape splicing), selecting the new sounds, and organizing them into a piece of music recorded on another tape.

Subsequently, electronically generated sounds (synthesizer) became common, first in classical music, then in rock music and jazz. Now, synthesizer keyboards as well as guitar and drum synthesizers are purchased through music stores as traditional instruments.

Electronic technology includes computer applications, MIDI technology, and sampling. MIDI (Musical Instrument Digital Interface) is the technology that allows an electronic musical instrument to "speak" to a computer, and vice versa. The sampling feature can be found on many small, inexpensive electronic keyboards as well as highly sophisticated, expensive models. One can digitally record and store in memory one or more sounds, and these "samples" are stored in memory to be retrieved as a sound source for later playback on a synthesizer or other electronic instrument. The quantity of sound samples is limited only by the capacity of the computer memory.

Much electronic music today, whether in live or recorded performance, combines electronically produced sounds with those from traditional instruments.

Representative Electrophones

A. Keyboards
    1. Synthesizer
    2. Electronic organ
B. Guitars
C. Drum machine (drum synthesizer)

Descriptions of Representative Instruments

Accordion: A portable, free-reed aerophone with keyboard for melody and buttons for chords. Its wind is supplied by bellows worked by the player's arm that compress and expand the air supplied to the reeds.

Autoharp: A zither that has a series of chord bars that lie across all the strings. Grooves in the bars are placed to allow strings that produce pitches in the chosen chords to vibrate while other strings of nonchord tones are damped to prevent vibration. The autoharp is commonly used in elementary school music programs and in the performance of folk music of the southern mountains.

Banjo: A plucked chordophone of black African origin, with a long guitarlike neck and a circular, tightly stretched parchment of skin or plastic against which the bridge is pressed by the strings.

Baritone: *See* euphonium.

Bass fiddle: *See* double bass.

Bassoon: A double reed tenor or bass instrument made of a wooden tube doubled back on itself. It dates from the seventeenth century. Also, there is a contrabassoon that plays one octave lower than the bassoon.

Bongos: An Afro-Cuban, single-head, membranophone usually played in pairs. The two are of the same height but of different diameters and are joined. Bongos are often played in jazz and rock groups featuring Latin American rhythms.

Cello: *See* violoncello.

Charango: A small guitar from South America. It is made of dried armadillo shell or carved wood and used mainly by the Indians and mestizos in the Andean mountains. Most models have 10 strings tuned in pairs.

Clarinet: A single-reed woodwind instrument dating from the late seventeenth century. The clarinet family consists of the soprano in E♭, soprano in B♭ and A, alto in E♭, bass in B♭, and contrabass in B♭. The soprano B♭ clarinet is common in many parts of the world and is an important melody instrument in western European (and American) bands, symphony orchestras, and chamber music ensembles and jazz groups.

Claves: Idiophones consisting of two cylindrical hardwood sticks that are clapped together. They are usually used in the performance of various Latin rhythms.

Cornet: A trumpetlike instrument that has a bore and bell slightly different than the common trumpet and achieves a more mellow tone quality. In earlier decades of the twentieth century, it was the main melodic high brass instrument in European and American concert bands and American Dixieland groups.

Cymbal: An idiophone of indefinite pitch. It is a round metal plate that can vary in size that is hit with a stick or played in pairs (clapped together: crash cymbals). The high hat and ride cymbals are common in jazz.

Double bass: The bass instrument of the violin family. It is the standard bass instrument of the symphony orchestra (the bass section). At least one is found in many symphonic bands, and it is standard in any traditional jazz combo or big band. In modern jazz and rock, it has largely been replaced by the electric bass or bass guitar. The double bass is often known as the bass, bowed bass, stand-up bass, acoustical bass, bass fiddle, or string bass.

Drum machine: A drum synthesizer used in modern jazz and rock groups. Some groups will carry the traditional drum set and the drum "synth."

Dulcimer: A name applied to certain zither-type instruments. Certain dulcimers are plucked with the fingers. Others are hammered (strings struck with curved mallets).

Electronic organ: *See* organ.

English horn: An alto oboe that looks similar to an oboe but is larger and has a bulb-shaped bell. It has a slightly more mellow sound than the oboe.

Euphonium (baritone): A valved brass instrument that has the same playing range as the trombone.

Fiddle: A generic name for a bowed instrument having a neck. It is the common name for the violin, particularly when used to play folk or country music.

Flügelhorn: Similar to the trumpet but with a bore and bell that gives it a more mellow, sweeter tone. It is a favorite melody instrument among some jazz artists.

Flute: A woodwind instrument generally made of either wood or metal. There are two types of flutes: vertical flute (recorder, panpipes) and transverse flute (the flute in general use today in American bands and orchestras).

Gong: An idiophone in the form of a circular, shallow, metal plate that can vary in size that is hit usually with a soft-headed beater. It is hung vertically, and its tone characteristically swells after the gong is struck.

Guitar: A flat-backed, plucked chordophone of Spanish descent. It is traced from the thirteenth century and is now used worldwide in folk, jazz, popular, and classical styles of music.

Guitarrón: A bass guitar used in Spain and throughout Mexico and Latin America. It is common in modern mariachi groups.

Harmonica: A free-reed aerophone. The reeds are placed in a small rectangular box. Grooves lead from the reeds to openings on one of the long sides of the box into which the player exhales or inhales air. The player changes pitches by moving his or her mouth back and forth along the side of the box.

Harp: A chordophone with ancient heritage. Its strings are placed perpendicular to the soundboard (sound resonator). Generally, they are triangular in shape and are placed on the floor and played vertically. Concert harps have pedals to play chromatically altered tones and all the major and minor keys. Folk harps typically are smaller and do not have these pedals and the tonal flexibility.

Harpsichord: A keyboard instrument characterized by a mechanism whereby the strings are plucked rather than struck as with the piano. It will have one or two manuals and less capacity than the piano for expressive contrasts. It dates to the Renaissance and was a popular baroque keyboard instrument.

Horn: A generic name for a variety of lip-vibrated wind instruments of the trumpet variety, with or without valves. It is also a name for a specific brass instrument whose bore spirals and culminates in a large, flaring bell. This instrument is sometimes known as the French horn.

Kalimba: See mbira.

Kettledrums: See timpani.

Koto: A long zither with 13 strings, each with a movable bridge, traditionally placed horizontally on the floor. It is sometimes considered the national instrument of Japan.

Lute: An ancient plucked or bowed chordophone with a round back and a neck (the guitar family of instruments has flat backs). The tuning pegs in many versions were placed perpendicular to the neck. The lute family includes the Arabic ud, the Japanese *shamisen*, the mandolin, and instruments of the viol and violin families.

Mandolin: A plucked chordophone of the lute family. It dates from the early eighteenth century and is in common use today, mainly in Italy and in the United States. Although it is chiefly used in folk and country music, it occasionally is used in classical compositions.

Maracas: A pair of gourd rattles, most commonly oval gourds usually containing dried seeds or beads. They are originally of South American Indian cultures but are now commonly used in playing Latin American dance rhythms.

Marimba: An idiophone (xylophone) comprised of tone bars under which are gourd or tubular resonators. The bars are hit with sticks (mallets). Its antecedents are instruments from sub-Sarahan Africa.

Mbira (thumb piano, *kalimba, sansa*): An African, plucked idiophone comprised of tuned metal tongues (as are common in music boxes) and sometimes gourd resonator boxes. The ends of the tongues are free to vibrate as they are depressed and released (plucked) by the thumbs of the performer.

Oboe: A double-reed, woodwind instrument whose tone can be described as nasal and piercing. The oboe is often used as a solo instrument in the classical symphony orchestra, modern symphonic bands, and woodwind chamber ensembles.

Organ (pipe organ, electronic organ): The pipe organ is a wind instrument consisting of one or more ranks (sets of pipes) of individual wooden or metal pipes. Each pipe produces a specific tone color at a specific pitch. Each rank is comprised of a set of pipes for each tone quality. An organ usually has from two to four manuals (keyboards). The larger organs will have thousands of separate pipes. The tones are generated from air supplied by a blower supported by action that is dictated by the organist at the keyboard and that directs the air to the appropriate pipes. The various tone colors of the electronic organ are generated by electrical circuitry rather than air pressure. These sounds are similar to those of the pipe organ. In fact, some electronic organs, by means of computer technology, now nearly duplicate pipe organ sounds.

Panpipes: Sets of end-blown flutes of different pitches combined into one instrument. There are no finger holes, since the player changes pitches by blowing air across the end-holes of the different pipes. Panpipes are used in all regions of the world. They often are associated with the Inca civilization of the Andes mountains in Peru and Bolivia.

Piano: A keyboard instrument whose 88 strings are struck by rebounding hammers. Its origin dates back to the early eighteenth century. In the second half of the eighteenth century, the piano replaced the harpsichord as the popular keyboard instrument in Western classical music.

Piccolo: A small, transverse flute. It sounds an octave higher than written and often doubles the flute part an octave higher.

Pipe organ: *See* organ.

Rattles: Any shaken idiophone.

Recorder: An end-blown, vertical flute used from the Middle Ages until the eighteenth century but has seen a resurgence in popularity in modern times. Often, recorders come in sets that consist of descant (soprano), treble (alto), tenor, and bass recorder.

Sanza: *See* mbira.

Saxophone: A single-reed, woodwind instrument made of metal. The family of saxophones includes the soprano in B♭, alto in E♭, tenor in B♭, baritone in E♭, and the less common bass in B♭. The alto and tenor saxophones are the most common and are integral to band instrumentation and to jazz ensembles. They are occasionally used in symphony orchestras.

Shakuhachi: An end-blown Japanese flute usually made of bamboo with five finger holes. With roots in China dating back to the tenth century, it is used today as a solo instrument and as part of various instrumental ensembles, sometimes with koto and *shamisen*.

Shamisen: A three-stringed, long-necked Japanese lute. It is used as part of ensembles, sometimes with koto and perhaps the *shakuhachi*, and is used also to accompany traditional Japanese songs.

Sitar: A large, fretted, long-necked lute. It has from four to seven metal strings, movable frets, and several drone strings. The sitar is the main melody instrument in music of northern India.

Snare drum: A side drum with a set of snares (wires) stretched across the lower head. The tension of these wires can be adjusted to change the quality of sound.

Sousaphone: A type of tuba used in marching bands. It is distinguished by its shape that wraps around the body for ease in carrying and its overhead, widely flaring bell.

Steel drum: A tuned idiophone usually made from an oil drum. Steel drum bands were first popular in the Caribbean, particularly Trinidad, and are now popular in the United States.

String Bass: *See* double bass.

Synthesizer: An electronic instrument capable of generating and processing a wide variety of sounds (drums, keyboard, and guitar).

Tablā: A pair of small, tuned, hand-played drums of north and central India, Pakistan, and Bangladesh. They are used to accompany both vocal and instrumental art, popular, and folk music. They are particularly well known in music of northern India as a frequently intricate accompaniment in rāga performances.

Tamburā: A long-neck, plucked lute of India. It has four wire strings used only for drone accompaniments in both classical and folk styles.

Timpani (kettledrums): A single-headed drum consisting of a large bowl-shaped resonating chamber or shell (usually of copper). The large head can be tightened or loosened to produce different pitches. It is struck with a pair of mallets. A band or orchestra usually uses a pair of timpani of different sizes. Some music calls for four timpani, with the additional ones extending the pitch range higher and lower.

Trombone: A brass aerophone characterized by a telescopic slide with which the player varies the length of the tube, thereby manipulating the pitch. It is a common harmony and melody instrument in the tenor range used in bands, orchestras, brass chamber music, and jazz ensembles of all kinds.

Trumpet: A treble brass instrument played with a cup-shaped mouthpiece. Its brilliant tone makes it an ideal melody instrument in bands, orchestras, chamber music ensembles, and jazz groups. It is found frequently in Mexican and Latin American popular music groups. Various versions of the trumpet, many made from animals' horns, date from ancient times and are found in many cultures. The invention of the valves in 1813 as a means of changing pitch has made it the versatile and popular instrument it is today.

Tuba: The bass instrument of the brass family.

Ukulele: A small guitar originally from Portugal but popularized in America through Hawaiian music.

Vibraphone (vibraharp or "vibes"): A xylophone with metal bars and metal resonator tubes suspended below each bar that help to sustain the tones. An electric motor drives propellers affixed at the top of each resonator tube that produces its characteristic pulsating pitches (vibrato).

Viol: A bowed string instrument with frets usually played vertically on the lap or between the legs. The viol was built in three sizes: treble, tenor, and bass (viol da gamba). It flourished in Europe in the sixteenth and seventeenth centuries and subsequently became one of most popular Renaissance and baroque instruments.

By the middle of the eighteenth century, it was replaced by the more resonant violin family of instruments.

Viola: The alto or tenor member of the violin family. The viola is slightly larger than the violin and creates a slightly more mellow sound.

Violin: The soprano and most prominent member of the violin family. Its versatile, expressive quality is unequaled. The history of the violin dates to the early seventeenth century in Cremona, Italy. It was here that the first great violin makers worked: Niccolo Amati, Antonio Stradivari, and Guiseppe Guarneri. The violin is the main melody instrument of the Western symphony orchestra and of chamber music ensembles such as the string quartet. The violin is also used in folk music (fiddle), jazz (both acoustic and electric versions), and in music of many other cultures.

Violoncello (cello): The tenor or bass instrument of the violin family. Its beautiful, lyrical quality makes it ideally suited to play melody as well as harmonic and bass lines.

Xylophone: A percussion instrument consisting of two or more wooden tone bars of varying lengths to produce varying pitches. The bars are struck with knobbed sticks. Modern versions have the bars laid out similarly to a piano keyboard with each bar having a metal resonator suspended below it. With roots in Asia, the xylophone was introduced in the Americas by Africans.

Zither: A folk instrument, but also a class of chordophones whose strings are stretched between two ends of a flat body, such as a board or a stick. The hammered dulcimer, piano, and harpsichord are board zithers.

Appendix B
Architectural and Audio Acoustics

Attaining proper acoustics in an auditorium, recording studio, or home requires knowledge, skill, and planning. Acoustical characteristics must be designed into such facilities. The size, shape, wall and ceiling material, structure, and type of seating must be consistent with the purpose of the room. Also, different physical characteristics are required depending on the needs—whether it is to be used for speech, chamber music, large performing groups, home listening, or professional recording. Characteristics that acoustical engineers (professional or amateur) can consider include blend, brilliance, clarity, ensemble, fullness, intimacy, liveness, reverberation, and warmth, each of which will be briefly defined, particularly in the context of home listening.

Blend

The sounds of the music blend properly if they are well balanced and are heard at appropriate loudness levels throughout the ensemble (in a studio or concert performance) and throughout the room or hall. The blend of sound refers to the mixing of the sound from all the instruments or voices in the ensemble over all points in the room. In a concert hall having poor blend, an audience member may hear one section or player louder than another in ways that were not intended by the composer or performer; in this case, people in different parts of the hall will hear the sound differently. The simplest technique for achieving proper blend is to use appropriate reflecting structural surfaces surrounding the performance area. The purpose is, in effect, to mix the sound on stage before distributing it to the audience.

Brilliance

The high frequencies are predominant. It is the opposite of warmth and exists if the reverberation time for high frequencies is larger relative to that of the low frequencies.

Clarity

Sounds do not run together; all lines (parts) are heard distinctly. It is the opposite of fullness. This is obtained when the intensity (loudness level) of the reflected sound is low relative to the intensity of the direct sound. Great clarity is required for optimum listening to speech and is particularly important when performing orchestral music. In general, greater clarity is achieved from shorter reverberation times.

Ensemble

Good ensemble playing is determined by the extent to which a performing group plays together with precision. To do so, the musicians must hear each other. To achieve good ensemble playing, reflections must not prolong the sound beyond the duration of the fast notes in the music being performed.

Fullness

A room will have fullness if the intensity of the reflected sound is high relative to the intensity of the direct sound. In general, greater fullness requires longer reverberation time.

Intimacy

Sound has intimacy if the live or recorded sound seems close to the listener. This is a situation easily found in small halls where reflected sound reaches the listeners very quickly. For large halls, intimacy can be enhanced by placing a reflecting canopy above the performers, directing the reflected sound toward their audience. A canopy is sometimes used in large cathedrals above the pulpit to achieve intimacy of the speaker's voice in relation to the congregation. A canopy also forms the basic part of the structure of a band shell, helping to increase the sound level by reflecting the upward sound out toward the audience.

Liveness

The longer the reverberation time, the more live a room is.

Reverberation (Echo)

The length of time a sound will bounce around a room (reverberate) determines the reverberation time. A live room will have long reverberation time, whereas the sound waves in a dead room will be absorbed immediately without time to reverberate. Reverberation time is one of the more important acoustical considerations in room design.

Warmth

A room is considered to have warmth (as opposed to brilliance) when the reverberation time for low frequency sounds is somewhat greater than the reverberation time for high frequencies.

Other Acoustical Factors

In the construction of auditoriums or in designing rooms for home listening, there are several factors that influence the sound:

1. Type of building materials used, whether hard surfaces (reflective) or soft (absorptive).
2. Size and shape of room, whether rectangular with all corners at 90 degrees or having corners at angles other than 90 degrees.
3. Types of rugs, drapes, and furnishings.
4. Quality of audio equipment, especially speakers.
5. Placement of speakers as recommended by the manufacturer.

In most cases, one cannot do much to alter the size or shape of a room without great expense. If the room needs to be deadened, it may be possible to install absorbent tiles or to hang rugs on the walls. If the desire is to retain as much liveness as possible, furnishings can be obtained that offer little absorption of sound. Placement of speakers can be of considerable importance, particularly in listening to stereophonic music or surround sound. The distance between speakers is critical: in larger rooms, the speakers need to be farther apart. An average home listening room, for optimal sound, would require stereo speakers to be placed six to eight feet apart. The listening area should begin some distance back from the speakers. Space is required for sound to spread out evenly. Equalizers can be used to "tune" the sound to fit the room. If certain frequencies are lost due to the construction of the room, they can be boosted by means of a graphic equalizer.

Purchasing a turntable, compact disc (CD) player, tape deck, speaker system, or microphones can be confusing because of the quantity and types of equipment from which to choose and the language used to describe the equipment. A good strategy for understanding such language as *wow* and *flutter, signal-to-noise ratio, impedance, harmonic distortion*, and *frequency response* is to look at specifications (specs) in a high-quality audio store and ask questions of a salesperson. Recommendations, test reports, and specs on the latest equipment can be found in current magazines such as *StereoReview's Sound and Vision, Mix, Stereophile, Electronic Musician*, in selected issues of *Consumer Reports*, and online at www.audioreview.com.

Audio Equipment

Glossary

Absolute Music   Music created for its own sake without extramusical connotation. It is characteristic of such genres as the sonata, symphony, concerto, and string quartet as well as preludes, fugues, études, and other works whose titles depict only form or function. Program music depicts images, moods, stories, characters, and other nonmusical associations. It includes all music with text and many instrumental forms common during the romantic period, including the symphonic poem and some symphonies that were created with programmatic associations.

Accent   A stress or emphasis on a particular tone.

Acculturation   The blending of cultures. The process by which a culture assimilates or adapts to the characteristics and practices of another culture.

Acoustics   The science of sounds and the physical basis of music.

Aerophone   A wind instrument. The sound-producing agent is air set in vibration either within the body of the instrument or outside of the instrument. *See also* Appendix A.

Aesthetics   The study of the emotional and expressive aspects of music.

Airplay   The number of times a popular song is broadcast on radio. Airplay can generate record sales and can contribute to making a song a hit.

Aria   A lyrical song found in operas, cantatas, and oratorios. It may comment on the text presented in a recitative that preceded the aria.

Arrangement   A setting (rescoring) of a piece of music for a genre or ensemble for which it was not originally intended, such as a pop song arranged for big band or an orchestral piece arranged for wind ensemble.

Art music   Music that is formal, sophisticated, urban, and appreciated by an educated elite. It is music derived from a cultivated tradition based largely on notated music. Therefore, it requires a certain amount of musical training to be able to create and perform art music.

Art song   *See miniature.*

Assimilation   The process whereby immigrant groups gradually adopt the characteristics of the host society. It is also the process by which a primitive culture is modified by contact with an advanced culture.

Atonality   The avoidance of tonal centers and tonal relationships in music. This is highly chromatic, dissonant music without traditional, functional chord progressions, modulations, and tuneful melodies. Dissonances stand alone, without the need to resolve to consonances as in traditional music.

Avant-garde   Experimental composers who are in the forefront of musical developments and who are the leaders in the development of new and unconventional musical styles. They experiment with untried techniques, forms, timbres, or concepts in developing new approaches to composition, new aesthetic notions, or a new language for expressing music.

Ballads   Songs with a story having a beginning, middle, and end. The music is strophic and may have many stanzas. A ballad singer is a storyteller.

Ballet   Stage production featuring formal, stylized dance performances with story or unified theme. It has, at times, been part of opera, but also developed popularity as an independent genre in the nineteenth century.

Bar   *See meter.*

Bebop   A combo jazz style that emerged in the 1940s. It is characterized by high energy, virtuoso solo improvisation, complex rhythmic patterns, and more novel and chromatic harmonies than were used in previous styles.

Big band jazz   Music for a large jazz ensemble, usually from 12 to 20 musicians. It is notated music (charts) that may be original compositions but more frequently are arrangements of preexisting songs. Arrangements are scored for the brass section (trumpets and trombones), the sax section, and the rhythm section.

Binary   *See* form.

Black gospel   *See* gospel music.

Bluegrass   A style of country music that combines a return to the rural, folk traditions of hillbilly music and the urban, commercial music that is part of our national, popular culture. The typical bluegrass instrumentation includes the acoustic guitar, fiddle, mandolin, bass fiddle, and banjo—no electric instruments.

Blues   A style of music that has exerted considerable influence on jazz, rhythm and blues, soul, rock, and other forms of recent American popular music. Blues can refer to a three-line poetic stanza, a 12-bar musical structure with a specific chord progression, a scale having the flatted blues notes, or a melancholy, soulful feeling.

Boogie woogie   A piano jazz style popular in the late 1920s and 1930s. It is characterized by a left-hand ostinato figure underlying a rhythmically free and highly syncopated right-hand melodic texture. Most boogie woogie pieces are based on the standard, 12-bar blues chord progression.

Bossa Nova   A popular music of Brazilian origin that is rhythmically related to the Samba but with complex harmonies and improvised jazzlike passages.

Break   A stop of the music in a jazz piece during which a soloist will improvise, usually for two bars. A break will occur at the end of a phrase, providing transition to the next phrase.

Broadside   A song written on one large piece of paper with or without music notation. These songs, which flourished during the eighteenth and nineteenth centuries, described current events and function somewhat as newspapers in communities and regions. Originally written down, many broadsides were eventually passed on by word of mouth, thus becoming part of the oral tradition.

C

Cadence   The ending of a musical phrase.

Cadenza   *See* concerto.

Cantata   An extended solo or choral work that flourished during the baroque era. It was intended for the German Lutheran worship service, although some cantatas have secular texts. Choral cantatas, particularly those by J. S. Bach, include harmonized chorales, polyphonic choruses, arias, recitatives, solo ensembles, and instrumental accompaniment.

Cantus firmus   A term meaning "fixed melody" that denotes a preexisting melody, often a Gregorian chant, which a composer from the Renaissance used as the basis of a polyphonic composition.

Chamber music   Works for solo instruments performing together in small ensembles, such as a string quartet, a woodwind quintet, or a piano trio. Each part is played on one instrument (no doubling). In the classic era, the string quartet (first and second violins, viola, and cello) became the standard chamber music genre. The quartet typically was a four-movement work with a fast-slow-dance-fast pattern, although many exceptions exist to this pattern exist.

Chance music   A compositional technique whereby a composer does not control all the details of a composition, allowing the performer to make creative choices through improvisation or other means of selecting sounds within the structure of the composition. John Cage was a major influence in developing chance music.

Chant   A simple song found in many cultures and traditions. It is a monophonic song without accompaniment, of relatively short duration, of limited melodic range, and with a fluid pulse reflecting the rhythm of the text. Gregorian chants, sung in Latin, are those used in the Liturgy of the Roman Catholic Church. They date from the end of the sixth century A.D., when Pope Gregory was thought to have ordered a collection and classification of chants used throughout the far-flung Roman Church.

Character piece   *See* miniature.

Chart   A weekly record of sales of songs in a variety of categories, such as rock, jazz, rhythm and blues, and country. It is used to measure a song's popularity. The most widely used charts are produced by *Billboard*. Also, the written or printed arrangement of a popular song or a jazz tune for an ensemble, such as a rock group, studio orchestra, or a jazz band.

Chorale   Originally a hymn tune of the German Lutheran Church sung by the congregation in unison and in the German (rather than Latin) language. It was an outgrowth of the Reformation and the rise of the Protestant Church. Chorale tunes, especially during the baroque era, were used as the basis for other compositions: they were harmonized in four-part settings for singing by choirs and congregations; they were used as the basis of sacred polyphonic compositions for trained choirs; and they formed the basis of organ pieces known as chorale preludes.

Chord   A meaningful (as opposed to random) combination of three or more tones. The primary chords in western European harmonic practice are the tonic (I chord), the subdominant (IV chord), and dominant (V chord).

Chordophone   A stringed instrument. The sound-producing agent is a stretched string that is plucked or bowed. *See* Appendix B.

Chromatic   Proceeding by half steps, using sharps or flats. Notes outside of a standard major or minor scale. A melody is chromatic if many of its pitches are not derived from the standard major or minor scale.

Combo jazz   A small jazz group, usually from three to six musicians.

Comping   The syncopated chords and melodic figures played by a jazz pianist while accompanying a solo improvisation, adding rhythmic punctuation and vitality.

Concerto   A three-movement work for solo instrument and orchestra that emerged during the baroque period and has been a common instrumental genre ever since. The concerto grosso was an important genre of this period that featured a small group of soloists with orchestra. The arrangement of the movements is fast-slow-fast. Many concertos since the baroque era include a cadenza, an unaccompanied passage in free rhythm in which the soloist displays his or her greatest virtuosity.

Conjunct   *See* melody.

Consonance   A relatively stable, comfortable sound that seems to be at rest as compared with a dissonant, restless sound.

Consort   A group of like instruments, such as soprano, alto, tenor, and bass recorders, that provide a homogenous sound.

Context   The social, economic, and political circumstances prevalent in a society that may influence the nature of a creative work.

Continuo   A technique for providing a harmonic basis in the new homophonic music of the baroque period. It was a style of accompaniment for a singer or one or two solo instruments. The bass line provided the underlying structure for the harmonies, and it usually was played on a cello. The chords were not completely notated and were improvised on a keyboard instrument, usually a harpsichord. The performer determined what chords to play from the bass line and the figured bass. The figures were numbers below certain notes of the bass line that served as a musical shorthand to indicate the harmonies.

Contrast   A departure from that which has been presented. A phrase or section that is different from that which preceded it. To achieve contrast, the music will have different tonality, rhythm, melody, tempo, dynamic level, articulation, or mood.

Cool   An outgrowth of and reaction to the bebop style. Cool jazz arrangers and performers strived to maintain the musical qualities of bebop while making their music more accessible to their audience. They adopted many elements from classical music, including the use of orchestral instruments not commonly used in jazz, such as the flute, oboe, and French horn.

Counterpoint   The compositional technique of creating polyphonic texture. It is frequently used as a synonym for polyphony. Imitative counterpoint is the creation of two or more independent melodic lines, with each entrance beginning with the same melodic shape at the same or a different pitch level.

Culture   A group of people, a society, characterized by the totality of its arts, beliefs, customs, institutions, and all other products of work and thought.

Dance suite   A multimovement work for keyboard or orchestra. It includes contrasting, stylized dances popular in the baroque period. The principal ones are the allemande, courante, sarabande, and gigue.

Diatonic   The eight tones of a standard major or minor scale. A melody is diatonic if most of its pitches are derived from these eight tones.

Disjunct   *See* melody.

Dissonance   An active, unstable sound. *See* consonance.

Dixieland   The first popular jazz style. It was characterized by group improvisation (clarinet, trumpet, and trombone) supported by a steady ragtime rhythm.

Dominant   A chord built on the fifth degree of the major or minor scale.

Duple meter   *See* meter.

Duration   The length of time a pitch sounds. *See* rhythm.

Dynamics   The level of loudness. *See* loudness.

Electrophone   Electronic instruments. The tone is produced, modified, or amplified by electronic circuits. *See also* Appendix A.

Ethnic   Pertaining to a group of people recognized as a class on the basis of certain distinctive characteristics, not part of mainstream, such as their religion, language, ancestry, culture, or national origin.

Ethnomusicologist   *See* Ethnomusicology.

Ethnomusicology   A study of music in culture, considering the context of music in a society, music as it relates to human behavior, and the general attitudes of a people about their music. Ethnomusicologists undertake the research of music in a culture and teach others about that culture's music.

F

Fasola System   A system in which the initial letters of four syllables—fa, sol, la, and mi—are placed on the staff, each representing a different pitch. The fasola system was used in nineteenth-century America to aid in the immediate recognition of scale degrees and to help people read musical notation.

Fiddle tunes   A song from oral tradition used to accompany country dances. The song has a shape and character more appropriate for playing on the fiddle than for singing. Fiddle tunes are frequently played by string bands, bluegrass groups, or solo fiddlers.

Field recording   A scholarly or professional recording of folk or traditional music made in the environment where the performers typically make music, rather than in a professional recording studio.

Figured bass   *See continuo.*

Fill   Melodic movement and embellishment in jazz while the main melody sustains a tone, such as at the end of a pattern or a phrase.

Folk music   Usually of unknown origin and enjoyed by the general population, it is informal, aesthetically and musically unsophisticated music that communicates directly and obviously to large groups within a culture or a subculture, such as a nation or an ethnic minority. It is usually preserved and transmitted by memory (oral tradition).

Follies   *See vaudeville.*

Form   The shape or structure of a piece of music. Form is determined primarily by patterns of contrast and repetition. A two-part form is binary (a b)—no repetition. A three-part form is ternary (a b a)—the first theme is followed by a contrasting section, after which the first phrase or section is repeated. A 32-bar song form is a a b a—four phrases with the third in contrast to the first two phrases, after which the first phrase is again repeated. Other forms include the 12-bar blues, the verse-chorus or verse-refrain forms, sonata form, minuet and trio, theme and variations, and rondo.

Forward energy   The tendency in some music to have momentum, that is, to move from one point to the next, such as from the beginning of a phrase to its conclusion.

Free jazz   A style that is almost pure improvisation without adherence to predetermined chord structures, meter, or melodic motives. Musicians interact musically with each other, build on what others in the group are doing, and are free to create according to their musical instincts.

Frequency   The rate of speed of sound waves.

Fugueing tune   *See psalm singing.*

Fugue   An imitative polyphonic composition that originated as a keyboard genre during the baroque period. It is, however, a compositional technique used during and since the baroque in both choral and instrumental music. A fugue is built on a single theme whose entrances appear imitatively in several voices (melodic lines at different pitch levels), usually three or four, and then are developed in intricate contrapuntal interplay.

Funk   A distinctive style using polyrhythms, syncopated bass lines, and short vocal phrases.

Fusion   A synthesis of elements of jazz and rock. A style of modern jazz.

G

Gagaku   An instrumental music genre of the imperial courts of ancient Japan. It is the oldest documented orchestral music in the world.

Gamelan   An Indonesian orchestra, particularly from the islands of Bali and Java, that is comprised of various sized drums, metal xylophones, and gongs. Gamelan music has a long history and has influenced composers of Western classical music as well as jazz and rock performers.

Genre   A category of music, such as a symphony, hymn, ballad, march, or opera.

Global perspective   A worldwide point of view, including an awareness of and respect for the life-styles, traditions, values, and arts of nations and cultures.

Gospel music   Protestant religious music usually associated more with rural, folk roots than with urban, European traditions. American gospel music has evolved in such a way that distinct stylistic differences exist between the gospel music of white and black Americans. We now refer to the black gospel and the white gospel styles. White gospel includes camp meeting songs, hymns and songs for revival services, and music from the pentecostal tradition.

Gregorian chant   *See chant.*

H

Hard Bop   The bebop style of the 1950s and 1960s. Hard bop retained the intensity, complexity, harmonic imagination, and speed of the bebop of Charlie Parker and Dizzy Gillespie. Counted among this second generation of bebop musicians are John Coltrane, Sonny Rollins, Clifford Brown, Ornette Coleman, and Cannonball Adderly. Some musicians and scholars use "hard bop" to describe any of the jazz styles that followed bebop, including the funky, gospel jazz of Horace Silver, Art Blakey, and Herbie

Hancock, and the cool jazz of Miles Davis, Gerry Mulligan, and the Modern Jazz Quartet. None of these musicians, however, played in only one style.

Harmony   Pitches heard simultaneously in ways that produce chords and chord progressions.

Hillbilly   A style of popular song derived from the rural, southern folk tradition and from sentimental songs of the late nineteenth century. It represents a merging of rural and urban influences and a regional, ethnic music made popular nationally and successful commercially.

Homophony   *See* texture.

Homorhythmic   Multiple horizontal lines moving with the same rhythm in all parts.

Hymnody   The hymns of a time, place, or church.

Idiophone   Percussion instruments that are struck, shaken, plucked, or rubbed. *See also* Appendix B.

Impressionism   A style of music, exemplified in the works of Debussy, that avoids explicit statement and literal description, but instead emphasizes suggestion and atmosphere, evokes moods, and conveys impressions of images and feelings.

Improvisation   The process of simultaneously composing and performing music.

Instability   *See* tension.

Intensity   The energy that generates the amplitude or height of sound waves.

Interval   The difference in pitch between two musical tones.

Jam session   Where jazz musicians gather, usually "after hours," to improvise and enjoy making music. Because the musicians are not obligated to an employer or a paying audience, they have the freedom to explore and share their musical ideas.

Kabuki   A Japanese theatre style with music that is considered a genre of traditional Japanese music. Important components of Kabuki music are the narrative *gidayu* songs with *shamisen* accompaniment, and the *nagauta* ensemble of drums, a flute, several *shamisens*, and singers. The *nagauta* became an important concert genre, independent of Kabuki theatre.

Lead   The soloist in a jazz arrangement or performance.

Lead sheet   A notated melody with chord symbols, usually of a popular song or jazz tune, on which a musical performance is based. A means of structuring a performance in lieu of notating all parts for the entire piece.

Libretto   The words to an opera or other musical stage production. The person who writes the story is the librettist.

Lied (plural: lieder)   *See* miniature.

Lining out   A style of hymn singing whereby a minister or song leader sings one line at a time followed by the congregation singing it back, usually by adding its own individual or collective embellishments and often at a much slower tempo. Lining out is derived from rural, folk traditions and was brought to the United States from the British Isles.

Loudness   The degree of intensity or energy producing a sound. The loudness or softness of a tone.

Lyrics   The words to a popular song. The person who writes the lyrics is a lyricist.

Madrigal   A Renaissance secular contrapuntal work for several voices that originated in Italy and later flourished in England.

Mainstream   The prevailing characteristics of a society.

Mariachi   A type of popular Mexican folk music ensemble that includes a harp, violins, various sizes of guitars, and sometimes trumpets.

Mass   The Roman Catholic worship service. It may be a High Mass or a Low Mass. The High Mass is composed of the Proper and the Ordinary. The Proper varies from Sunday to Sunday throughout the church year. The Ordinary remains the same and is comprised of the Kyrie, Gloria, Credo, Sanctus and Benedictus, and Agnus Dei. Much choral literature has been derived from polyphonic settings of various parts of the Ordinary.

Measure   *See* meter.

Melisma   A setting of a text to music wherein one syllable of text is given a series of notes of music. A syllabic setting is one in which one syllable of text is given one note of music.

Melody   A succession of musical tones usually of varying pitch and rhythm that has identifiable shape and meaning. A melody may be characterized by its smooth, conjunct shape that moves mostly stepwise or its disjunct, angular shape resulting from frequent use of wide intervals (skips). It may be comprised of a wide or a narrow range of pitches.

Membranophone   A percussion instrument whose sound is produced by the vibration of a stretched membrane, either skin or plastic. *See also* Appendix B.

Mestizo   Natives of Mexico and Latin America having mixed Indian and Spanish blood.

Meter   The organization of rhythm into patterns of strong and weak beats. A pattern in which alternate beats are stressed (strong-weak-strong-weak) is duple meter. A pattern in which the first of every three beats is stressed (strong-weak-weak-strong-weak-weak) is triple meter. Each pattern comprises a bar (a measure in notated music). Each strong beat is the downbeat of the bar. Groups of patterns can comprise a phrase (an eight-bar phrase). Combinations of duple and triple (shifting strong beats) are mixed meter. Music is nonmetric if no regular pattern can be perceived.

MIDI (Musical Instrument Digital Interface)   MIDI is a means for providing electronic communication between synthesizers and computers or other synthesizers. It enables sounds to be stored in memory until needed.

Miniature   A small-scale composition that became popular in the romantic era, perhaps as an alternative to the massive size and sounds of the symphony orchestra. It includes the art song (a solo song with piano accompaniment) and the character piece (a one-movement work for solo piano). The art song (commonly known by the German word, *lied*, or its plural, *lieder*) is exemplified by the songs of Schubert that he set to German poetry. The character piece is exemplified by the works of Chopin, such as his impromptus, nocturnes, mazurkas, études, polonaises, and preludes.

Minimalism   A style of composition whose creator attempts to achieve the greatest effect from the least amount of material. It is typically based on many repetitions of simple patterns, creating slow, subtle changes in rhythm, chord movement, or other musical elements. Phillip Glass, a contemporary American composer, has been considered the leading exponent of minimalist music.

Minstrel Show   A variety show, popular in the nineteenth century, that included songs, dances, and comical skits. Lively, syncopated minstrel songs formed the nucleus of the minstrel show. A product of the merging of rural American folk traditions with urban, composed music, the minstrel song can be considered the first distinctively American musical \ genre.

Minuet and trio   A stately dance in triple meter in a b a form. It is found most often as the third movement of a

symphony, sonata, or string quartet. A scherzo and trio form is similar, but it has a faster tempo and increased rhythmic energy. The form and function are the same as the minuet and trio.

Mixed meter   *See* meter.

Modulation   To change from one tonality to another, frequently by harmonic progression.

Monophony   *See* texture.

Motet   A sacred, polyphonic composition with a nonliturgical text. It flourished during the Renaissance and was sung without accompaniment (a cappella) in Latin by trained choirs, typically in four or five parts. Polychoral motets were written for multiple choirs or choirs divided into two or three distinct groups performing singly (in alternation) and jointly in the full ensemble.

Motive   A short melodic pattern or phrase that is used for further development and sometimes as the basis of a section of music or a complete composition.

Motown sound   A style of black popular music derived more from black gospel than blues or jazz traditions. It featured a studio-controlled sound (Motown Records) designed to make black music widely popular and profitable.

Musique concrète   The compositional technique of manipulating tape-recorded sounds of existing natural resources. The sounds of recorded instruments, voices, or other sound sources are altered by changing tape speed or direction and by cutting and splicing the tape. These altered sounds, perhaps combined with original sounds, serve as the sound source for an electronic music composition. Edgar Varèse pioneered *musique concrète*, which predated electronically generated or synthesized sounds.

Nagauta   An ensemble that provides the basic accompaniment on stage in Kabuki theatre, a highly stylized Japanese form of music drama. The ensemble includes perhaps a dozen musicians, including three drums, a flute, several *shamisen* players, and singers.

Nashville sound   The sound of hillbilly music produced by sophisticated recording techniques and arrangements controlled by the recording studios to assure the popularity and commercial success of their songs. It minimized the country twang of the singers, reduced the emphasis on fiddle and steel guitar, and included background singers.

Nationalism   Concert art music that reflects national or regional rather than universal characteristics. The music may describe something derived from the folk or popular traditions of a nation; its history, tales, or legends; its cultural characteristics; or a place that is important to the nation or region. *Americanist music* or *American nationalism* refers to composers who sought to develop a distinctively American musical style. They frequently would incorporate familiar patriotic, folk, or religious tunes, or at least fragments of these tunes, in their classical compositions.

Neoclassicism   A style of modern composition that is based on established forms and structures of the past and particularly on the aesthetics and musical values of the classic era.

Nonmetric   See meter.

Notation   The use of written or printed symbols to represent musical sounds. The notated tradition provides for the preservation and dissemination of music by means of written or printed music, rather than by memory as in the oral tradition.

Octave   See interval.

Opera   A dramatic stage production that involves soloists who sing arias and recitatives, solo ensembles, choruses, dancing, dramatic action, costumes, staging, and orchestral accompaniment. It began at the beginning of the baroque era and evolved into a genre that continues in popularity throughout the Western world, particularly in Italy.

Oral tradition   Music learned and passed down by word of mouth as opposed to that which is conveyed in writing.

Oratorio   An extended, sacred choral work intended for concert performance. It emerged during the baroque era and has been a common genre since. It is of large proportions, lengthy (many lasting up to three hours), and dramatic in nature, sometimes including the character of a narrator as a soloist. Polyphonic choruses, arias, recitatives, solo ensembles, and orchestral accompaniment are common components of oratorios.

Ostinato   A rhythmic and/or melodic pattern repeated many times.

Overture   A festive opening to an opera or other musical stage production. It sets the tone, sometimes identifies principal themes and characters, and prepares an audience for the opening scene. Overtures have become popular concert pieces, sometimes achieving popularity and subsequent performances where the stage production did not. Because of this popularity, many composers have composed overtures as independent concert pieces. In the baroque era, the French overture was a popular instrumental genre, and in the romantic period, the concert overture assumed even greater popularity.

Patterns   Groupings of notes having an identifiable character that, when used repeatedly, help to give form and style to a musical work.

Pentatonic scale   A five-tone scale that serves as the basis of much music throughout the world.

Perceptive listening   Listening to music attentively and analytically in an attempt to understand the musical processes and structure that give the music its characteristic qualities.

Phrase   A section of music with a recognizable beginning and ending. A complete musical thought.

Pitch   The highness or lowness of a tone produced by a single frequency. Clusters of frequencies produce sounds perceived as registers: high, middle, or low. A melody will have a range of pitches: the lowest pitch to the highest.

Polychoral motets   See motet.

Polyphony   See texture.

Program music   See absolute music.

Psalm singing   Rhymed, metrical settings of the psalms to hymn tunes suitable for congregational singing. Psalm singing was prevalent in early America. Psalters were the hymn books in which the settings were published with words only or with hymn tunes. A fuging tune was a form of psalm singing popular throughout the eighteenth century. A typical fuging tune was a four-part hymn with a short middle, fugal section where each voice enters at a different time.

Psalter   See Psalm singing.

Pulse   The recurring beat of the music.

Raga   The basic means by which the melodic or pitch aspects of the classical music of India are determined. Ragas convey not only melodic shape but mood and aesthetic character, and they provide the basis for extended improvisations. The moods they represent usually are related to temporal elements, such as seasons of the year or times of day (morning or evening ragas).

Ragtime   A style of music first popular in the first two decades of the twentieth century. It is characterized by a strongly pulsated, nonsyncopated bass line that supports a highly syncopated right-hand melody. Ragtime remains popular today.

Range   See pitch.

Rap   A style of black popular music that, in the 1980s, emerged from the inner city to become mainstream—an ethnic style becoming nationally popular. Rhythm is highly repetitive, including the poetry which is recited in a highly rhythmic manner. Electronic keyboards, sampled sounds and rhythms, drum machines, and prerecorded tracks are common in rap records.

Recitative   A vocal solo in opera, cantatas, and oratorios that declaims the text in a sung-speech manner, in free rhythm with minimal accompaniment, so that all listeners can understand the words. It frequently introduces an aria.

Reggae   A synthesis of rock, rhythm and blues, and Latin American and African rhythms. Reggae originated in the poor sections of Jamaican cities and has become an internationally popular music genre. Many of the songs reflect black nationalism and social reform and are rooted in Rastafarianism and its spiritual leader, Haille Selassie, late emperor of Ethiopia. The original superstar of reggae is Bob Marley.

Register   See pitch.

Repetition   A return to previously stated material. A pattern, phrase, or section that is presented again either exactly or modified but retaining basic characteristics.

Resolution   See tension.

Revues   See vaudeville.

Rhythm   The organization of time in music, creating patterns of long and short durations of pitches to achieve desired degrees of rhythmic energy—the rhythmic impulse.

Rhythm and blues (R&B)   A style of black popular music that originally featured a boogie-woogie-style piano accompaniment in blues form, a blues singer, and electric guitar. Later, R&B symbolized any blues-based black popular music.

Riff   Short, syncopated patterns usually written for specific groups of instruments in a big band jazz arrangement. Riffs provide punctuated background material while another section or soloist is playing the melody or improvising. Occasionally an entire chorus will be comprised of riffs without a recognizable melody.

Rock and Roll   An underground, antiestablishment, and protest music that emerged in the 1950s and evolved into a phenomenally successful commercial product. It was derived primarily from a merging of black and white traditions (rhythm and blues and hillbilly) and was a music that appealed mostly to teenagers for both listening and dancing. Influenced by the Beatles, Rolling Stones, Pink Floyd, and other British groups, rock and roll assumed a new character (now known as rock) that featured advanced electronic technology, sophisticated arrangements, and extreme visual impact and on-stage behavior. Rock transformed American popular music and created the study of popular culture.

Rockabilly   The form of popular music in the 1950s that resulted from the influence of hillbilly singers on the new rock and roll music.

Rondo   Based on two or more contrasting theme areas, each followed by a return of the opening theme. Common forms of the rondo may be depicted as a b a c a or a b a c a b a. It is commonly used as the spirited final movement of a classic era sonata, symphony, or string quartet.

S

Salon music   A type of piano music popular throughout the Western Hemisphere during the nineteenth century. Reflecting European practices, salon music was comprised of short, simple pieces published as sheet music. Often it was created in the style of marches or dances, such as the tango, habanera, conga, polka, bolero, or waltz.

Salsa   A popular music of Latin American origin that has absorbed characteristics of rhythm and blues, jazz, and rock.

Sampler   Using MIDI technology, samples of sounds can be recorded and stored in memory to be recalled and performed. The sampled sound is expanded for performance to include the entire range of the keyboard.

Scale   An ascending or descending series of tones organized according to a specified pattern of intervals.

Scat singing   Improvised jazz singing using a variety of vocal sounds rather than lyrics. Its purpose is to improvise a vocal solo line in the manner of a lead instrumentalist.

Score   A printed version of a piece of music. Often refers to the version used by a conductor that depicts the music to be played by all performers—the full score.

Sections   See big band jazz.

Sequence   A melodic pattern repeated several times either a step lower or a step higher than the preceding statement.

Serial composition (12-tone technique)   A set of nonrepeated pitches—a tone row—used as the basis for organizing the vertical and horizontal arrangement of pitches throughout a composition. A system created and refined by Schoenberg, rows originally were comprised of all twelve tones of the chromatic scale. Serialism was created as an alternative to the major-minor tonal system, and it was a means for organizing the chaotic chromaticism prevalent in late nineteenth-century German romantic music and early twentieth-century atonal music. An extension of the 12-tone technique includes the serialization of note values, timbres, or dynamics. Music in which all these aspects are serialized, including pitch, is known as *totally controlled music*.

Shape-note system   An aid in learning to read music

popular in nineteenth-century America. Each pitch of a hymn tune was represented on the staff by a note whose head had a distinctive shape. Each shape represented a specific pitch of the scale.

Singing schools   Established to introduce and teach singing from musical notation. Their primary purpose was to improve the state of hymn singing in America, that is, to elevate the rural, folk-based hymn derived from oral tradition to the urban, European, notation-based hymn sung in a refined style.

Sonata   Since the classic era, a multimovement work for piano or for a solo instrument with piano. The typical order of movements is fast, slow, dance, fast. In the baroque period, the sonata was a multimovement work written for a solo instrument and continuo, and the trio sonata was written for two solo instruments and continuo.

Sonata form   A structure that composers from the classic era and since have commonly used for the first movement of a sonata, symphony, concerto, or string quartet (or other similar chamber music work). It includes three main sections: the exposition, development, and recapitulation and often begins with an introduction and ends with a coda. The exposition has two theme areas in contrasting keys. The development is based on material from the exposition. The recapitulation is a return to previous material stated in the exposition.

Song form   A 32-bar a a b a chorus (verse). *See also* form.

Soul   An extension of rhythm and blues that has come to symbolize any popular music performed by blacks for black audiences. It combines elements of R & B, jazz, and black gospel.

Sound source   Any elastic substance capable of generating sound waves that can be perceived as music, such as any conventional band or orchestral instrument, any instrument identified in Appendix B, or any material in the environment used to generate sounds to be incorporated in a piece of music. This material may include pots and pans; taped sounds of water, fire, birds, or whales; or things that people become aware of in a classroom that can be used in an original piece of music.

Spiritual   A religious song usually of a deeply emotional character that was developed especially among African Americans in the Southern United States.

Stability   *See* tension.

Standard   A song that has sustained popularity through decades and generations, transcending changing styles and tastes.

Stride   Originally a solo piano style growing out of ragtime. Its most predominant characteristic is the strongly pulsated, "boom-chick," left-hand rhythmic and harmonic foundation over which, in the right hand, is usually a highly syncopated dazzling display of improvisation with fast runs

and arpeggios. Fats Waller is well known for his stride style. Later pianists such as Art Tatum were rooted in the stride style but incorporated a more advanced harmonic vocabulary and, with both hands, covered the entire range of the piano with their dazzling displays.

Strophic   A musical structure in which the same music is used for each stanza of a ballad, song, or hymn.

Structure   The way in which parts are arranged to form a whole. The form of a piece of music.

Style   External characteristics of music developed through the creative process that distinguish one piece from another, characteristics that are determined by the composer's use of musical elements, formal design, and emotional expression.

Subdominant   A chord built on the fourth degree of a major or minor scale.

Swing   A manner of performance that, in part, separates jazz from other styles of music. It is a manner that generates heightened energy and rhythmic vitality.

Syllabic setting   *See* melisma.

Symphonic poem   A programmatic, one-movement work for symphony orchestra with contrasting moods. It became popular during the romantic period.

Symphony   A multimovement work for symphony orchestra. The typical order of movements is fast-slow-dance-fast. This pattern was standard in the classic period but less adhered to in the romantic and modern eras.

Syncopation   The occurrence of accents in unexpected places, usually on weak beats or on weak parts of beats.

12-bar blues   A musical phrase of 12 bars, usually divided into three 4-bar segments using a specific set of chord progressions. Some blues melodies have 8 or 16 bars.

12-tone technique   *See* serial composition (12-tone technique).

Tāla   The basic means for organizing the durational aspects—the rhythm and meter—of the classical music of India. They involve cycles of counts with regular or irregular subdivisions. For example, a 16-count cycle may be subdivided 4 + 4 + 4 + 4, or a 14-count cycle may be subdivided 5 + 2 + 3 + 4.

Tempo   The rate of speed at which music is performed.

Tension   A perception of instability in traditional Western music that suggests the need for release of tension or resolution. It is often marked by increased harmonic or rhythmic complexity, dissonance, modulation away from the tonic, or a rise in pitch or dynamic level. A lessening of complexity or loudness, a lowering of pitch, a decrease in complexity, and a return to consonance or tonic can create stability, resolution, or release of tension.

Ternary   *See* form.

Tex-Mex   A style of music originating in Southern Texas.

Texture   The density of sound. The number of simultaneously sounding lines. Music can have a full, thick texture or a thin, transparent texture. Also, the manner in which the horizontal pitch sequences are organized determines musical texture. A single line melody with no accompaniment or other horizontal or vertical sounds has a monophonic texture; two or more independent, simultaneously sounding melodies having equal emphasis have a polyphonic texture; and a melody that is dominant with other lines supporting the main melody has a homophonic texture.

Theme and variations   An instrumental form based on a stated theme followed by a series of variations on that theme.

Timbre   The characteristic quality of the sound of a voice or instrument.

Tin Pan Alley   A period of popular song writing that began in the 1890s and whose most productive years were in the 1920s and 1930s. Many of America's most beloved songs—the standards—are part of the Tin Pan Alley tradition. Also, Tin Pan Alley symbolized that part of the music industry devoted to the sale of popular songs. The name is derived from the street in New York City where virtually every publisher of popular music was located in the early part of the twentieth century.

Tonality   The gravitational pull of the music toward a tonal center. The key of the music.

Tone clusters   Three or more adjacent tones sounding simultaneously.

Tone painting   A technique common in the baroque period of conveying in the music the moods, emotions, images, and meanings suggested by a text, that is, to mirror the text as literally as possible.

Tone quality   *See* timbre.

Tonic   The first and most important note of the major or minor scale. The tonal center of a piece of music.

Totally controlled music   *See* serial composition (12-tone technique).

Trio sonata   *See* sonata.

Triple meter   *See* meter.

Unity   Music that does not ramble, is cohesive, and has variety and contrast along with repetition by returning to previously stated material.

Variety   *See* unity.

Vaudeville   A variety show that was comprised of a sequence of unrelated acts by singers, dancers, comedians, jugglers, child performers, trained animals, and actors. It replaced the minstrel show as America's most popular stage show. New York City was the center of vaudeville, with the more sophisticated shows produced on Broadway. These shows were variously known as revues, vanities, scandals, and follies, of which the most famous were the Ziegfeld Follies produced from 1907 through 1932.

Vernacular   The most familiar and most used language of the people of a nation, region, or a cultural group. Vernacular music is the common musical language of a people.

Verse-chorus   A form in which there are different texts to each verse and a return to the chorus after each verse. *See also* form.

Vibrato   An oscillating variation of pitch that enhances a tone, providing a richness and warmth, particularly to sustained pitches or a slow, lyrical melody.

Vocables   Words in native-American songs having no meaning and intended only as vocal sounds.

Walking bass   A jazz bass line played on each beat, frequently with some embellishment and emphasizing the main tones of the underlying chord structure.

Western swing   A style of country music that became popular as the popularity of hillbilly music moved westward. It features a larger instrumental ensemble that includes saxes, brass, and a standard jazz rhythm section.

White gospel   *See* gospel music.

𝒵

Zydeco   The popular dance and entertainment music of the black Americans living in southwestern Louisiana. Their songs, often sung in a French dialect, combine the Cajun music and the blues. Common instruments include the button accordion and rub board (washboard) in addition to electric guitar, bass, and drums. It has become nationally popular from appearances in the 1970s and 1980s by zydeco artists at folk and blues festivals nationally. The original superstar of zydeco is Clifton Chenier.

Bibliography

American Music—General

Crawford, Richard. *The American Musical Landscape*. Berkeley: University of California Press, 1993.

Ferris, Jean. *America's Musical Landscape*. New York: McGraw-Hill, 2002.

Hamm, Charles. *Music in the New World*. New York: Norton, 1983.

Heintze, James R. (ed.). *Perspectives on American Music since 1950*. New York: Garland, 1999.

Hitchcock, H. Wiley, and Stanley Sadie (eds.). *The New Grove Dictionary of American Music* (4 vols.). New York: Grove's Dictionaries of Music, 1986.

Kingman, Daniel. *American Music: A Panorama*. New York: Schirmer Books, 1998.

Southern, Eileen. *The Music of Black Americans: A History*. New York: Norton, 1997.

Stewart, Earl L. *African American Music: An Introduction*. London: Prentice Hall International, 1998.

American Vernacular Music (chapters 4–7)

Boyer, Horace Clarence. *How Sweet the Sound: The Golden Age of Gospel*. Washington, DC: Elliott and Clark Publishers, 2000.

Campbell, Michael. *. . . and the Beat Goes On*. New York: Schirmer Books, 1996.

Cantwell, Robert. *When We Were Good: The Folk Revival*. Cambridge, MA: Harvard University Press, 1996.

Cusic, Don. *The Sound of Light: A History of Gospel Music*. Bowling Green, OH: Bowling Green State University Popular Press, 1990.

Filene, Benjamin. *Romancing the Folk: Public Memory and American Roots Music*. Chapel Hill, NC: University of North Carolina Press, 2000.

Garofalo, Reebee. *Rockin' the Boat: Mass Music and Mass Movements*. Boston: Allyn and Bacon, 1997.

George, Nelson. *Hop Hop America*. New York: Viking, 1998.

Harris, Craig. *The New Folk Music*. Crown Point, IN: White Cliffs Media, 1991 (Distributed by Talman Co.).

Kernfield, Barry (ed.). *The New Grove Dictionary of Jazz* (2 vols.). New York: Grove's Dictionaries of Music, 1988.

Lewis, George H. *All That Glitters: Country Music in America*. Bowling Green, OH: Bowling Green State University Popular Press, 1993.

Lornell, Kip. *Introducing American Folk Music*. New York: McGraw-Hill, 2002.

Neal, Mark Anthony. *What the Music Said: Black Popular Music and Black Popular Culture*. New York: Routledge, 1999.

Nicholson, Stuart. *Jazz Rock: A History*. New York: Schirmer Books, 1998.

O'Meally, Robert G. *The Jazz Cadence of American Culture*. New York: Columbia University Press, 1998.

Oliver, Paul. *The Story of the Blues*. Boston: Northeastern University Press, 1998.

Peretti, Burton W. *Jazz in American Culture*. Chicago: Ivan R. Dee, 1997.

Porter, Lewis. *Jazz: A Century of Change: Readings and New Essays*. London: Prentice Hall International, 1997.

Reagon, Bernice Johnson. *We'll Understand It Better By and By: Pioneering African-American Composers*. Washington, DC: Smithsonian Institution Press, 1993.

Robinette, Richard, and Thomas Pasqua. *Historical Perspectives in Popular Music: A Historical Outline.* Dubuque, IA: Kendall/Hunt, 1993.

Roberts, John Storm. *Latin Jazz: The First of the Fusion, 1880s to Today.* New York: Schirmer Books, 1999.

Van der Merwe, Peter. *Origins of the Popular Style: The Antecedents of Twentieth-Century Popular Music.* New York: Oxford University Press, 1989.

World Music (chapters 8–9)

Bender, Wolfgang. *Sweet Mother: Modern African Music.* Chicago: University of Chicago Press, 1991.

Broughton, Simon, et al. (eds.). *World Music: The Rough Guide.* London: Rough Guides, 1999.

Ewens, Graeme. *Africa O-Ye! A Celebration of African Music.* New York: Da Capo Press, 1992.

Garland Encyclopedia of World Music (9 vols.). New York: Garland, 1998.

Lornell, Kip, and Anne K. Rasmussen. *Musics of Multicultural America.* New York: Schirmer Books, 1997.

Malm, William P. *Music Cultures of the Pacific, the Near East, and Asia.* Englewood Cliffs, NJ: Prentice Hall, 1996.

Manuel, Peter. *Cassette Culture.* Chicago: University of Chicago Press, 1993.

Manuel, Peter. *Popular Musics of the Non-Western Worlds.* New York: Oxford University Press, 1990.

Manuel, Peter, et al. *Caribbean Currents: Caribbean Music from Rumba to Reggae.* Philadelphia: Temple University Press, 1995.

Roberts, John Storm. *Black Music of Two Worlds: African, Caribbean, Latin, and African-American Traditions.* New York: Schirmer Books, 1998.

Roberts, John Storm. *The Latin Tinge: The Impact of Latin American Music on the United States.* New York: Oxford University Press, 1999.

Schechter, John M. (ed.). *Music in Latin American Culture: Regional Traditions.* New York: Schirmer Books, 1999.

Stewart, Gary. *Breakout: Profiles in African Rhythm.* Chicago: University of Chicago Press, 1992.

Taylor, Timothy D. *Global Pop: World Music, World Markets.* New York: Routledge, 1997.

Titon, Jeff Todd (ed.). *Worlds of Music: An Introduction to the Music of the World's Peoples.* New York: Schirmer Books, 1996.

Western European–American Classical Music (chapters 10–15)

Briscoe, James R. (ed.). *Contemporary Anthology of Music by Women.* Bloomington, IN: Indiana University Press, 1997.

Duckworth, William. *20/20: 20 New Sounds of the 20th Century.* New York: Schirmer Books, 1999.

Grout, Donald Jay, and Claude V. Palisca. *A History of Western Music.* New York: Norton, 1996.

McCutchan, Ann. *The Muse That Sings: Composers Speak about the Creative Process.* New York: Oxford University Press, 1999.

Morgan, Robert P. *Twentieth-Century Music: A History of Musical Style in Modern Europe and America.* New York: Norton, 1991.

Pendle, Karin (ed.). *Women and Music: A History.* Bloomington, IN: Indiana University Press, 1991.

Schwartz, Elliott, and Daniel Godfrey. *Music since 1945: Issues, Materials, and Literature.* New York: Schirmer Books, 1993.

Stolba, K. Marie. *The Development of Western Music.* New York: McGraw-Hill, 1998.

Music Business and Technology (chapter 16)

Fries, Bruce. *The MP3 and Internet Audio Handbook.* Burtonsville, MD: TeamCom Books, 2000.

Krasilovsky, M. William, and Sidney Shemel. *This Business of Music: The Definitive Guide to the Music Industry.* New York: Billboard Books, 2000.

Sanjek, Russell, and David Sanjek. *Pennies from Heaven: The American Popular Music Business in the Twentieth Century.* New York: Da Capo Press, 1996.

Williams, David Brian, and Peter Richard Webster. *Experiencing Music Technology.* New York: Schirmer Books, 1999.

Credits

Photo Credits

Chapter 1

1.1: Ravi Shankar © AP/Wide World Photos; **1.2:** Eric Clapton playing guitar © Corbis; **1.3:** Joan Baez and Bob Dylan © Peter Simon/Stock Boston; **1.4:** Guitarron player © Albert Copley/Visuals Unlimited; **1.5:** Andres Segovia © Bettmann/Corbis

Chapter 2

2.1: The interior shapes of walls, floors of a concert hall © Red Diamond Stock Photos; **2.2:** big band, jazz © Jack VartoogianFrontRowPhotos, NYC; **2.3:** chamber music © Jack VartoogianFrontRowPhotos, NYC; **2.4:** L7 in concert © Matthew Mendelsohn/Corbis; **2.5:** children singing, moving, playing with instruments © David Young-Wolff/PhotoEdit; **2.6:** Composing with pen and paper © Richard Wood/Picture Cube; **2.7:** Composing electronically © P. Gontier/The Image Works

Chapter 3

3.1: Sweet Honey in the Rock © Denise Sofranko/Michael Ochs Archives, Venice, CA

Chapter 4

4.1: Field recording of folk music in North Carolina, 1941 Courtesy of the Frank and Ann Warner Collection. Rare Book, Manuscript & Special Collections Library, Duke University; **4.2:** Peter Seeger in concert © AP/Wide World Photos; **4.3:** Fisk Jubilee Singers Music Division, New York Public Library for the Performing Arts/Astor, Lenox and Tilden Foundations; **4.4:** Son House © Michael Ochs Archives, Venice, CA; **4.5:** Leadbelly © Bettmann/Corbis; **4.6:** Taj Mahal © Michael Ochs Archives, Venice, CA; **4.7:** Bob Dylan at the Newport Folk Festival, 1965 (w/electric guitar) Photo by Diana Davies, courtesy of the Center for Folklife and Cultural Heritage, Smithsonian Institution; **4.8:** Newport Folk Festival, performers holding hands and singing to close show, 1963 © David Gahr; **4.9:** Bessie Smith © Bettmann/Corbis; **4.10:** BB. King © Ebet Roberts; **4.11:** Aaron Copland conducting (rehearsal or performance) © Hulton-Deutsch Collection/Corbis

Chapter 5

5.1: Jean Ritchie © Michael Ochs Archives, Venice, CA; **5.2:** Doc Watson © Jeff Albertson/Corbis; **5.3:** Gospel choir Courtesy Community of St. Sabina Church; **5.4:** Thomas A. Dorsey in performance in church 1980 Photo by Joel Richardson/© 1980 The Washington Post. Reprinted with permission; **5.5:** Mahalia Jackson singing © Underwood & Underwood/Corbis

Chapter 6

6.1: The George Williams Brass Band in New Orleans © Ray Avery; **6.2:** Louis Armstrong © AP/Wide World Photos; **6.3:** Benny Goodman band © Bettmann/Corbis; **6.4:** Duke Ellington © Bettmann/Corbis; **6.5:** Charlie Parker playing sax © Bettmann/Corbis; **6.6:** Dizzie Gillespie © Steve Kagan/Photo Researchers, Inc.; **6.7:** John Coltrane playing sax © Bettmann/Corbis; **6.9:** Gerry Mulligan © Sherry Suris/Photo Researchers, Inc.; **6.9:** Miles Davis (circa 1970) © David Redfern/Redferns; **6.10:** Thelonius Monk © AP/Wide World Photos; **6.11:** Billie Holliday © Ray Avery; **6.12:** Ella Fitzgerald © AP/Wide World Photos; **6.13:** Toshiko Akivoshi © Michael Ochs Archives, Venice, CA; **6.14:** Marian McPartland Louis Ouzer

Chapter 7

7.1: sheet music: Jeanie with the Light Brown Hair/Music Division, New York Public Library for the Performing Arts/Astor, Lenox and Tilden Foundations; **7.2:** "I'm Just Wild About Harry" campaign song/poster Charles

Klamkin; **7.3:** Irving Berlin & Ethel Merman ©
Bettmann/Corbis; **7.4:** Bill Monroe and his Bluegrass Boys
© Cheryl Higgins/Light Sources; **7.5:** Hank Williams ©
AP/Wide World Photos; **7.6:** Barbara Mandrell ©
AP/Wide World Photos; **7.7:** Randy Travis © Bob
Daemmrich/The Image Works; **7.8:** James Brown ©
AP/Wide World Photos; **7.9:** Tina Turner © AP/Wide
World Photos; **7.10:** Stevie Wonder © UPI-Bettmann/
Corbis; **7.11:** Little Richard © Michael Ochs Archive,
Venice, CA; **7.12:** Beatles © AP/Wide World Photos;
7.13: The Rolling Stones (early performance) ©
Bettmann/Corbis; **7.14:** Amnesty International concert
(showing all singers at the end of show singing together) ©
Neal Preston/Corbis; **7.15:** Willie Nelson at Farm Aid ©
Neal Preston/Corbis; **7.16:** Peace Sunday concert ©
Henry Diltz/Corbis

Chapter 8

8.1: Santa Clara Pueblo Indians © Robert Alexander B.
Grunzweig/Photo Researchers, Inc.; **8.2:** Tito Puente ©
Jack VartoogianFrontRowPhotos, NYC; **8.3:** Flaco Jiminez
playing accordion © Stills/Retna, Ltd.; **8.4:** Mexican
ensemble © Peter Menzel/Stock Boston; **8.5:** Klezmer
Band called Nisht Geferlach © Lionel Delevingne/Timepix;
8.6: Tahuantinsuyo ensemble © Jack VartoogianFrontRow-
Photos, NYC

Chapter 9

9.1: a classic Indian ensemble © Silverstone/Magnum
Photos; **9.2:** Indian women meeting weekly to sing
bhajanas © 1983 Carol Reck. All rights reserved.; **9.3:**
Geisha and a shamisen player © Horace Bristol/Corbis; **9.4:**
nagauta musicians on stage © Jack VartoogianFrontRow-
Photos, NYC; **9.5:** musicians playing a koto and shamisen ©
Bettmann/Corbis; **9.6:** a child playing a mbira © Elsa
Petersonj/Stock Boston; **9.7:** Miriam Makeba © Mitch
Wojanarowicz/The Image Works; **9.8:** Fela Kuti ©
S.I.N./Corbis; **9.9:** Thomas Mapfumo in concert © Nigel
Crane/Redferns; **9.10:** Youssou N'Dour © Jack
VartoogianFrontRowPhotos, NYC.; **9.11:** King Sunny Ade
© Jon Sievert/Michael Ochs Archives, Venice, CA; **9.12:**
Indonesian gamelan orchestra and dancer © Jack
VartoogianFrontRowPhotos, NYC; **9.13:** Mickey Hart ©
Redferns

Chapter 10

10.1: crucifixion of St. Andrew . . . vellum Courtesy St.
Louis Art Museum Purchase; **10.2:** Notre Dame (exterior
photo) © Foto Marburg/Art Resource, NY; **10.3:** Basilica of
St. Mark's © Alinari/Art Resource, NY; **10.4:** Singers with
lute and viola da gamba © Giraudon/Art Resource, NY

Chapter 11

11.1: person playing harpsichord © Jan Lukas/Photo
Researchers, Inc.; **11.2:** Santa Fe Opera's production of
L'incoronazione di Poppea © Hans Fahrmeyer; **11.3:** Santa
Fe Opera House Courtesy Santa Fe Opera House © Hans
Fahrmeyer; **11.4:** Singers with lute and viola da gamba ©
Stock Montage

Chapter 12

12.1: Haydn leading a rehearsal of a string quartet ©
Bettmann/Corbis; **12.2:** Emerson String Quartet in
concert © Jack VartoogianFrontRowPhotos, NYC; **12.3:**
The minuet © North Wind Picture Archive; **12.4:**
Beethoven holding his Missa Solemnis © Superstock, Inc.

Chapter 13

13.1: a scene from Tchaikovsky's Swan Lake © Linda
VartoogianFrontRowPhotos, NYC; **13.2:** Chopin playing in
the salon of Prince Radziwill © Bettmann/Corbis; **13.3:**
Brahms © Bettmann/Corbis

Chapter 14

14.1: A scene from Stravinsky's The Rite of Spring © Jack
VartoogianFrontRowPhotos, NYC; **14.2:** Jean Cocteau's
ink sketch of Stravinsky © Bettmann/Corbis; **14.3:** The
Ondes Martenot © Bettmann/Corbis; **14.4:** John Cage &
piano © New York Times/Getty Images

Chapter 15

15.1: Leonard Bernstein © AP/Wide World Photos; **15.2:**
Luciano Pavarotti; © Jack VartoogianFrontRowPhotos,
NYC; **15.3:** Echoes of Time and the River *Echoes of Time
and the River,* by George Crumb. Copyright © 1968 EMI
MILLS MUSIC, INC. All rights reserved. Used by
permission. WARNER BROS. PUBLICATIONS INC.,
Miami, FL 33014; **15.4:** Ethel Leginska/Music Division, New
York Public Library for the Performing Arts/Astor, Lenox
and Tilden Foundations; **15.5:** JoAnn Falletta/Reprinted by
permission of JoAnn Falletta/Courtesy Women's
Philharmonic, San Francisco; **15.6:** The Kronos Quartet ©
Jack VartoogianFrontRowPhotos, NYC

Chapter 16

16.1: recording studio © Michael McGovern/Picture
Cube/Index Stock Imagery; **16.2:** Merce Cunningham
Dance Co © Jack VartoogianFrontRowPhotos, NYC; **16.3:**
a radio disc jockey © Batt Johnson/Unicorn Stock Photos;
16.4: a symphonic band concert © Peter Menzel/Stock
Boston; **16.5:** Charles River concert © Kevin
Flemming/Corbis; **16.6:** Street musicians © Susan
Kuklin/Photo Researchers, Inc.

Index